MW00640293

reader on a journey that is almost as good as being there. For those who love road trips, *A Cast Away in Montana* is a trip well worth taking."

—Jerry Kustich, author of *At the River's Edge*, *A Wisp in the Willow*, and *Around the Next Bend*

"Tim Schulz's journey of discovery leads him deep into the Missouri headwaters of Lewis and Clark, but his corps features angling companions and waters whose names we know, or wish we did, and a sense of perception and humor that is transformative for him as well as for us. Accompanied by the ghosts of his past and a giddiness toward exploration of the fabled rivers of Montana, Schulz draws advice from Jerry Kustich, Todd Tanner, Kelly Galloup, and other guides to fellow travelers. Despite the apprehension that haunts us all as we set out from the beloved to the adventure, he sweeps us up in his awe of new places and their stories. With humor well tended by insightful analogies, Tim Schulz's journey of discovery is a worthy companion to our own."

—Kathy Scott, author of *Changing Planes*, *Brook Trout Forest*, and *Moose in the Water—Bamboo on the Bench*

A Cast Away in Montana

A CAST AWAY IN MONTANA

TIM SCHULZ

Illustrations by Bob White

Foreword by Jerry Dennis, author of *The Living Great Lakes*

LYONS
PRESS

Essex, Connecticut

An imprint of Globe Pequot, the trade division of
The Rowman & Littlefield Publishing Group, Inc.
4501 Forbes Blvd., Ste. 200
Lanham, MD 20706
www.rowman.com

Distributed by NATIONAL BOOK NETWORK

British Library Cataloguing in Publication Information available

Library of Congress Cataloging-in-Publication Data Available

ISBN 978-1-4930-8434-0 (cloth)
ISBN 978-1-4930-8435-7 (ebook)

♾️™ The paper used in this publication meets the minimum requirements of American National
Standard for Information Sciences—Permanence of Paper for Printed Library Materials, ANSI/
NISO Z39.48-1992.

For the woman who gave me life and taught me to love fishing nearly as much as I loved her.

Marie Holliday

August 28, 1921–May 16, 1981

CONTENTS

FOREWORD

Tim Schulz is good at many things. He's a professor of electrical engineering at a prestigious technological university and an expert on optics whose papers on the subject are understood by a few brilliant people, of which I'm not one. But I'm told they're very good.

He's a good guitar player, singer, and songwriter and performs on weekends with a band popular in some corners of the Upper Peninsula of Michigan called Uncle Floyd.

He plays hockey, too, on what he says is the slowest hockey team in the world, and though he might not be especially good at scoring goals or passing the puck or, really, skating, I bet he can chirp at opponents with the best of them, though probably in a good-natured, inoffensive manner.

He's a very good angler. Let me amend that. He's a damned fine angler. He fishes with focus and finesse. He's observant. He's patient. He's a problem solver. He casts like a dream. And he catches fish.

He is also good company. For one thing, the conversation never lags. It's not that he's a chatterbox, it's that he is smart and has much to say. When I say "smart" I mean very, very smart, but he carries it lightly. You'll find no Mensa bumper stickers on Tim's truck.

I remember one late night riding home in his truck after fishing something like sixteen hours on three rivers. We were tired in that restless way that makes the synapses snap and can make you a little giddy. Somehow the conversation turned from the mysteries of trout behavior to the mysteries of the infinity between numbers. Tim's an advanced mathematician of the PhD variety and a veteran college professor. He explained in what I'm sure were Math-101 terms that the infinity of rational numbers between 0 and 1 differs greatly, mysteriously, incomprehensively from the infinity of irrational numbers between 0 and 1. I might not have it right. The words were flying over my head, but Tim's such a good teacher that for a moment, just a flash, I understood. I saw the vast distances between integers. I saw lines of numbers rolling away into infinite space. Tim said, "Do you see why it's such an important question?" I said I did, but I didn't, and anyway by then I was thinking about us shimmying through tag alder bottoms to remote stretches of rivers and how happy I am that we can still get lost in the world.

Another thing about Tim: he's generous. Once while exploring a warmwater river, he stumbled upon a spring-infused stretch where large trout fed regularly and aggressively on the surface, *and nobody knew about it*. Here's the kind of guy he is: he took me there. Swore me to secrecy, then showed me a calm, ice-cold flat where tiny bulges on the surface were made by big-ass browns sipping midges. In the faster water we came upon bulging rises, head-and-shoulder rises, head-and-tail rises, splashing rises, slurping rises, and we caught and released more trout over fifteen inches than I can remember catching in a single day anywhere east of Montana. At dusk he led me to a section of still water under leaning cedars that he called the PhD Pool, placed me at the prime ambush point, and was delighted when I hooked and he netted my best trout of the year.

Tim can testify to it. He has the photos. He is also a good photographer.

And, best of all, he's a good writer. A few years after we started fishing together, Tim called to say shyly that he had been "playing around" with some essays and wondered if I would look at them. Of course. Other friends have asked the same favor, and I'm always happy to see what they're doing. But Tim was different. He had chops. His work was fluent, it was smart, it was funny in the right places, it rang with a distinctive voice—all the qualities that writers can spend years trying to develop and never achieve. Tim nailed it right out of the gate and has been getting steadily better ever since. You'll know what I mean when you read the pages that follow.

Over the years we've talked often about writing and fishing. We agree that one reason so many anglers write so well is because sharing their stories allows them to double the pleasure they get from fishing. But I would argue that there's more to it. Fly fishing is complex. It requires giving our full attention to the fish, water, weather, insects, our flies and how they're tied, our rods and how we cast them, the weight of the line, the diameter of the tippet, the state of the world, the social and genetic history of humanity since the Pleistocene—and the more attention we give to it, the greater the quotient of the universe we draw upon. It requires a complex response, and only written language—imperfect as it is—is up to the challenge. Calculus is probably not much help in this case.

Though if anyone could express it mathematically, I bet Tim Schulz could.

I've never fished with him in Montana, but I've read this book twice and feel like I have. I was with him on every mile of highway, at every campsite and restaurant, on every river and lake. I mourned his dog with him and watched over his shoulder as he cast to difficult trout and sometimes fooled them. And I stood beside him grinning while he made new friends everywhere he went.

It turns out, Tim's company is just as good on the page as it is on the river.

—Jerry Dennis

CHAPTER 1

Beginning

The beginning is the most important part of the work.

—PLATO

GREAT ADVENTURES OFTEN EMERGE FROM UNEXPECTED BEGINNINGS. Meriwether Lewis met William Clark after being court-martialed for getting drunk and challenging a lieutenant to a duel. Ernest Shackleton reputedly gathered his crew in response to a want ad promising small wages, bitter cold, and the unlikely prospect of a safe return. Life itself ofttimes begins with the caress of a hand, a suggestive smile, or the incandescent spark from an anxious eye. But even something as modest as an aging angler fishing in Montana for the first time has to start somewhere. And for me, it began alongside the Au Sable River in Grayling, Michigan.

Providing direct access from your car to your room, Gates Lodge is more like the roadside motor inns I loved as a kid than something my wife, Roxanne, would call a lodge. With a gravel parking lot and low-profile, barn-shaped sign flaunting playful sayings like, "Eat an early dinner, fish the evening spinner," or "The best surprises are spring rises," this rustic motel eight miles from a town with a population under two thousand wouldn't likely be on her list of top romantic weekend get-aways. Still, I told her we'd stay in a *lodge* if she came along on my trip to speak at the "Celebrate Michigan Rivers" event on the last weekend of September 2018.

"Maybe," she said.

From the perspective of a traveler looking for a place to sleep, Gates Lodge is a motel. A door with a metal kick plate opens to the parking area, just like the doors at so many classic Route 66 motels with neon signs boasting television and 100 percent refrigerated air. But another door on the back side of the room—or the front side if you prefer to think of it that way—is a narthex to the Holy Waters of the Au Sable River, complete with pew seating for streamside worship. So from the perspective of an angler looking to experience one of the most storied rivers in the history of American fly fishing, Gates Lodge is a lodge, and you can make a convincing case it is *the* lodge among all midwestern fly-fishing destinations. Rusty Gates set this standard long ago. Josh Greenberg maintains it today.

Positioning another nugget of bait behind my snare, I told Roxanne our good friend Jerry Dennis would speak at the event too—although he'd stay in a cabin on the North Branch of the Au Sable and wouldn't join us at the lodge. But another speaker and friend of Jerry's—Bob DeMott—would be at Gates, and Jerry passionately assured us meeting Bob would be a great treat.

"Anyone good enough for Jerry is good enough for me," she said.

"Does that mean you'll come along?"

"Yes."

In some sense, Roxanne and I were like the blind men in the fable, and Gates Lodge was our elephant. Although we touched the same doors and walls, she saw a motel everywhere I saw a lodge. During dinner at Gates's restaurant, where the menu described dishes like chicken papri-kash, steak au poivre, and parmesan-crusted whitefish, the playing field tilted in my direction.

"Well, that's lodge-like," she said.

For me, the lure of this place was the famous river in its backyard. For Roxanne, it was the proximity to Petoskey and its historic Gaslight

District. And because Bob and I would be stranded while she was away on Saturday morning and afternoon, we hired a guide to pole us down the Au Sable River. What else were we to do?

—◆—

Three months earlier, in June, I had floated the big water of the Au Sable with my friend David McMillan during the Hex hatch. Because these mayflies are half the size of a hummingbird, sizeable brown trout abandon their inhibitions to fill their stomachs with the closest thing to fried chicken they'll ever see—unless they get to eat a baby duck at some point. We fished from a classic McKenzie-style drift boat, which, for a fly angler, is the equivalent of using a moving walkway in an airport. You just stand there like a homecoming queen in a parade and let the boat and guide do all the work. Our guide was in his early thirties, and—like most guides on the river that night—he frantically exchanged text messages with his colleagues.

Bzzt Bzzzt . . . Bzzt Bzzzt . . . Bzzt Bzzzt

"Adam says three boats are posted below us on Angel Bend."

Bzzt Bzzzt . . . Bzzt Bzzzt . . . Bzzt Bzzzt

"Oh no. Gunner says two boats are rowing like crazy a couple of bends above us. They'll probably catch us soon, so we better post up here. This is good water."

We were on good water, and when night fell, the ravenous trout crammed the hatching bugs into their mouths like Bonnie and Clyde filling their bags with swag. The armada settled, and we had plenty of room on our stretch of the river. Still, electrons soared from phone to phone, conveying messages of anguish and aggravation over the crowds. I understood and appreciated how our guide wanted to enhance our experience, and I detest crowds as much or more than anyone. Nevertheless, I wanted to hijack the guide's phone and broadcast a message on his behalf:

"Guys, we aren't fighting the crowd. We *are* the crowd."

—◆—

Bob and I floated the river in a different kind of boat with a different sort of guide. His name was Jimmy Calvin, and he wore a ragged cotton

3

baseball cap instead of the millennial guide's fashionable mesh-back trucker hat. And while Jimmy backed his wooden riverboat down the ramp at Keystone Landing, Bob answered a call on his cell phone.

"Oh, hi Nick, how are you?"

"I'm great. I'm here with Tim Schulz. We're floating down the Au Sable River this afternoon before we speak at an event this evening. Jerry Dennis is here too . . . yes, yes, I'll tell Jerry you said hello."

Wouldn't that be something, I thought, if the Nick on the other end of Bob's call was Nick Lyons? It wouldn't be that crazy, really. Nick has a blurb on the cover of one of Bob's books that says: "DeMott's *Angling Days* is a rare treat. It is intimate, brilliant, bone honest, and memorable." Still, I couldn't be a Nosy Parker and ask Bob to tell me who was on the phone.

"Hey, Tim, that was Nick Lyons," Bob said when the call ended.

"We're standing beside the Au Sable River, and you're talking to Nick Lyons? Really?"

"Yeah. Nick doesn't fish much anymore, but he lives vicariously through his friends, and I like to keep him posted."

Jimmy put us on the seats of his wooden riverboat, then skillfully poled us through the Holy Waters while Bob and I cast small dry flies with our bamboo rods. Bob's a certified casting instructor, so, unlike my prosaic casts, his loops unrolled like poetic strokes of calligraphy above Michigan's river of sand. I wore my usual waxed cotton packer hat, and Bob wore a hunter-green wool beret, ensuring no one would mistake us for millennials. One of the several people who overtook us in a kayak yelled out as he passed:

"Boy, a picture of this would look like you gentlemen were in the nineteenth-century fishing for grayling."

None of us took offense, and I'm pretty sure Bob and Jimmy were pleased, like me. Especially for being called—or, in my case, mistaken for—a gentleman, and for the fanciful notion that, in another time, we might have been fishing for grayling.

Just after we floated past a man walking an oversized tabby cat on a leash, I asked Jimmy the question everyone seems to throw at the guides.

"I'm sure most of your clients are good folks, but you must get some tough ones sometimes, right?"

We ask that question, hoping the guide will affirm we are the good clients. Many guides appropriately brush the question aside by saying, "Oh, most people are great. The river has a way of neutralizing the knuckleheads." But Jimmy gave a slightly different response.

"Well, the guys who get most of their information from the internet and are constantly yapping about the big fish they caught in Montana can be annoying, but most people are okay. Except for the lawyers. You guys aren't lawyers, are you?"

"No, we're not. What's up with the lawyers?"

"Well, if you tell a lawyer to cast to the left side of the boat, they'll always cast to the right because they think you're lying."

"That's a joke, right?"

"What do you mean?" Jimmy said.

Later, I asked Jimmy about cooperation among guides.

"With so many guides on the river these days, do you share information about where, when, and what? At least with the ones from your shop?"

"Well, many guides talk and text continuously on their cell phones. I don't do that, so I'm not in those circles. I do okay, though. You have to stop worrying about all that stuff and just fish," Jimmy said. "A few months ago, on the big water, a couple of guys spent so much time stressing about where all the other boats were, I don't think they ever settled down. I find some good water and let my clients fish. It's pretty simple. Plus, I don't own a cell phone."

"No cell phone?"

"Yeah, everyone seems surprised. I don't need one of those things and all the complications it brings.

"We had a guide meeting with the boss a few days ago. He told us he had to return a client's money because he complained that the guide was on his phone the entire trip. The constant buzzing from text messages had pissed him off. The other guides were silent and fidgety, worrying they had pissed off their clients. After a few minutes, I broke the silence: *Well, it sure as hell wasn't me.*"

At dinner the night before, Bob told Roxanne and me that he and his partner, Kate, would—as he had done for thirty years—rent a house for the entire month of August in a small community along the bank of Montana's Madison River. They go there to fish for trout in Montana's most storied rivers, places I'd never seen, let alone fished—a fact at odds with my lifelong admiration of western waters.

It's a longing I gained as a young boy when my mom took me to Colorado to visit a distant cousin who never seemed to anticipate our visits with the same enthusiasm we did. Leading up to one particular trip, though, the cousin sent us tourism brochures from the State of Colorado describing rivers with names like Frying Pan, Gunnison, Animas, and Roaring Fork. Night after night, I'd fall asleep with those brochures on my chest, listening to the roaring water I heard in the photos, my mind canceling its regularly scheduled dreams about the pretty girls in my seventh-grade class, replacing them with documentaries of me fishing in a torrential flow in some Rocky Mountain canyon, holding tight to a spinning rod that strained to contain a wild trout desperately fighting to reclaim its freedom around the downstream bend.

Once we got to Colorado, my mom drove our old Plymouth to the bank of some roadside pond and paid a per-fish fee for us to catch trout that would literally fight for the right to wrap their lips around our baited hooks. The water in these ponds didn't roar. There were no amnesty-granting bends for the fish to race toward freedom. But I caught rainbow trout in the west, and as my mom said after she'd implanted the stench of fried fish deep into the fabric of every curtain and upholstered item in the cousin's house, those Colorado trout tasted pretty damn good.

At breakfast during our last day at the lodge, Bob invited me to join him and Kate in Montana. Roxanne reacted swiftly and with conviction. "This kind of opportunity doesn't come along every day," she said. "You need to go." I'd canceled trips to Montana twice before because of things that might or might not have warranted the cancelation. Because of that, Roxanne firmly believed I should—and would—go this year. Later, when Bob reaffirmed his invitation, Roxanne told him I'd be there. And as happens more often than not, she was right.

In his travelogue *Travels with Charley: In Search of America*, John Steinbeck wrote, "I'm in love with Montana. For other states I have admiration, respect, recognition, even some affection. But with Montana it is love. And it's difficult to analyze love when you're in it."

Indeed, but Livingston, Montana—the northern gateway to Yellowstone—is about twelve hundred miles from my home in Michigan's Upper Peninsula. That's a long drive for a first date. But Roxanne and I lived over twice that far apart when we first dated, and wedding rings have banded our fingers for over three decades since. All I need to do is head south, make a right turn at Wisconsin, and then drive west until I see mountains. If my friend Jerry Kustich is right—and he usually is—the opportunity to plug into the magical world of Montana far outweighs any inconvenience of getting there. So it was settled. I'd load the truck and drive west, looking for love in all the right places.

But you don't just drive to Montana and say, "Hello, my name is Tim. I'd like to catch some trout, please." You need a plan that answers two fundamental questions: Where will you fish? And where will you sleep? Bob graciously offered a place to sleep for a few nights, but I needed an itinerary for three weeks. So I called on some friends I'd corresponded with but never met. They'd be matchmakers of sorts, and because a first date is an event from my distant past, I needed all the advice and guidance they could share.

Dave Delisi directed me to the Big Hole, where he said I might find "brook trout of prodigious size, cutthroats, rainbows, grayling, and of course, our beloved native whitefish." I bought my first bamboo fly rod from Dave when he worked at Sweetgrass Rods, and through that experience I learned to listen to his advice and trust his judgment. "Anywhere up there is just stunningly pretty," he told me. "And the fishing can be great throughout the stretch that extends for thirty miles upstream from Divide." Like my adolescent self, I studied maps and imagined driving along a highway for thirty miles, stopping nearly anywhere along the way to fish for all the species of trout I've come to love, plus cutthroats, whitefish, and grayling. My sweet dreams returned.

The accomplished outdoor writer and *School of Trout* founder, Todd Tanner, prefaced his advice with this: "My thoughts are going to be colored by the type of fishing I enjoy. In general, I like to find big rising trout, target them, and try to catch them. I enjoy doing that in pretty places. It doesn't much matter to me whether there are other people around as long as there are enough fish, and enough space, to scratch my itch." Exactly the preface I hoped to get. Then he told me about rivers with big fish, rivers with elusive fish, rivers with rattlesnakes, and rivers with bears. As a warning, he told me August could be hot, dry, and windy.

I expected sage advice from writer and bamboo-rod builder Jerry Kustich about a state he'd lived in and fished for decades, but I didn't expect him to guide me on a journey that would mean nearly as much to him as it would to me. Yet he did. On the day I'd leave for Montana, Jerry would summarize our connection in a short essay for the Sweetgrass Rods newsletter:

> Sweetgrass friend and Michigan writer Tim Schulz contacted me a month ago about a several-week road trip he planned to take by himself to fish various waters around Montana. Since he has never been to the Big Sky State before, he was seeking my advice for an itinerary that would give him a good sampling of the Montana experience. In an instant flash of reverie, his request got me thinking about good ole times and the many road trips I once took to the Big Hole River and Rock Creek in the late 70s before moving to Montana in 1983. I close my eyes and still feel the excitement of sleeping in my truck and waking up to the whisper of flowing water humming an alluring tune like a siren beckoning me to dance with trout from sunup to sundown for days on end. There were few people around back then, so the sound of solitude overwhelmed my senses, inspiring a mood of introspection that has remained core to my fishing pursuits. Oh . . . the memories!
>
> Since Tim was going to be camping out of his truck, I naturally directed him to the Big Hole River. Maybe it was wishful thinking on my part to be back there again or a wish for a friend to experience something special, but I suggested to Tim that he start there. A visit to the Big Hole last fall forged for me the realization that the entire valley had not changed substantially in forty-some years, and though fly fishing has become glamorized over the past couple of decades, hiding in the riffles and runs of the Big Hole are ghosts from bygone days when fly fishing was still a solitary endeavor of quietude and reflection.

Although these types of journeys are not likely in my future, I figured I could vicariously relive those magical Big Hole days through Tim's ventures.

And with that, I was set. Like a spaniel with its teeth sunk in the left-rear tire of a Corolla, it was time for me to figure out why I'd been chasing this thing. I'd begin my first date with Montana in late July and end in late August. I'd bring a bouquet of red roses, a box of Godiva chocolates, and a bottle of Beringer Private Reserve cabernet. I'd comb my hair, shave my cheeks, and put a nice crease in the sleeves of my newest plaid fishing shirt. I'd try to do all the right things at all the right times. Most of all, though, I'd navigate that awkward first glance, first smile, first touch, and—dare I say—first kiss with the guidance and support of gracious friends who, before me, had all surrendered parts of their hearts to this mysterious maiden named Big Sky.

CHAPTER 2

Goodbye

How lucky I am to have something that makes saying goodbye so hard.
—A. A. MILNE, *WINNIE-THE-POOH*

EVER SINCE BOB PLANTED THE SEEDS FOR THIS TRIP LAST SEPTEMBER, Roxanne has watered and weeded until roots have taken hold and sprouts have pushed through the soil. Now the crop is mature, the fruit is ripe, and it's time for me to go to Montana. I've packed the truck with all the pots, pans, blankets, pillows, and tackle I'll need to eat, sleep, and fish for the next three weeks. Enough stuff, really, to stay twice as long if I want. I planned to leave around 8 a.m., but it's close to noon, and I'm pacing the house like a child delaying bedtime, pretending I need to find one more thing for the trip. Roxanne knows I should have left hours ago. It doesn't take Nancy Drew's eye to decode my tactics, and she also knows why I haven't. My stalling routine this morning is as transparent as the clear Montana sky will be tonight. So when I take the leash from its hook, she smiles and says, "Just one more time." Saying nothing in return, I fasten the clasp to Sunny's collar and take him for our third—and final—morning walk.

I hate to say goodbye. Whether to a person, an animal, a place, a thing, or simply an idea, I don't like to do it. I've been like this since I was a kid. Most notably, I dreaded how Sunday brought its abrupt farewell to the weekend. I never wanted to go to school the way kids with straight teeth and brand name shoes did. I didn't like what it was—a place where I had to sit still and pretend to listen. Or what it wasn't—a place without cornfields, oak trees, and bluegill ponds. My issue with Sundays went further than that, though. On that day—while watching an episode of *Bonanza*—I first realized everyone and everything I knew would die: my mom, my dog Brandy, Uncle Floyd, Aunt Gladys, and, yes, even me. I don't remember what it was about that show that did it. Maybe Little Joe got bushwhacked in the desert. Perhaps Ben said something profound about life and death. I'm not even sure it had anything to do with the show. I only know I didn't want to watch *Bonanza* again after that night.

When I was in college, a friend and I, who both lived in the dormitory, always showed up at some friends' nearby apartments on Friday afternoons and stayed until Sunday. We did it every weekend, and when the guys who lived there went to bed, we crashed on their couches like the Sooners in the panhandle plains because, I guess, neither of us wanted to say goodbye. Even now, as a supposedly mature adult, I'm often the last to leave a party, and when the second-to-last person departs, I close the door behind them and exclaim, "Gee, I thought they would never leave!"

The eight guys who lived in the two college apartments never formally invited my friend and me to stay the night. They just accepted that we'd imposed our version of squatters' rights on them. They had a pretty friendly attitude about it, though, and at some point, they printed a couple of T-shirts with *The Things That Wouldn't Leave* on the front. The back of mine said *Thing 1*; the back of my friend's said *Thing 2*. I hadn't thought about this much until last year when I learned *Thing 2*—a guy we called Fish because he drank like one and, I suppose, liked to catch them—had died. I found that out on a Sunday.

Earlier this summer, I said goodbye to my old fish truck, a 2010 Ford Expedition with enough miles to make me and—more importantly— Roxanne nervous about my trip. My replacement plan was simple. I'd find a similar model with ten to twenty thousand miles on its odometer, buy it, then sell the truck I called "The Great White Whale" to a private buyer. I traveled a lot of back roads, escaped several snares, and slept many nights in that vehicle. It took me where I wanted or thought I needed to go and always brought me home safely, even when I bounced its undercarriage off the tops of boulders and stumps. Saying goodbye would be difficult, but I'd get to approve the new owner, which assured The Whale would go to a suitable home where they'd change its oil on schedule and rub Armor All on its seats. Somehow, though, I stopped at the local Chevrolet dealer, and, after some transactional details with a neighborly lady named Jennifer, I signed the adoption papers for a brand new Suburban and gave the guy behind the counter the keys to The Whale. With that, I had a shiny new green ride that my friend Cam immediately christened, "The Green New Deal."

Sunny, the yellow dog on the end of my leash, is the third dog Roxanne and I have had in our family. The first was a cocker spaniel named Linus that she bought for my birthday the year after we married. Linus was an affectionate dog around anyone who knew him or, more importantly, anyone whom he knew. But as happens with many breeds, the cocker spaniel's popularity incentivized a rash of selfish breeding practices. Linus inherited an irrational fear of everyday items like grocery bags, trash cans, open ovens, open refrigerators, and—most tragically—unfamiliar people, especially small ones. For a time, we controlled his encounters with people in general, and small people in particular, by using leashes, fences, and crates. But we needed a more reliable plan after Roxanne gave birth to Daniel. Although Linus took to Daniel pretty well, little people attract other little people, so we hired outside help. Our dog made good progress until the day someone left the gate to our yard unlatched, and the neighbor kid found Linus roaming the streets. Everything was fine when the boy brought the dog to the front door. But something in Linus snapped when the kid turned and walked away from our house, and Roxanne watched in horror as our dog charged into the street and sunk his teeth into the boy's arm.

After a tearful goodbye to Linus, the dog psychologist told us the best medicine would be a new dog. She said we deserved a friendly one and recommended a place called *Leader Dogs for the Blind*. Dogs in that program would have excellent temperaments—the sort you could trust with someone's life. But because their standards are so high, some fail the curriculum and get offered for adoption. The guy on the phone laughed when I told him we were moving to the Upper Peninsula the next week and I wanted to adopt a dog to take with us. He said the waiting lists were two to three years, but he took my number and promised to get back to me if the Mississippi River started flowing north. Two days later, though, he called and told me about a dog they hadn't trained because of heartworm and cataracts. If we would take on the expense of completing the heartworm treatments and refrain from making any "blind leading the blind" jokes, the dog could be ours. And that's how Sampson, a yellow Lab the same age as Daniel, moved with us to Houghton.

Sampson's cataract-clouded eyes watched over the growth of our children for twelve years. He was their pillow and blanket, both literally and figuratively. A big brother and best friend who protected them from the creatures of the night or, at least, made them feel protected. They paid him with stolen cheese, chicken, and other scraps from the table, pats on the head, and plenty of belly rubs. Sampson had a dash of a vagabond heart, causing a few sleepless nights when the voices in his head called him to the road. But he always returned. After he died, the heartbroken kids insisted we replace him with another yellow Lab. Roxanne preferred a smaller dog, but we'd furnished all the rooms in our home with carpet and couches in either a dark or light shade of a color we called "yellow Lab," so another yellow dog made good sense. At least that was the case I made. And so it was that an undersized yellow Labrador retriever named Sunny joined our family in the summer of 2005.

The kids picked Sunny's name before seeing the dog, and their choice was perfect. From the first day in our home, he found immediate comfort in the glow of even the slightest patch of sunshine. As a small puppy, he circulated about the house like a hairy high-energy sundial: mornings by the east-facing windows, evenings by the west-facing ones. With age, Sunny perfected the art of sunbathing and taught himself the difference between a sunbeam's leading and trailing edge. He used that knowledge to maximize his time under the beam and minimize the number of moves he'd need to make from window to window. "What do dogs do on their day off?" the comedian George Carlin asked. "Can't lie around. That is their day job."

I mean none of this to portray Sunny as a lazy dog. The "puppy crazies"—those moments in life when something deep inside compels us to run like hell in circles for the sole purpose of running like hell in circles—were encoded permanently into his DNA. Mine too, I suppose. When he was happy, which was any time he didn't hear the frightening sound of thunder or anger in a human voice, his tail would wag every inch of his muscular body. He had no limit to how many times he could chase a stick into Lake Superior's frigid water. But time is a relentless bandit who has gotten his hands on both of our strongboxes. We've slowed, and neither of us can deny that. The gray hairs on our faces signal sprains, strains, and worn-down joints that will never have that new-car feel again. When either of us gets that urge, though, we still drop just about anything we're doing to take twenty or thirty laps around the coffee table. Or at least we give it one hell of a try.

Now, with over fourteen years in the mirror, it's hard not to notice how every day behind is one less in front. Sunny's arthritic hips don't navigate the stairs and trails with the linebacker's power and gymnast's grace they once did. His old ears don't respond to commands and calls, not even in the selective way they used to, partly because he's lost most of his hearing, and partly—as Jimmy Buffett once put it—because "he don't care what most people say." Several tumors—mostly those benign fatty ones that plague so many dogs—have misshaped his body. But the cancer tumor on his back is more massive than his heart. And that—being the heart of a Labrador retriever—is enormous.

Still, we walk the trail we've walked together countless times. He stops to smell every daisy and black-eyed Susan his failing eyes see. I've never needed to tell Sunny to stop and smell the roses, or another dog's poop, for that matter. He marks his favorite oaks and maples to warn the other dogs—especially the younger ones—that they are still guests in his woods. A gray squirrel crosses the trail before us, but Sunny doesn't chase. Instead, he cocks his head to the side, just the way he does when someone says "please" and he thinks they've said "cheese." Then, after a few seconds, he gives the squirrel a deep "in my younger days" bark and limps his way on with our walk. The trails here have names from *The Lord of the*

Rings: Troll, Ring, Ent, Gnome, Elf, and Hobbit. Maybe—just maybe, I hope—if we walk the Elf loop one more time, Sunny can be immortal.

Toward the end of Sampson's life, his worn-out hips barely supported his body on level ground. So I carried him up the stairway to the bolster bed in our room each night and back down each morning. Everyone except me saw his pain, but I believed my care was best for him, even though it wasn't. We prolonged his life because we—well, I actually—didn't want to say goodbye. How we take care of our pets at the end of their lives is equally important to how we care for them at the beginning. Even more important. So the day we brought Sunny, the mischievous puppy, home with us, Roxanne told me she couldn't—and wouldn't—let that happen to him. When it was time, she said, we would do what was best for *him*, not what we—meaning I—thought was best for *us*. I told her I understood. But understanding something like this is easy when your puppy is young and full of piss and vinegar. Fourteen years later, when time has taken most of the piss and all the vinegar, it is not.

When we get home, I remove his leash and return it to its hook. Sunny pushes his head between my legs, which is his way of asking me to scratch his ears and rub his back. Based on fourteen years of data, there is no limit to how long he will stay if I keep scratching and rubbing. But I also know that when I stop, he'll back his head out and limp to a familiar and comfortable place to curl up for a nap. "It's time for you to go now," Roxanne tells me. I hug her, kiss her, tell her I love her, and promise to be careful. Then, with tears welling in my eyes and a lump growing in my throat, I tell her that if the time comes while I'm gone, I know she'll do what's best for Sunny. Then I say the same thing to my dog.

Out at the Suburban, I inspect my gear one last time. I have a cooler, portable stove, camp chair, rods, reels, waders, nets, sleeping bag, pillows, battery-powered fan, mosquito netting, and boxes of clothes and food lashed together and stacked nearly up to the roof—a modern-day covered wagon readied for a six-month journey on the Oregon Trail. Still, I tell myself I need to scrutinize the contents one more time. I might have forgotten to pack that thirteenth fly rod, that ten-year-old pair of socks Roxanne threatens to throw out every time she sees them, or some other gizmo or gadget I won't use even once on the trip. But I know it's all there. Every little circle on my packing list has a checkmark on it. I don't need Roxanne to tell me I'm stalling this time.

In *The Lord of the Rings*, the half-elf Arwen tells Aragorn, "I would rather share one lifetime with you than face all the ages of this world alone." Our dogs love us more than they love themselves. They lick away our tears, fetch us from burning buildings, and protect us from intruders—real and imagined. In return, they expect only an encouraging smile, a loving pat, and an occasional slice of bacon. Dogs don't dwell on the concepts of the future and the past the way we do; instead, they live fully in the here and the now. Still, I think Sunny understands something about the finiteness of life. Unlike me, though, I don't think he consciously considers it. For him, life is likely both simple and straight-forward. We are all immortal until that one day when we aren't.

I start the Suburban, back out of the garage, and look at the vertical sidelight window beside our front door. There, in the first pane at the bottom, I see the nose, the gray muzzle, and the dark eyes of a faithful friend who—for fourteen years—has watched me drive down this road, always returning for another walk in the woods or mad dash around the coffee table. I smile at my friend the way I would if I planned to return in a few hours, guiltily knowing I won't. At the end of our driveway, I set the navigation tool on my phone for Bozeman. The screen shows a little over twelve-hundred miles to my destination. I don't know where I'll go first when I get to Montana, but I know I'll be able to get there from Bozeman. I pull onto the street, and as the first tear rolls down my cheek and onto my lip, I think of something I've said to Roxanne many times before.

"The only thing sadder than seeing that face in the window is seeing that window without that face."

Lord knows I hate to say goodbye.

CHAPTER 3

Doing the Right Thing

Do what you can, with what you've got, where you are.
—SQUIRE BILL WIDENER (AS TOLD BY THEODORE ROOSEVELT)

EACH TIME I'VE CONSIDERED CANCELING THIS TRIP, ROXANNE HAS CON-
vinced me to go. I see myself as our family's logical, rational mind—a
cross between John von Neumann and Mr. Spock. And because of her
compassion and empathy, I think of Roxanne as our emotional one. I also
like to think I'll get a call from the Nobel Committee in Stockholm one
day, but I'm equally wrong in all those ruminations. When I suggested
postponing the trip for another year, Roxanne reminded me about the
bookings with guides, commitments to friends, and the ticket our son
Daniel bought to fly from San Francisco to Bozeman for a few days while
I'm there. She told me we don't know what will happen with Sunny—he
could still be with us when I return. I know she's as right as the water is
wet, but I still feel I'm doing the wrong thing.

As I drive south on Highway 26, I tell myself I can't—or won't—turn
back once I cross the Wisconsin border. That's a two-hour drive through
the Ottawa National Forest. If I avoid stops in Wisconsin, I'll be in Minnesota two hours later. In four more hours, I'll hit North Dakota. And
if I make "good time"—like my father-in-law always did—I'll wake up

tomorrow in a motel between Fargo and Bismarck, five or six hundred miles from home. Like Amelia Earhart crossing the Atlantic, I must stick to my plan.

To make good time, I'll need to avoid distractions along the way, of which there are more than you might expect in northern Wisconsin and Minnesota. In the 1920s and '30s, upper Wisconsin's rural cities made popular destinations for Chicago gangsters on the run, or the lam, as they liked to say. The border town of Hurley—home to Al Capone's older brother Ralph—was, for example, a hotspot for bootlegging, gambling, and prostitution. John Dillinger and Baby Face Nelson had a bloody shoot-out with FBI agents thirty-five miles south at a lodge called Little Bohemia. Remnants of that era still stand in the Silver Street district of Hurley, with establishments like the Full Moon Saloon and Tails N Trails still lining the roadway. To my good fortune, though, and to that of the people who depend on me, I'm not the sort of gentleman who frequents a gentleman's club, so I drive on.

Just past the Minnesota border, I think about diverting north to drink some water from the small town of Hibbing. Roger Maris, the first player to break Babe Ruth's single-season home run record, and Robert Zimmerman—better known as Bob Dylan—the Nobel laureate who wrote the soundtrack for a generation of change agents, both grew up in Hibbing. And Judy Garland—Dorothy from *The Wizard of Oz*—lived a few miles down the road in Grand Rapids for the first four years of her life. Whatever elixir enhanced the groundwater of Minnesota's St. Louis and Itasca counties, though, is likely too weak to counteract the thousands of gallons of unenhanced southern Illinois water I drank during my youth. So even with a couple of swigs from Hibbing's water, home-run records, Nobel prizes, and Academy Awards will probably remain out of my reach. So again, I drive on.

The roads from Duluth to Fargo take me through a sequence of nondescript towns with names like Remer, Whipholt, Ah-gwah-ching, and Akeley, though Akeley claims to have the world's largest Paul Bunyan statue. The route also takes me along the Viking Trail for fifty miles—supposedly, the same path Vikings used to explore the region in the 1300s. When I reach Fargo, it's 9 p.m., and my eyes are haggard and heavy from the strain of driving and crying. Nevertheless, I keep going, finally stopping for the night in Valley City. With a population of sixty-five hundred, it's the thirteenth most populous city in North Dakota, which says more about the state than the city. After checking into my motel, I order a jalapeño burger for dinner at a nearby restaurant, with a beer from the Fargo Brewing Company. Other than me, the clientele comprises two couples at the bar and four construction workers at a table by the window. While I eat my burger and drink my beer, the construction guys flirt with the barmaid and drink "one more beer" five more times, confirming the lore that construction hard hats take the edge off hangover headaches.

When I return to my room, I tie a few flies, hoping the tedious work of wrapping thread around a hook will release emotional energy. Jerry Kustich told me to focus on grasshoppers and caddisflies, so I do. After I tie four bugs, I pull the curtains tight, spin the air conditioner's dial to its coldest position, and set my alarm for 5 a.m., Mountain Daylight Time.

I wake up Sunday morning with confusional arousals or—as some call it—sleep drunkenness. A sliver of light from the parking lot shines through a small gap in the curtains, and I can't understand why the window is on the wrong side of the bed. I check for Roxanne's body beside mine, but she's not there. A slight panic sets in, and I feel as though someone has locked me in a stateroom on a ship and set me to sea. Eventually, the air conditioner's steady hum calms me, and I remember where I am. I'm somewhere in North Dakota, near a place where four hungover road workers are patching holes out on the highway. And with the most certainty I've felt since Roxanne told Bob DeMott I'd accept his invitation, I realize I'm going to Montana.

Sometimes, I tell people my home in Michigan's Upper Peninsula doesn't get as cold as they think. It's simple science. Water in liquid form can't get below 32°F, and Lake Superior's water is usually in liquid form. So during the winter months—while our upper midwestern neighbors fight trench foot in Minnesota and frostbite in North Dakota—we bask in the relative warmth of our great lake's shadow. But in return for keeping our air warmer than it would otherwise be, colossal clouds of steam rise from the lake and drop ghastly piles of snow on our peninsula. It's a trade-off we welcome. The lake sometimes freezes, though, and because water in solid form doesn't warm the polar air like water in liquid form, it gets colder than a brass toilet seat in northern North Dakota. At least that's the joke I like to tell.

As I drive across North Dakota, the joke seems to be on me. Not because it's cold, of course, because even North Dakota isn't cold in late July, but because the rolling and twisting two-lane highways that carried me through the gentle hills and peaceful forests of Michigan, Wisconsin, and Minnesota have morphed into a straight stretch of interstate promising to bore the life out of me for the entire three hundred fifty miles between borders. After four hours of this seventy-five miles per hour monotony, a sign announces the visitor center for Theodore Roosevelt National Park. I look to both sides of the road, and all I see is a dull landscape with a few modest buttes and mesas. "I guess every state gets a national park," I think. But I need a bathroom break, so I put on my blinker and take the exit.

Abruptly, and as if the ghost of the Rough Rider himself had set me up, the relatively flat sprawl of North Dakota transforms into a seemingly endless canyon painted in goldenrod, avocado, slate, and soft amber. Although my first look at the Grand Canyon inspired more awe, and my first drive across the Mackinac Bridge delivered more surprise, nothing I'd seen before provided a more intense combination of awe and surprise. This park, where I casually and callously stopped for a pee, is the top attraction in North Dakota. A prepared traveler who studied a map and, perhaps, a little presidential history, rather than simply punching their destination into a GPS, would know something like this was on their route. Blissfully ignorant road trippers like me are, I suppose, the reason "getting there is half the fun" is more than just a saying.

Our country has named no other national parks after a person. This one spreads across more than seventy thousand acres and contains a cabin Roosevelt used on his bison hunts in the nineteenth century. Bison still roam the place, along with feral horses, elk, pronghorn, white-tail and mule deer, and prairie dogs. Prairie dogs aren't dogs, of course. They're more like ground squirrels, with two distinctive features. They're known to build underground towns, the largest believed to cover more than twenty-five thousand square miles, housing about four-hundred million residents. And the female prairie dog is only in the mood one day a year—for only one hour. You learn things like this when you stop for a pee in North Dakota, half an hour before the Montana border.

I enter Montana about thirty-two miles past the visitor's center. Evidently, central North Dakota shares its patents on dry, flat, isolated land with eastern Montana. But according to a study by the *Washington Post*, eastern Montana owns all the rights to those patents. Using data from Oxford's Big Data Institute, the *Post's* staff examined all the places in the continental United States with more than one thousand residents. They then computed the distance from those places to the nearest metropolitan area with over seventy-five thousand people. According to this metric, the three most isolated communities are, in order, Glasgow, Scobey, and Wolf Point, all in eastern Montana. When I enter Montana on Interstate 94, those three cities—each about fifty miles from the others—form a tidy little triangle about one hundred crow miles to the northwest. Without exaggeration, I am as close to the middle of nowhere as I've ever been. Not knowing how far it will be between places to fill and empty my tanks, I make a mental note to stop at every gas station and bathroom I see.

As recently as 1999, the speed limit on most Montana highways was "reasonable and prudent." Now it's just eighty miles per hour—fast enough, though, to make good time as I've never made it before. It took more than ten hours for the first six hundred miles from Houghton to the capital city of North Dakota. The remaining six hundred miles will take about eight. The hills in eastern Montana are mostly barren, but as the Suburban hurls me westward, I see a few stands of ponderosa pines. Based on the little research I did for my trip, I remember this is the official state tree of Montana, and that reminds me that the official state fish is the westslope cutthroat trout, which reminds me why I'm here.

I stop to send a message to Jerry Kustich. "I'll be in Billings around 2:30 or 3:00," I type on my phone. "Should I try the Bighorn in the evening or push on?"

"At this point, push on," Jerry replies. "If you have time at the end of the trip, maybe. Logistically, it will take more time than it's worth. Once you get to Livingston, check out the Yellowstone River at any access point for the evening. It may still be off-color, but there could be caddis activity. You'll keep in a better time frame for getting to better options."

The drive from Billings to Livingston takes a little under two hours. I first learned about Livingston from Jimmy Buffett's "Livingston Saturday Night," a song from his album, *Son of a Son of a Sailor*, that also appeared in two movie soundtracks: *FM* and *Rancho Deluxe*. The Montana novelist Thomas McGuane wrote the screenplay for the latter and played mandolin in the band when Buffett sang the song in the film. Then, two years later, McGuane married Buffett's sister. As poorly as I prepared for this trip to Montana, I'm surprised I know these things.

I search on my phone for "fly shops in Livingston" and find that the Sweetwater Fly Shop will be open when I arrive. The shop is about two miles south of the interstate, and when I walk in, I see a kid—most people who work in fly shops look like kids to me now—helping some people buy fishing licenses and teaching them the difference between a nymph and a dry fly. When my turn comes, I say, "Hi, my name is Tim, and I'd like to catch some trout, please." I tell him I just drove from Michigan, and he recommends some flies that look like they could imitate a stonefly or hopper, assuming stoneflies and hoppers in Montana are purple. He also suggests a smaller mayfly pattern, similar to a parachute Adams, except with a purple body. I buy them all, of course, because buying flies is how you say "please" and "thank you" when you ask a fly shop worker for advice. And equally important, I don't want to stand in some Montana river watching other anglers catch fish with the purple flies I was too cheap to buy.

I give the kid my credit card and ask about places to fish. He recommends access to the Yellowstone River, about thirteen miles south of the shop. "Stay until dark," he says, "and you should get into some fish, especially if you use those purple flies." I thank him and drive toward the access. To my left is Livingston Peak and the Absaroka Mountain Range. Farther to my right is the Gallatin Range. I'm going through a vein in the heart of Paradise Valley, one of Montana's high-rent districts. Famous actors, artists, authors, and musicians—like Russell Chatham,

Jeff Bridges, Peter Fonda, John Mayer, Thomas McGuane, and Jim Harrison—have made their homes here. Many still do.

To my great surprise, I find the access. The kid annotated a map for me, with some lines directing me where to go and others showing me where not to go. Still, I've screwed up less complicated directions and could have easily wound up at the Yellowstone entrance in Gardiner. Even more surprising, I'm the only one here. I walk down to the Yellowstone from the parking area and take a close-up look at my first Montana river. From bank to bank, it's about two-hundred-fifty feet wide. The river's surface bounces with gentle riffles as far as I can see in either direction. The afternoon sun lights up the mountains to the north, creating an illusion of snow-covered peaks. I feel as if I'm standing before the backdrop for a *Greetings from Montana* postcard.

I return to the Suburban, and a truck pulls into the area just after I lace my boots. "Damn it," I think, "it's another fisherman."

"Timothy Schulz, Timothy Schulz," a driver yells from the truck. It's the kid from the fly shop.

"Yeah, what's up?" I ask.

"I have your credit card. You left the shop before I gave it back."

"Wow, thanks for driving it out here."

"No problem. Man, it would suck to drive from Michigan and lose your credit card on your first day." Then the kid drives away.

Stunned, I walk toward my truck and think about what had just happened. This kid drives a twenty-six-mile round trip to return my credit card, and I don't give him a tip. He just did the right thing, and somehow, just when I needed to perform, I dropped the ball like a fourth-string quarterback in the Super Bowl.

The recording on the fly shop's answering machine tells me they're closed when I call, hoping to get the kid's name and arrange a way to get him a tip. I gather my gear and walk to the river in a daze, overwhelmed by guilt. Guilt about the kid, of course, but now—as I stand beside my first Montana river—I think about Jerry Kustich. "The Big Hole from Melrose up is the ultimate trout river," he told me. "My heart and soul still haunt those waters." Through all our correspondences, Jerry made it clear that the Big Hole is extraordinary, and because of that I had decided my first Montana trout—my first date and first kiss with Big Sky—should come from that river. But here I am about to fish in a different river because I can't wait a little longer to get to the Big Hole valley. And, on top of that, I just stiffed a kid who pulled my rear from a roaring fire.

I put my gear in the truck and speed to the fly shop, hoping to find the kid. When I arrive, the place is dark, and the sign on the door says "closed." I consider leaving money in an envelope, but I don't remember the kid's name and I want to thank him in person. I decide to return on my way home in three weeks and give the kid a signed copy of my book with some twenty-dollar bills for bookmarks. So I get back on Interstate 90 and motor through Bozeman, Three Forks, and Butte. Just past Butte, I take Interstate 15 south and exit at Divide. As I drive beside the Big Hole River on my way to the Dickie Bridge Campground, there is just enough light to see my first Montana trout rise to a fly. Several of them, actually. I find an open site at the campground, and two guys from Oregon and Washington invite me to their campfire.

I make a tuna sandwich and pour two fingers—the pinky and the index—of Bulleit Rye into a tin cup with ice. The guys are in Montana to see the Big Hole National Battlefield. But they both like to fly fish, so they've been camping along the river. I tell them I drove from Michigan in two days. "Holy shit," one guy says, "you were pushing some asphalt." We talk for another half hour, and when the mosquitos chase the guys to their camper, they tell me I'm welcome to use their fire until it burns out. My legs are bare below the same shorts I wore when I left Michigan. These guys don't know what it means to be run off a fire by mosquitos. When the last red ember fades, I crawl in the back of the Suburban and go to bed. I think about Sunny, Jerry, and the kid at the fly shop. My air mattress floats on an ocean of emotion, and I try to convince myself I'm doing the right thing.

CHAPTER 4

Indecision

Would you tell me, please, which way I ought to go from here?
That depends a good deal on where you want to get to, said the Cat.
—LEWIS CARROLL, *ALICE'S ADVENTURES IN WONDERLAND*

LAST NIGHT AT THE CAMPFIRE, THE GUYS TOLD ME THE TRICOS weren't hatching. The word trico is short for *Tricorythode*, the Latin name for tiny dark-bodied and light-winged mayflies resembling flecks of black pepper and specks of salt on the water's surface. In the air, they can be so thick, they suggest clouds of smoke billowing above the river. I might find some farther downstream, they said, but not here. Still, my campsite is within casting distance of the river—a Steve Rajeff cast anyway—so I crawl out of my truck at 7 a.m. and pull on my waders. It's one of the rare times they'll be dry when I put them on here in Montana. Later today, the temperature will rise into the mid-to-high eighties, but this morning I need a jacket over fleece to stop shivering. Jerry Kustich warned me about this. The Big Hole, he said, would be cool enough to fish in the morning and early afternoon but often too warm in the mid-to-late afternoon. Starting the day with the air temperature forty degrees below the forecasted high, I understand how that can happen.

I want to catch my first Montana fish—every Montana fish, really—on a dry fly, but I don't see any bugs. No tricos, midges, or pale morning duns in the air. Just the vapor from my breath, dancing in the breeze before disappearing into nothingness. Jerry said hoppers might work throughout the day, and I've heard about nocturnal stoneflies on the Montana rivers. So I search through my stonefly and hopper boxes before remembering the plastic container of flies I bought from the kid in Livingston. Some of those flies look like they could imitate a hopper or a stonefly, and the kid said they would work. So I select a big purple one and tie it to my leader.

The river is about one-hundred-fifty feet wide and relatively shallow. Stones—most between the size of a softball and a basketball—cover the bottom and the bank. The rocks on the bank have a distinct characteristic I like: they don't offer many places for rattlesnakes to hide. A few weeks ago, Roxanne told me to ask Jerry about the chances of being eaten by a bear or bitten by a rattlesnake. "Funny you should mention rattlesnakes," he replied. "Another friend just posted a picture of one on the Big Hole. Although not extremely common, I always watch where I step and listen for the buzz." I didn't want to hear that. My attitude about snakes—especially those that don't live in reptile houses—comes from an old railroader friend of my mom's. "I ain't afraid of what snakes might do to me," he used to say. "No, I'm afraid of what those sons-ah-bitches might make me do to myself."

The rocks *in* the river have a distinct characteristic I *don't* like and, unfortunately, won't know about for about five more minutes. A few weeks before I left Michigan, the sole on one of my felt-soled wading boots came partially off. Those boots—and the tube of contact cement I plan to repair them with—are in a luggage box on top of the Suburban. In their place, I'm wearing boots with worn-out rubber soles and worn-down metal cleats. I stand on the dry bank for my first few casts, but the best place for a fish is in a riffle behind a distant boulder. I give it a few tries but can't cast to that spot without getting in the water.

People often quote Mark Twain—or slightly misquote him—as saying, "A man who carries a cat by the tail learns something he can learn in no other way." When I started skating and playing ice hockey, I once stepped onto the ice with protective guards on my blades. A memorable cat-by-the-tail moment on par with stepping into the Big Hole River without realizing how much moss covers the rocks in the water. Moss that is slicker—as that same old philosophical railroader from my youth used to say—than snot on a doorknob. I blame it on the awkward jitters of a first date. There's no other excuse for an experienced wader to walk into a trap the way I walk into this one.

I fall without puncturing my waders or frightening every fish and pocket gopher between Wise River and Wisdom. As falls go, it's not too bad. I get back on my feet, check for blood, and look around to see if anyone witnessed the show. All the theater seats are empty. The only mark is on my ego, and that fades with my first cast to the riffle. When the fly lands at the base of the boulder, I mend the line upstream to make it float like it's edible and not just a mannequin made of foam, fur, and fiber. Five feet into the drift, the water erupts, signaling the rise of my first Montana fish. It's a brown trout around ten or eleven inches long, colored like buttered asparagus with dark jungle-green freckles.

Brown trout aren't native to Montana, nor anywhere else in North America. The first browns stocked in the United States came from Germany in 1884 and were released into Michigan's Baldwin River. Montana stocked them into their rivers a few years after that. So for a few seconds, and a few seconds only, I'm disappointed that I've caught a brown trout instead of a native fish. The irony of this moment is so thick I could nail it to a tree. A guy from Michigan—with a German surname—has a tinge of regret because the ancient ancestors of his first fish weren't born in this state. The State of Montana hasn't stocked brown trout in the Big Hole since 1954, and they have put no trout in this river since 1989. All the trout in the Big Hole—brown or otherwise—are wild and, as far as they know, native. The fisherman from Michigan who fell on his stern a few minutes ago is the only alien in this scene. Back in control of my sensibilities, I release the fish into the river of its birth and give this event the approving nod it deserves.

I soaked my right sleeve during the fall, and now I'm as cold as a penguin's chuff. When I begin to shiver, I return to the Suburban to change jackets and drive to another downstream spot. After about nine miles, I pull into the parking area for a boat ramp at Jerry Creek bridge. I catch a brook trout on my first cast, but the rocks are slicker than the ones at Dickie Bridge. Plus, I'm looking for more solitude than this spot a hundred feet from the highway affords. So I drive another fifteen miles downstream to Maiden Rock. There, I park my truck on the south side of the railroad tracks where, in contrast with Dickie Bridge, the streamside rocks present plenty of places for rattlesnakes to hide. I grit my teeth and run the gauntlet to the river just before a train roars through the canyon. The pale-peach-colored engine blasts a thundering warning before stampeding through the crossing. The tracks loosely follow the river from Glen to Divide, but in Maiden Rock canyon, they stay shoulder-to-shoulder through every bend. I find a few fish rising to a sparse hatch of tricos and catch one rainbow trout, making my morning a grand slam of sorts. When the hatch stops around noon, I leave the river.

The temperature is rising toward eighty, so I drive to the fly shop in Melrose rather than check another spot. The guy behind the counter says hello, but I ignore him to pet his dog. It's the first dog I've petted since I said goodbye to Sunny, and the exchange clearly means more to me than it does to the pup. I ask the guy—who is too old to call a kid—if he has any felt-bottom wading boots in my size. He doesn't. I also want advice about fishing, so I ask him to recommend flies. He suggests some purple stoneflies and a trico pattern that—to my surprise—isn't purple. The smallest tippet on the wall is 5X, so I ask where he keeps the smaller tippet to use for tricos. He laughs and says, "There are some big fish in this river. I wouldn't use anything smaller than 4X. Use a bigger fly if you can't get that through the eye. The current is fast, and the fish aren't that picky." This guy's advice is nothing like Josh Greenberg's the summer he convinced me to use 8X fluorocarbon for the trico hatch on the Au Sable River in Michigan. "Toto," I say to the guy's dog, "I don't think I'm in Michigan anymore."

This morning I moved from Dickie Bridge to Jerry Creek to Maiden Rock without thinking much about it. Now—planning my next move— I'm thinking about it. Dickie Bridge to Maiden Rock is about twenty-five miles, and altogether I fished about three hundred feet—or 0.2 percent— of the water between those spots. Unfettered and untethered, I can fish anywhere I want. But I know I can't fish everywhere I want. I need to make some deliberate decisions. Like a political candidate at a two hundred dollars per plate fundraiser, I'm in danger of shaking everybody's hands but not getting to know anyone.

Jerry recommended I fish either the Ruby River, Poindexter Slough, or the Beaverhead River in the late afternoon and evening after the temperature rises on the Big Hole. Before I do that, though, I need to eat and find a new pair of boots. Butte is thirty-three miles to the north; Dillon is thirty-one miles to the south; Twin Bridges is twenty-two miles to the east. I can take Interstate 15 to either Butte or Dillon, but as Jerry told me, the drive to Twin Bridges is on "a shitty twenty-mile dirt road . . . slow going." I decide to take the smooth highway to Dillon, but when I get to the shitty dirt road to Twin Bridges, I take it. Like Jimmy Buffett's Frank Bama once said, *the best navigators are not quite sure where they're going until they get there, and then they're still not sure.*

About a half-hour later, I get a note from Jerry while eating a BLT at the Wagon Wheel Steakhouse. He says there could be a caddis hatch in the evening on the Ruby and directs me to one of his favorite places to fish that river. After lunch, I drive there to check it out, but it's mid-afternoon, and the water looks dead. With time to kill, I decide to go to Dillon and look for wading boots, then return to fish in the evening. I strike out at the first two shops. In the third—I find three golden retrievers sleeping in the doorway, a giant of a kid named Josh tying flies in the corner, and a pair of felt-soled Simms G3 wading boots in my size. After selling me the boots, Josh gives me a hand-drawn map that shows places to access Poindexter Slough and the Beaverhead. One of those spots is close to one of Jerry's suggestions, so I refine my plan again. I'll fish the Beaverhead tonight, drive back to a campsite near Divide and return to the Big Hole in the morning.

The hike into the Beaverhead is slightly over a mile. The air smells like rain when I pull on my waders, and on the walk to the river, I encounter my first Montana storm, which forces me to scramble to shelter under a highway overpass. Even there, I strain to keep a biblical wind from ripping the hat off my head. The storm passes in about a half hour, just like the weather app promised. I get to the river around 5:30 p.m.

and am surprised by how much it reminds me of the Brule River on the Michigan-Wisconsin border, except for the mountains on the horizon. Will Rogers said, "You never get a second chance to make a good first impression," and the Beaverhead River isn't wasting its first. I sit in the dense brush on the bank with my feet in the current and monitor a few seams where I believe fish will eventually rise. Especially if the caddisflies hatch the way Jerry said they might.

A few minutes past 6 p.m., a slight disturbance attracts my attention to a current line against the far bank. At first, the fish pokes its nose through the surface. But after a few halfhearted rises, it porpoises with a purpose. Mouth first, followed a foot later by the dorsal fin, then another foot later by the tail. I haven't tied on a fly yet, so I search my box for a caddis emerger that works well for me back in Michigan. I pick a size 16 with an olive body and push the 5X tippet through its eye. My left hand shakes from buck fever, so I leverage my wrist against my chest and secure the fly with a Davy knot—the easiest one to tie when my hand behaves like this.

I tell myself this Montana trout isn't different from any big trout I've caught in Michigan. Still, I left my dog and wife to drive nearly two thousand miles for this moment, and now that it's here, I'm overwhelmed. I pull some line from my reel, false cast twice, then put the fly exactly where I want it to be. But my line forms a "Z" shape, the result of three conflicting currents I didn't consider. Although the fly drags, the big fish keeps eating, impervious to my mistake. I wade upstream to a spot where I should be able to mend enough line to account for the chaotic flow on the river's surface. Using a slack-mend cast, I point my rod upstream just before the line lands. When the bug arrives, I beg the fish to take it. My heartbeat races when the trout's nose cuts through the surface.

The trout makes a mad rush for the deepest water in the middle of the river. I get the line onto the reel and apply upward force, but the fish resists my pressure with the grit of an oak tree in the wind. I bend the rod toward the water, pulling to my left and right, but we're in a deadlock. The fish ignores both requests, and suddenly, without warning, the tension is gone. In just an instant, the trout and I are eye to eye. No dancing tail. No shaking head. Just two feet of brown trout suspended in the air, taunting me like the blue marlin taunted Santiago. When the fish falls back into the water and sprints downstream, my reel squeals, and the bamboo fibers in the rod strain to protect my line from snapping under the pressure of this fight. Then the fish turns, swims straight toward me and launches from the river for another eye-to-eye encounter. We repeat this scene twice before I coax the trout into a position where I can net it. For reasons I still can't explain, though, I have my smaller net with its sixteen-inch opening instead of the one with the twenty-inch opening I should have brought. The fish doesn't fit. I try to cradle it in my hand, but as I do, the hook pulls loose, and the mighty trout swims away.

I wanted to cast to that fish, see it take the fly, bring it to my feet, control it, and then let it go. That's pretty much what happened, so why am I so disappointed? The only thing I could have done differently was to contain the fish in my larger net and capture it in a photograph. But I don't show those photographs to anyone anymore. I just use them to help me remember, and I don't need one to remember this trout. What compels me to fool these fish into taking the bait, drag them to my side, and exert complete control over their lives, even for only a short time? I think it's a primal survival instinct to bring a fish to hand, kill it, then eat it. Years of catch-and-release have conditioned me to ignore this blood lust or at least constrain it. So when I pull a fish within reach, but it escapes before I control it, something deep inside screams that my existence is at risk. All this is a conjecture from a guy without formal human psychology training. So it's possible, maybe even likely, it's caused by a souped-up angler's ego.

Clouds of caddisflies float above the river and interrupt my moping. Several fish feed, and I do my best to fool them into taking my bait. Four of them do, and all but one escapes. When I net the one that doesn't, I feel a rush of adrenaline as old as human existence. With that fish in my net, I will survive. At dusk, a fast-moving storm pushes me off the river, the sky a mix of salmon, lavender, and chambray, like a pastel-colored quilt hung over the horizon. I hurry to my truck, where I meet a young man with a young son who talks with me between lightning flashes and thunderclaps. He's a guide on the Beaverhead, and he says I should fish with nymphs in the water below the dam. "It's fishing great now," he says, "and the fish are huge." I tell him I'd prefer to catch fish with dry flies. "I understand," he counters, "but when you're this close to Clark Canyon Dam, you should give it a try. When in Rome, you know." He directs me to a campground in Barretts and tells me the names of some popular access points for the river. I decide to sleep in that campground and fish with nymphs below the dam in the morning. Indecision, I suppose, is no longer my problem. At least not now. Maybe.

CHAPTER 5

I've Been There

We can only be guided by what we know,
and our only source of knowledge is experience.

—ARTHUR J. PILLSBURY

LAST NIGHT, I COULDN'T FIND A CAMPSITE IN THE DARK AND RAIN, SO I parked and slept in the day-use lot at Barretts Park Campground. When I crawl out of my truck this morning, I'm about two hundred feet from the Beaverhead River, which flows beside a four-hundred-foot-wide and sixty-foot-high rock formation Lewis and Clark called "Rattlesnake Cliff." The cliff's granite, platinum, and charcoal-gray face forms a towering bank, shielding the river from the harsh morning sun. Heightening the surreal charm of this park, cars and trucks speed atop Interstate 15, three hundred feet to the west, just beyond a frontage road and a pair of train tracks. Another small mountain rises about one hundred feet on the other side of the highway, forming a narrow gateway from Dillon into Beaverhead Canyon.

During last night's storm, the guide in the parking area told me the Beaverhead wouldn't fish well until 9 or 10 a.m. So I grill a pancake for breakfast, heat some water to wash my face, and walk through a sparse stand of cottonwoods to the river, hoping to see a trout feeding, despite what the guide said. But the greenish-brown water flows north toward Dillon with no sign of life. A bronze plaque erected by the Daughters of the American Revolution in 1935 says an ancient Indian trail, the great Beaverhead wagon road, and the first railroad into Montana all passed through this site. My thoughts drift back to when the smell of livestock hung heavy in the air, sparks flew from the locomotive smokestacks, and iron wheels clanked on iron tracks. But soon, the raucous chorus of AC/DC's "Highway to Hell" blasts from a campsite, yanking me back to the now.

I break camp, which only entails folding my aluminum table, rinsing out my stainless steel pot and pan, and stowing my single-burner butane stove. When I reach the dam, a flotilla of drift boats lines up for the launch. The guides prepare their vessels for departure, checking and rechecking to ensure they have all the rods, reels, and flies they'll need for the day. The clients fidget the way we do when our job is to stand around and watch someone else do the work. For many of us, it's the most awkward part of hiring a guide. We know they neither want nor need our help, but we can't escape feeling we should do something. Unable to help, we stand around like misplaced props on a movie set.

Today I'm on my own, and I don't know where to start without someone to show me. The guide from last night mentioned High Bridge, Henneberry, and the Slick, but I'm disoriented and overwhelmed, so I drive to a fly shop near the dam. It's a little A-frame building with a generic, banner-style sign over the door that simply says, "Fly Shop." Inside, they have a few pairs of waders for sale, a well-stocked bin of flies, several stickers and tee shirts with pigs and toads painted to look like rainbow, brown, and brook trout, and a pegboard display with some leaders, tippets, sinkers, and tools. The guy behind the counter recommends two tiny candy-red midges, another with black and white stripes like a zebra, and some pheasant tail nymphs he says always work. When I ask for advice about where to fish, he says, "No secrets here. Just find an empty spot. The fish are everywhere."

I drive north on High Bridge Road and park in the first empty pull-off. The river is forty feet from my truck, down a well-worn footpath through some rocks between clusters of sagebrush. I assemble my rod, pull on my waders, and take the short hike to the river. It's still cold, so I tell myself the snakes will stay in the gopher holes and crevices until the sun warms the rocks. I don't know if that's true, but I make it to the river without being shaken, rattled, or rolled. I sit on a boulder and prepare a leader for my nymphs by squeezing two split shots on its end. Above that, I tie two flies on droppers that extend at right angles from the leader. Ahead of all of that, I attach a small balloon-like thingamabob that is actually called a *Thingamabobber*.

━ ◦ ━

I caught the first fish of my life with a worm suspended below a bobber. In my early years, I didn't know any other way. My rod was a two-section cane pole, which might explain my love of bamboo fly rods today. The fish was a sunfish, most likely a bluegill, pumpkinseed, or red-ear, about the size of a baseball card. A tiny spring gadget held the bobber on my line, and—even though the red and white float was plastic—my mom and I called it a cork. Mom gathered our bait from the worm farm she made from an old bathtub in our backyard. Besides my cane pole, my only other gear was a bright red Folger's coffee can filled with dirt and worms.

Sitting still when told to do so—in church, school, or the back seat of our '68 Plymouth—was never one of my childhood talents. Away from those places, though, I could sit beside a pond for hours and stare at that cork. My mind drifted the way young minds do, but my eyes focused like a laser on the bobber, alert for any suspicious movement, even the slightest bounce or wiggle. Anything telling me a fish was making its move on the worm at the other end of my line. My heart raced when the cork tilted and skimmed across the surface like a tiny speedboat, followed a moment later by my favorite sight of the day: that glorious place in the water where the bobber used to be.

After graduating from cane-pole school, my mom gave me a black plastic Zebco 202 reel with a short fiberglass casting rod. It wasn't as sophisticated as the rod and reel she used, but it opened up a wonderful new world of opportunities. I could fish in the same places the adults fished and catch the same fish they caught. One summer afternoon, when my mind drifted more than my eyes watched, I failed to notice the cork sink two seconds before my rod and reel launched into the pond from its makeshift rod holder. In two or three heartbeats, my rod, reel, and the biggest fish I'd ever hooked were gone. I started crying and couldn't stop. I was sure my mom would deliver a swift and unjust punishment for my offense. But when she ran over to see what I was crying about, she smiled—laughed, actually—and said it must have been a big fish.

Eventually, I progressed to open-face spinning reels and artificial lures. Our local sporting goods store displayed aisles and aisles of spinnerbaits, jigs, plugs, spoons, and plastic worms. The smell of molded plastic was the aroma of possibility. I got a job in the summer, bought a fancy tackle box, and filled it with all the lures I could afford. But no bobbers. I was a sportsman, and we sportsmen didn't use bobbers. Then colleges and jobs in un-fishy places put my angling on hold for over a decade. I started fishing again when I moved to Michigan—using spinning reels at first—but a new chapter in my angling biography began when Roxanne bid on fly-casting lessons at an auction for a local art gallery. Pandora's box flew open.

I started with an entry-level Cortland rod-and-reel outfit with a small plastic box of Royal Wulff flies. I didn't catch big trout, but I got a lot of them. Steelhead smolt that shined like prisms in the sun, and brook trout painted like mottled autumn leaves. The small streams close to my home were all I knew about this new way of fishing. Then, on a business trip to New Mexico, I rented a car in Albuquerque, drove three hours north to Navajo Dam, and hired a guide to take me fishing. He didn't have any Royal Wulff flies. Instead, his flies looked like worms, eggs, and tiny un-baited hooks wrapped with colorful thread. And after he tied one of the worms on my leader, I watched in awe as he put a bobber on my line. I'd come full circle.

If I ignored the click-and-pawl reel and the thick PVC-coated line, I felt like a kid with a cane pole again. But this wasn't the same. These fish didn't suck worms into their gullet and make the bobber dance across and under the surface. The guide told me they'd make quick decisions about the fly's authenticity just a fraction of a second after drawing it into their mouth. If I paid attention, I'd notice a slight movement of the bobber, which was a clump of chartreuse yarn he called a strike indicator. He said I'd need to react quickly, or I wouldn't hook the fish. After I missed my first several opportunities, I compensated by yanking harder. "You can't make up for being late by doing that," he told me. "And when you're on time, you'll rip that tiny hook from their lip if you pull that hard. These aren't Eagle Claw bait hooks, and you're not fishing for sunfish."

Every trout I landed on that trip was larger than any I'd caught back in Michigan. At first, I thought it was a Michigan versus New Mexico thing, and I said something like that to the guide. "Michigan has plenty of big fish. The issue is your presentation, not your place." He taught me how to attach the yarn indicator to the line. I felt like a fool when I screwed it up, but when I got it right, I felt like a magician. The flies I thought were un-baited hooks wrapped in thread were called nymphs. The ones we used were called midges, but he said when I returned to Michigan, I could use bigger ones that looked more like the bugs I was used to seeing. Pandora's door swung open even wider.

A drift boat floats downstream toward me while I finish preparing my leader. The clients flip their flies tight to my side of the river, and when the guide sees me, he tells them to cast toward the other bank. Unknowingly, they gifted me a valuable clue. I planned to step into the river and fish in the deeper water, but after seeing how they would have fished tight toward my bank, I stay on the rocks and cast just beyond where I can see the bottom. I flip my rig upstream, watch the little bobber float back, then pick it up when it drags below me. With the cadence of an intermittent wiper, I toss the rig back upstream. The bobber shakes each time the split shots bounce off the bottom. I lift the line when one shake looks slightly suspicious, and the rod bends.

I think I'm snagged until I feel the familiar shake of a hooked fish. I can't move it upward, so I extend my rod to pressure the trout toward the middle of the river. It dawdles initially, then uses the faster mid-stream current to propel downstream. A boat floats by with two men fishing toward both banks. Their guide gives me a nod, but neither of the anglers seems to notice—or care—that I'm fighting a fish. Two more boats do the same thing, reducing what I believe to be a noteworthy event into some mundane business as usual. I see myself as the Cardinal's David Freese hitting the walk-off homer to force game seven against Texas in the 2011 World Series. They see me as a backup catcher taking spring training batting practice. But I must be right about this: it's an eighteen-inch brown with a tail like a square-tipped canoe paddle. The fish hardly needs resuscitation—a sign that reveals it has headlined this show before.

I catch four more trout, each between fourteen and eighteen inches, then decide I've had enough nymph fishing. It's past 11 a.m., and a trout has risen steadily on the far bank for half an hour. I want to catch it, but the river is sixty feet wide and flows at several speeds across its span. I need to get closer before making a cast, so I sneak into the water. My first step sinks me knee-deep. My second puts the river's surface about ten inches below the top of my waders. I slide my foot forward until I feel the bottom fall away. I need to get closer, so I take another step and ask the fish gods to show mercy.

Swimming in waders is never easy. I use one hand like a five-pronged oar, the other to keep my rod safe above my head. A guide has anchored his boat about a hundred feet downstream, and I hear him and his clients laughing. Hell, I'm laughing too. But I'd like to get out of the Beaverhead River before I float down to them. About twenty feet into my swim, I grab onto some sedge and pull myself into a place where I can stand. The guide in the boat asks if I'm okay, and when I hold up my thumb as a sign of triumph, he holds up all eight fingers and two thumbs to give me a perfect score. I take an exaggerated satirical bow.

When another boat floats by, I'm standing beside my truck in my Venetian-red scotch plaid boxer shorts, holding my waders by the neoprene booties while water pours from the opening that used to be around my chest. "I've been there," says the guy in the back of the boat. After pulling on my jeans, I make a turkey and Swiss sandwich, open a Miller Lite, and stand in the sun to dry off. I don't usually have a beer with lunch, but I don't typically swim in my waders either. Unthreatened by my antics, the trout near the far bank continues to eat its lunch too. When another boat approaches, I ask the guys if they have a dry-fly rod rigged and ready to go. They do, and the guide anchors above the fish to position the man in the bow for a downstream cast.

Perhaps I should be upset to stand next to my SUV and watch these guys catch my fish, but I'm not. The clients tell me they're lifelong friends from New York who've been fishing together in Montana for twenty years. When I tell the guys what happened when I tried to catch that fish, the guide laughs and says these trout rise on the west bank in this stretch of the river precisely for that reason. Catching the fish will be challenging, even from a boat with a guide who can position it. The conflicting currents that deliver the real flies make it nearly impossible for an angler to fool the fish with a fake one. This trout seems to know this, and each time it rejects the counterfeit, it eats the next natural fly that floats by. Like a huckster in a shell game, the trout always knows which shell covers the pea and which ones don't.

I feel bad for the fisherman, but he stays upbeat. He puts the fly exactly where he needs to put it and sets the hook precisely when he needs to set it. This trout is tricky, and the *where* and *when* are not what they appear to be. The anglers switch places, and the other guy takes several shots at the fish. When he makes his first cast, I swat a gnat from the back of my neck. A few seconds later, I smack another one. When the next one lands on my shoulder, I grab it between my index finger and thumb. But it's not a gnat. It's an ant. And when I realize a hundred more are marching up my leg, I rip off my pants and madly shake the ants from them. For the second time in an hour, I stand on the bank of the Beaverhead River, displaying my taste in boxer shorts to everyone who floats or drives by. The guide in the boat laughs and tells me he's been there.

The guidebooks say the Beaverhead consistently produces more large trout than any other river in Montana, and I believe that. But I'm standing beside a relatively busy road where I'm buzzed by a Dodge Ram or Chevy Silverado every seven minutes, and an interstate highway on the other side of the river rumbles with Peterbilts and Freightliners hauling lumber, toilet paper, whiskey, and other vital goods to the fine people of Idaho and Montana. And in the river, drift boats float by with the frequency of rubber ducks at a carnival fair. The fishing and catching have been great fun, and I can't recall another time I've stripped to my skivvies beside a river twice on the same day. But half a day of this is enough, and I need to move on.

I drive back to the town of Barretts and stop at the truck stop beside the highway. My tank needs gas, my cooler needs ice, and my hygiene needs servicing. I ask the lady behind the counter if I can get a shower here, and she points to a sign on the wall that tells me how much money I need to pay and what rules I need to obey. I don't recall ever breaking a rule in a shower, and I can't imagine violating any of the ones I see on the sign, especially since I don't have a goat. Frankly, I can't envision anyone breaking these rules, but this truck stop is on Interstate 15, a major route connecting Canada to Mexico. So I try not to imagine anything at all.

I stop in Dillon to buy groceries, then briefly visit the Anderson and Platt fly shop. I don't really need anything, but I pick up some flies and a couple more *Thingamabobbers*. Mostly, I want to pet the dogs. About forty minutes after getting back on the interstate, I exit west onto Highway 43. The air temperature dropped after yesterday's storms, and I have a hunch that the Big Hole River will fish well this evening. If it does, I want to be there.

CHAPTER 6

Stages

My destination is no longer a place, rather a new way of seeing.
—MARCEL PROUST

ONE FISH, TEN FISH, BIG FISH, ZEN FISH. THAT'S HOW THEODOR GEIsel—Dr. Seuss from our child- and parenthoods—might have described the fly fisher's journey. In his excellent essay, "The Five Stages of Fly Fishing," Todd Tanner includes another phase between big and Zen, something Seuss might have called *finicky fish*. This stage is when *that* fish—the one that sips unrecognizable flies from an inaccessible lie—is the only fish we want to catch. We change flies, extend leaders, and push our casting skills against their ceiling, but—like Seuss's North-Going Zax—*that* fish refuses to change its ways. In defiance, we stand there like the South-Going Zax and fish until the entire world stands still.

For many of us, these stages link sequentially, like a prerequisite chain in education. First, we need to catch a fish, then a lot of fish, then some big fish, and finally, we need to catch *that* fish. Nothing as dramatic as Norman's Walter from *On Golden Pond*, but a fish we think might change our lives in some meaningful way. When we reach the end of this chain, need often gives way to want, and what we want is only to go fishing and, perhaps, watch someone else—a daughter, a son, a friend, or a stranger—catch a fish, a lot of fish, a big fish, or even *that* fish.

Like much of life itself, most chains have a beginning, a middle, and an end. Regarding this progression, Thomas Wolfe told us we couldn't go home again, and Heraclitus said we couldn't wade in the same river twice. But the fly-fishing chain is not so rigid, and we fly fishers can go back, especially if we blur the distinction between place and experience. After years of fishing, we can still catch a new fish in a new river, land a big fish in a small stream, or hook ten fish when we expect only one. And *that* fish can show up just about anywhere and anytime.

Here in Montana, I'm jumping from link to link like a frog in a thunderstorm. Yesterday, I caught my first fish in a Montana river. Then I discovered, hooked, and lost *that* fish on the Beaverhead. I landed several big fish with a bobber and a nymph this morning. Now I'm not sure what I want, but I know I want to find it in the Big Hole River. I've never caught a whitefish or a grayling, and they live here. And when I told Jerry Kustich I had landed a small brown, brook, and rainbow trout on my first day on the Big Hole, he said, "Don't let that fool you. There are big fish up there."

Fishtrap Creek flows into the Big Hole River halfway between Divide and Wisdom. There's a state campground where the creek joins the river and another campground—called Sportsman's—about three miles downstream from that. The campsites at Sportsman's are right on the river, so I pull in and check one out. The campground host tells me the camping is free, but they'd accept a donation if I want to give them one. I do. Several trailers and motor homes populate the main campground, but I'm the only one camping along a small gravel road that parallels the river, just to the west of the riverside hamlet. I park my truck, eat a late lunch, and then nap.

According to the Dalai Lama, "Sleep is the best meditation." I don't know how to meditate, and I'm not always good at sleeping, so I have apps on my phone to help me with those things. Soothing voices instruct me to block out negative thoughts and, instead, focus on breathing. Birds sometimes chirp and chatter in the background, depending on the theme. Regardless of the message, though, the sound of water is always there. It might be the pitter-patter of raindrops falling on leaves or the rhythmic brush of ocean waves rolling across sand. But it's always present in some form. Some scientists say the *white noise* aspect of these sounds masks out the alarming noises that might wake or excite us. Others say it's because our ancient ancestors lived in water. For whatever reason, when I stretch out on the air mattress and lower the windows, the Big Hole River does those things the scientists say it should.

Westslope cutthroat, Arctic grayling, lake trout, mountain whitefish, and several species of sucker, sculpin, dace, and burbot were native to the Big Hole drainage. The online stocking records for the river go back to 1933, and—during that time—the state has stocked Arctic grayling, brown trout, cutthroat trout, kokanee salmon, and rainbow trout. The kokanee experiment was short-lived: nine-hundred four-inch fish in 1950 and none after that. Brook trout are not native, nor do they show up in the stocking records for the Big Hole River. But they are abundant here.

I wake up, pull on my damp waders, and wade into the river. Some brook trout feed on tiny insects when the sun hides behind a cloud. The dimples they leave on the river's surface prompt me to cast. I can't tell what bugs they're eating, but brook trout aren't known for their discerning taste, so I tie on a size 18 Borchers Drake. None of the Montana fly shops I've visited carry this pattern. It's a Michigan fly created by an Au Sable River guide named Ernie Borchers to imitate the burly brown-drake mayflies. It works well in small sizes and in other states too, and when the tiny fly floats without dragging over one of these Montana brook trout, they attack it. None of the trout I catch are trophies—by Montana standards. But by the benchmarks of Michigan's small Upper Peninsula streams, they are excellent fish.

In *Brook Trout and the Writing Life*, Craig Nova writes of how the sides of brook trout have "a line of bright circles which are red or orange and bright, and they have the aspect of sequins, of a silver maple leaf in late fall." How, I wonder, can something as wary as a brook trout display such color on its body? The pale yellow freckles against the brownish-green hue of their skin fashion a sort of camouflage. But—to all the predators in the river—the gleaming red blotches encircled by brilliant blue halos seem to scream, "Hey, look at me!" Not getting eaten, though, is only part of the evolutionary game. The other part is finding the best mate, and—like the lavish tails on a peacock or a five-hundred-dollar Stefano Ricci silk tie—those spots might also say, "Look at me. I've got the right stuff." The spawning season has a way of bringing out the garish in all of us.

I stand in the river a little downstream from my camp, where a small island creates runs and riffles along its bank. The highway is about one hundred fifty feet behind me, but the traffic is sparse. The ground slopes upward on the other side of the river, the surface dense with pines. A man parks his truck near where I'm fishing, gets out, and gives me a friendly wave.

"How's the fishing?" he asks.

"Good," I say. "All brook trout so far."

"I got a nice rainbow here two nights ago, so don't let your guard down," he tells me.

"Do you want to fish this spot?" I ask. "It's my first time here, and I'll be fine fishing anywhere."

I don't know where this guy came from, but I don't want to take his spot if he drove a long way to fish.

"No, that's okay. I'm probably not going to fish this evening." Then he asks, "Have you seen any bears?"

"No," I say. "I heard they're mostly in the upper parts of the river, above Wisdom."

"Well, a friend of mine saw one on the bank across from you about a week ago. Big one too."

"Should I worry?"

"No, no, they have plenty of other things to eat at this time of year."

"Plenty of other things to eat" didn't have the calming effect the guy might have intended. Or maybe it got precisely the result he wanted. Either way, after the guy leaves, I keep one eye on my fly and the other on the wooded ridge across the river.

When the light dips below the hills and a single shadow blankets the water, I see a larger fish feeding behind a rock. A splashy commotion reveals each rise: the fish grabs the fly; its back breaches the surface; its tail froths the water. When I make a good cast and presentation, the fish rises to the fly, but I don't hook it. *The trout missed*, I think. But the trout never misses the real flies. My fly is probably too large, so I change to a smaller pattern. Yet I still can't catch it. I ensure the hook is intact and check its point on the nail of my thumb. Everything appears to be okay, so I make another cast. Finally, the fish rises to the fly, the bamboo rod arcs, and I hurry to get the excess line on the reel. *I've got a big trout*, I think.

At first, the fish swims toward the island, and I follow. The bottom isn't as slick as it was in the other places I've been on the Big Hole. But still, I move like a high-wire artist performing without a net. When the fish rolls and flops like a walleye, I'm convinced it's a large brook trout—possibly the largest I've ever caught. Then I see a red spot on its gill plate—the kind you see on a rainbow trout—but notice something peculiar about its body shape. Unlike a rainbow, this fish looks like a giant version of the minnows we used to pull from the Styrofoam bait bucket. When I get the fish close enough, I dip my net under its body. It's a Montana whitefish.

The whitefish tires quicker than a trout of its size would, but—once I have it in my net—it bucks like a Charbray bull. Fifteen inches of bone, muscle, and gristle make getting the hook out of its tiny sucker-style mouth nearly impossible. The river's surface is now boiling with rising fish. With the new patience I learned from the first whitefish, I catch four more, two of which suck the fly so deep in their mouth I have to cut the line. When it's finally too dark to fish, I return to the Suburban and make a chicken salad sandwich. I hear a few fish rising directly in front of my campsite, but I don't want to catch another whitefish. I'm content to sit at the picnic table and drink a Two-Hearted Ale.

I've heard some Montana trout anglers treat whitefish with the same violent disdain as some Michigan steelhead anglers reserve for suckers. I've seen the banks of a heavily fished Great Lake tributary lined with the corpses of redhorse, longnose, white, and other species of sucker. Some with a hook still in their mouth, having been interred into their grassy grave with a kick strong enough to snap the line. Montana whitefish sometimes meet with a similar demise. Like the suckers, the whitefish's capital crime isn't being who they are but simply being who they aren't. I have a list of fish I want to catch in Montana, and the native whitefish is on it. So I'm proud to put a check beside its name.

My aversion to catching another one of these fish is rooted in fatigue and fear, not prejudice. It's been a long day, and the guy's comment about the bear still echoes in my head. He didn't say, "Don't worry, the bear won't eat you." That would've been a comforting statement. Instead, he said the bear would have "plenty of other things to eat," which implies that I'm an item on a plentiful menu. My mother-in-law loved to tell a story about a hiker who came face to face with a seven-hundred-pound grizzly deep in Yellowstone Park. Sensing his imminent demise, the guy dropped to his knees, clasped his hands, looked to the heavens, and prayed. "Dear Lord, I've lived a good life and have asked for little. All I ask now is that this be a Christian bear." A look of calm came over the magnificent beast's face. Then it dropped to its rear knees, clasped its mighty paws, looked up toward bear heaven, and said, "Dear Lord, I thank you for this bountiful meal you've set before me today."

I lower the windows far enough for the river to sing me to sleep but not so far that a bear might reach in and pluck me out like a pickle from a jar. When I wake, a misty veil of fog blankets the river. I get out of the truck and look for paw prints but find no signs that a bear had visited in the night. I want to see some different scenery this morning, so I drive to the access near Fishtrap Creek. Boulders the size of refrigerators and ovens line the bank on my side of the river, and a mountain rises from the far shore, shading the water from the sun's first light. I sit on a sofa-sized rock and eat a cup of yogurt for breakfast.

Only a few fish feed from the surface, and the ones that do lack focus and commitment. I stay on the rock for over an hour, and—for the first time since I arrived in Montana—I think seriously about my dog. Last night, I dreamt about him. I was the fifty-seven-year-old man I am now, but Sunny was young and athletic. His body was in perfect shape: no tumors, scars, or growths. I threw a stick, but he didn't retrieve it. He just pawed at my hand until I petted his head. That was all he wanted. I wonder what a psychiatrist would tell me the dream meant. Something about getting old, dying, or regretting my relationship with my mother? When I look in a mirror, I don't see a fifty-seven-year-old man with thinning hair and a graying beard. I see a young man, barely out of adolescence. So maybe I just saw Sunny through that same mirror.

When the trico hatch is on, clouds of tiny flies will hover above the river. I drive along the highway, looking for those clouds, but the air is clear. It must be a few days too early still. When I drive over a bridge, I see hundreds of swallows dancing and darting like Messerschmitts in a dogfight. But they're not fighting each other; instead, they're in hot pursuit of tiny flies. I park beside the river, and the water is thick with rising fish in the bridge's shadow. More whitefish, I suspect, and even though I thought I was finished with whitefish last night, I pull on my waders and tie on one of the small purple mayflies I bought in Livingston. As expected, I don't hook the first fish that rises to my fly. I need a slight hesitation to catch these whitefish. So I whisper *God Save the Queen* before setting the hook on the subsequent rise. The fish is powerful. It hauls the loose line from the river when it swims for the deepest water under the bridge. "A big whitefish," I think. All the whitefish I caught yesterday had three stages of their fight. First, they bolted from the scene. Then, after a brief struggle, they went lifeless like a waterlogged stick, saving their energy for the final stage of bronco bucking in the net. This one doesn't enter stage two, and when it jumps from the river, I see a rosy spot on its gill plate and a spicy pink stripe along the entire length of its body. It's a rainbow trout and a large one at that. There's a lot of moss in this section of the Big Hole River, and the rainbow wraps several globs of this stuff around my line, causing me to worry that the added weight will impede the rod's ability to protect the tippet. But, somehow, I land this trout with about a pound of moss. I release the fish on the edge of the bridge's shadow, and when it swims into the light, its namesake stripe ignites into a brilliant fire-red.

I catch three more nice brook trout. Again, these are fine fish by Big Hole standards, but they'd be trophies by my small-stream, home-water benchmarks.

And then it happens. I see *that* fish rising next to one of the bridge's piers. It's a large brown trout, porpoising just like the one on the

Beaverhead two nights ago. I'm not as nervous as I was then, but I don't have the steady hands of a jeweler, either. My first two casts are short. The fish either doesn't see the fly or doesn't want to move to get it. When I cast to the right spot, the trout comes up for the fly, then pushes it to the side with its nose. It happens again, so I replace the little purple fly with a size 18 Roberts Yellow Drake, another Michigan fly that works well for picky fish. When the fly lands about three feet above the trout, I hold my breath as the yellow imposter drifts naturally toward the target. The big trout eats the fly without hesitating. I lift my rod too fast and too hard. The tippet snaps, and *that* fish is gone.

The birds have returned to roost under the bridge, and all the fish have stopped rising. There are no more flies for either of them to eat. The tricos probably won't hatch reliably for another day or two, so I reconsider my options. I could drive to the Ruby River, Poindexter Slough, or back to the Beaverhead. I've only peeled the outer layer off those onions. As an alternative, Jerry told me about another river named Rock Creek. He said I could get there by taking Chief Joseph Pass from Wisdom, then following Highway 93 north along Camp Creek and the Bitterroot River. Much like gravitational fields keep the planets in orbit, some invisible force at a distance draws me toward fresh adventures. Rock Creek will be the next stage of my trip.

CHAPTER 7

Missouri

I am from Missouri. You've got to show me.
                                    —WILLARD DUNCAN VANDIVER

I WADE FROM THE BIG HOLE RIVER, PUT MY ROD IN ITS CASE, THEN store my reel in a canvas bag with ten others—eight of which won't come out for the entire trip. Between bites of a tomato and cheese sandwich, I contemplate my next move the way a monk might contemplate his navel. A Subaru wagon with Missouri plates rattles down the rutted road, skids to a stop, and a guy with a tie-dye buff around his neck rolls out, pulls on his waders, and hurries into the river to cast. He doesn't look for rising fish, assess the current, or do anything else I think he should. He just flogs the water like it stole his wife.

Why bother to fish if you're going to do it like that? I think. But maybe someone or something did steal his wife. Or his job. Or his hope. I don't know the crosses he bears, just like he doesn't know mine. He doesn't seem mad or sad, but he doesn't seem intent on catching a fish, either. The scene advances like a Shakespearean problem play with no role for me, so I finish my sandwich and bounce back out through the potholes. When I turn from the rough road onto the highway, I see a sticker on the Subaru's bumper: VETERAN.

If I were a crow, the place on Rock Creek where Jerry Kustich suggested I fish would be a thirty-mile flight, mainly to the north and a little to the west. But I'm a man in a Suburban, so my shortest route is back to the east through Wise River and Divide, north toward Butte, and then west through Anaconda. Instead, I opt to head west and drive an extra fifty miles to see Chief Joseph Pass and the Bitterroot River. Later in the trip, when I'm bored and bothered by my own company, I might take the shorter route. But spending time alone and making some sense of a challenging year is one of the reasons I'm here.

Seeing the veteran from Missouri reminded me of my childhood, and now—as I drive toward Wisdom—I think about my mom. For the first eighteen years of my life, she and I lived in small Illinois towns within a few miles of the Mississippi River—just south of St. Louis, Missouri. My father left before I was old enough to know him, and after that, my mom remarried a World War II veteran who treated me like a son and taught me things little boys rarely get taught. War is nothing like the movies, for instance, and no matter how hard you try, you can never unsee a person die. I think he could have taught me many other things too, but he died when I was six years old, and—although my mom remarried—she basically raised me alone.

Growing up in the Great Depression, my mom abandoned school at fifteen, had her first child at sixteen, and learned most of what she knew through hard knocks and folklore. She liked to say the Mississippi was the biggest river in the world, and—when I was learning to spell—she taught me a song and a joke about the river's name.

"Mississippi is a big river," she'd say. "Can you spell it?"

"Em eye es es eye es es eye pee pee eye," I would sing.

"Wrong," she'd say. "Eye tee. That's how you spell *it*." Then she'd laugh so hard I could see the fillings in her teeth.

She owned a bar that catered to ironworkers and railroaders—men who smoked unfiltered cigarettes, cussed without regret, and shook salt into their beer because nobody trusted a man who didn't. One of those men worked on the Mississippi River bridges, and when he bragged about seeing catfish big enough to eat three kids of my size, I pestered my mom until she took me fishing there. The river was a magnificent, long lake, and the fishing and playing were best right after the wake from a large barge pushed water onto the bank. We caught catfish, carp, and drum, but none were big enough to eat even one kid of my size. Toward the end of the day, a whirlpool formed just offshore, and my mom told me to get my ass away from the bank. A week later, a kid from our town drowned in one of those things, and my mom never took me fishing in the Mississippi again.

Even though the Missouri River flows into the Mississippi just north of St. Louis, I didn't know—or think—much about that river when I was a kid. To me, it was just water under a bridge my mom and I drove over on our way to Colorado for one of our great trout expeditions. If I had paid better attention to my elementary school teachers—mainly the ones who tried to teach me about Lewis and Clark—I would have known then that the Missouri River comes from Montana. And I would have known that the Jefferson, the Madison, and the Gallatin are the rivers that form the Missouri. And perhaps today—as I drive into the tiny town of Wisdom—I would know that Lewis and Clark originally called the Big Hole River the *Wisdom* River to honor one of Thomas Jefferson's "cardinal virtues."

I buy fuel and ice at one of Wisdom's two gas stations and then stop at a small national park about ten miles out of town. Several wooden teepee frames mark a place where about eight hundred people of the Nez Percé tribe camped along the North Fork of the Big Hole River in August 1877. They were led by a chief named Looking Glass, and they fled from Idaho to escape forced confinement on a reservation there, seeking refuge here in the Big Hole Basin. They didn't want to fight with the men and women of Montana, and the men and women of Montana didn't want to fight with them. But a US Army battalion of about one hundred sixty men and one howitzer was on their track, and those men wanted to fight. They didn't want to negotiate, take prisoners, or do anything else compassionate people might. So on the morning of August 9, the Battle

of the Big Hole began, and—when the last gun fired the following day—
more than one hundred people were dead. Many were Nez Percé women
and children. As I look across the battlefield today, I wonder if any of
their blood flowed down the Big Hole into the Jefferson, the Missouri,
and, ultimately, into the Mississippi near the place I would one day be
born—a poetic yet ridiculous notion.

The Nez Percé survivors continued to migrate through Montana
and north toward Canada. Army troops caught them near the Bear Paw
Mountains, and it was there that a Cheyenne scout killed Looking Glass.
Shortly after that, Joseph—a Nez Percé chief who had long hoped for
peace—made his famous surrender speech:

> I am tired of fighting. Our chiefs are killed; Looking Glass is dead,
> Too-hul-hul-sote is dead. The old men are all dead. It is the young men
> who say yes or no. He who led on the young men is dead. It is cold,
> and we have no blankets; the little children are freezing to death. My
> people, some of them, have run away to the hills, and have no blankets,
> no food. No one knows where they are—perhaps freezing to death. I
> want to have time to look for my children, to see how many I can find.
> Maybe I shall find them among the dead. Hear me, my chiefs! I am
> tired; my heart is sick and sad. From where the sun now stands, I will
> fight no more forever.

About twenty minutes after leaving the battleground, I'm in Idaho. A
minute later, I'm back in Montana, where I stop at the Lost Trail Powder
Mountain rest area and park next to a car with Missouri plates. A mom,
a dad, three kids, and two dogs emerge like clowns from a Volkswagen at
the Shriner's Circus. The dad says *hey* to me, then tells the kids to *worsh*
their hands when they're done. One kid complains that the cooler *dudn't
have any orange sodies* left. I wonder if we are related.

The road north from Lost Trail cuts through the mountains, and—
for the first time on this trip—I grip the steering wheel with enough
pressure to make my knuckles turn chalky white. I wasn't always like
this. Things like driving through narrow switchbacks or across long, high
bridges weren't always stressful. But sometime during my thirty years of

mostly stress-free driving in Michigan's Upper Peninsula, I forgot how to forget about being afraid.

I stop for my second lunch in Hamilton, about two miles past the Skalkaho Highway. While trying to eat the most mountainous BLT sandwich in a state named for mountains, I look up the weather forecast on my phone: clear skies with little wind. When Todd Tanner counseled me on fishing in Montana, he said, "One last bit of advice. Find a good weather app and put it on your phone, then pay attention to it. Temps are important, and precipitation, but the wind is the biggest thing. Before you spend time driving to your next destination, check and make sure it's not going to blow and blow and blow."

Todd's advice was for Montana rivers in general, but especially for the Missouri River. To see what's happening there, I check the forecast for Craig, Montana: light wind for the rest of the day and the same for tomorrow and the day after. Indecision Tim—my alter ego who has peacefully slept somewhere in my head for the past few days—wakes up now and points out that Craig is about a three-hour drive from Hamilton. Fully awake and eager to work his sorcery, Indecision Tim calls a fly shop in Craig to ask if the fishing will be good this evening. The woman's answer is as positive as it is predictable. Indecision Tim tells her we'll be there around five-thirty.

I drive through Lolo and then Missoula, where I briefly travel over and beside the Clark Fork River. Then I wind off and on along the Blackfoot River on Highway 200 until I take the exit for Wolf Creek. When I get to Craig, the first three buildings on the right side of the road are fly shops, and drift boats outnumber the cars and trucks in their parking lots by three to one. I enter the shop I'd called and tell the woman I'm the guy who phoned from Hamilton. "I'm here to catch a trout," I say.

She sets me up with some dry flies, emergers, and a nymph to fish as a dropper just a few inches below the dry. She tells me to access the Missouri River from Craig Frontage Road, which runs along the east side for about five miles south of the bridge in town. The trout are everywhere, she says, so I can fish anywhere that looks good to me. When I ask about a place to camp, she directs me to a small campground in town but warns it can be a little rowdy at night. I tell her I have earplugs and bourbon.

I pull into a parking area about a mile and a half above the bridge. It's a spacious lot, but there's only one other car, and the people in it aren't fishing. I'm on a cliff overlooking the river, with a small trail descending through the rocks and shrubs. I see two trout rising near the bottom of the path, and—with that—I decide this spot looks good to me.

About halfway down the trail, I remember that I forgot to worry about rattlesnakes. But the woman in the fly shop didn't mention snakes, and the two trout are still rising close to the bank, about fifteen feet upstream from where the trail meets the river. So I forget about snakes again and focus on my breathing. And the trout. The vegetation in the water here looks like the moss I battled at the Big Hole, but when I pick a strand from the river, it's a leafy sort that shouldn't cause much trouble.

The river here is about four hundred feet across, and although it appears to be deeper, it feels like one of my favorite stretches on the Escanaba River back in Michigan. Instinctively, I tie on a size 18 Robert's Yellow Drake that works wonderfully there. Casting is different here, though. I must accommodate the rhythm of the trout's rises, like always, but I also have to place my fly in one of the irregularly spaced openings between the drifting vegetation. My first cast lands on a floating weed and drifts right by the trout as it takes a natural fly from a small patch of open water. My second cast does the same. I drive my third cast harder for accuracy, and the little fly smacks onto the water's surface in an opening between the weeds. The trout darts for the middle of the river, leaving a massive wake to reveal what might have been if I had made a better cast.

Another trout rises about twenty feet upstream and then a foot below that again. The fish drifts downstream, grabbing all the flies from the gaps between the floating weeds, much like a cedar waxwing cleaning them from the sky. I pick a relatively large opening about halfway between the trout and me, cast my fly into it, and wait. After the fish takes two more flies, its subsequent rise should be to mine, and it is. The fish reacts to the hook immediately, quickly deploying every trick it's learned to undo a predicament like this. The trout jumps twice, then pulls all the loose line through the rod's guides, followed by another twenty or thirty feet off the reel. Next, it swims a large arc downstream and back toward me. I can't keep tension on the fish with this much line in the water. The trout sheds the hook and swims away.

There are no more rising fish in the weeds along the shore, but a pod of trout feeds a little downstream from me, about thirty feet from the bank. I wade toward the fish, but two steps put the river's surface an inch below the top of my waders. I can't get far enough from the cliff to make a decent backcast, and the trout are beyond the range of my roll cast, so I'm stuck casting downstream and over my left shoulder. When my first few casts are short, I move down and out on my tippy toes, hoping the river bottom will rise enough for me to make a comfortable cast. My foot bumps into a boulder about half the size of a sofa footstool, and I use it to rise a few more inches out of the water.

I target the closest fish, using a reach cast to place the fly several feet above the trout with enough slack to get a drag-free drift over its head. The cast looks good, but the trout doesn't take the fly. I watch it eat two more real flies, and when I cast again, the trout makes a splashy rejection. Above the water, I see a swarm of caddisflies I hadn't seen before. The woman at the fly shop sold me a few low-wing caddis with CDC feathers and said I should use them instead of the more popular elk-hair style. CDC is a hyper-buoyant feather from the rear of a duck and an abbreviation for the French phrase *cul de canard* that translates loosely to English as *ass of duck*. Despite all the possibilities a duck-ass fly presents, I instinctively reach for a pattern I've had success with back in Michigan: the Henryville Special.

My first cast with the new fly is short but my second is on the mark, and the fish takes it. The trout bolts toward the middle of the river, and—to counter the counter maneuver I believe it has planned—I lift my rod high to get as much of the line out of the water as possible. As I expect, the fish loops back toward me, but this time my line stays tight. The rainbow leaps twice, swims straight for a drift boat about fifty feet downstream, then tires and follows my tugs toward shore. I net the fish in the weeds, roughly where I'd hooked the first one earlier. It's a light-colored female, with a silver-rose cheek and chrome-pink stripe along its side.

I lose two more fish and land one before an un-forecasted thunderstorm pushes me off the river. When I get back to the parking area, a guide is drinking beer and watching the storm light up the western sky like a photographer's strobe.

"How'd you do?" he asks.

When I say I hooked five fish and landed two, he slings far more praise than my performance deserves, but four empty bottles in a six-pack of Sierra Nevada Pale Ale on his truck's tailgate disclose the source of his exuberance.

The storm arrives in full force just as I get back to camp. I wait out the heavy stuff in the cab, then, after the rain ends, I sit at the picnic table and eat two boiled eggs with a small block of pepper jack cheese. I leave the liftgate on my SUV raised to provide some light, and when I go back to get another Miller Lite, I see hundreds—more likely thousands—of caddisflies have infiltrated the place I plan to sleep. When I finally lie down, I put two lanterns by my feet to lure the flies away from my face. Then I let the earplugs and bourbon do their work.

The following morning, I hook and land a large rainbow trout. I don't know it then, but I'll land only one trout larger than this during my entire trip, and that one will come on my last day of fishing in Montana. I release the fish, sit on the bank, and watch the twenty-one-incher glide into the darkest part of the river. Today's my fifth day in Montana, and I feel a rhythm building inside me. I haven't "kicked the river's ass" like the guys at the campground said they had last night, but the river hasn't kicked mine either. When I find contentment, I usually gain perspective; when I gain perspective, I usually find contentment. Like the chicken and the egg, I don't know which comes first. I'm just happy when one of them does.

Later in the day, an afternoon thunderstorm—another missed by the forecasters—rolls through Lewis and Clark County, leaving gale-force winds in its wake. Winds that blow so hard in the evening that my line extends at a perfect ninety-degree angle any time I hold my rod above my head. Twice I bury my fly into the back of my shirt while trying to cast, but luckily the hook never finds flesh. Somehow I fool one fish on the Henryville Special, but that one breaks off immediately after I set the hook. Perspective and contentment fight off a slight tinge of disappointment.

When I fish the following morning, two large trout break off the last of my size 18 Robert's Yellow Drakes with unstoppable runs down the river. "Such a hard problem to have," Roxanne says later when I tell her about it. The local fly shop stocks neither this fly nor the Henryville Special. They stock flies that work, but—more important for them—they stock flies that sell. I believe presentation, size, silhouette, and color—often, but not always, in that order—are the keys to dry-fly fishing. But when fly anglers fish a river as much as they do the Missouri here, it helps if your fly looks like one the trout often catch, but unlike one that often catches the trout. Perhaps that explains why over two evenings and two mornings—in between battles with un-forecasted winds—I hooked twelve fish and landed five with those foreign flies.

I didn't know what to expect from the Missouri River, but I let it show me, and I'm glad I did. Einstein taught us that time and space are interchangeable, and fifty years ago is just two-thousand river miles away from where I stand. And it's there, somewhere after this river joins the Mississippi, that a small boy sits on the bank and drinks an orange soda while his mom tells him about catfish big enough to eat him. He knows more about death than a boy his age should, and he worries you can't be uneaten by a catfish. But he's a fisherman who wants to catch a fish in this river. He doesn't know it, but one day he'll venture far upstream and catch some nice ones.

CHAPTER 8

Uniquely Portable Magic

Not that you have to be there;
books are a uniquely portable magic.
—STEPHEN KING, ON WRITING

WHEN I WAS A KID, OUR CAR AND MOBILE HOME SMELLED LIKE WIN-
ston cigarette smoke, and—by osmosis—so did I. My mom loved to
smoke, and most of her friends shared her passion for the game, especially Uncle Smokey. Uncle Smokey wasn't my uncle by blood or marriage, just a close family friend who wore a black captain's hat, drove a
Harley-Davidson cruiser, and called me Timothy J., as though I had one
of those southern double names. For my mom, Uncle Smokey, and their
friends, cigarettes were the smartphones of the day. Everyone had to have
one, whether it was good for them or not. So I lived my childhood in a
cloud of smoke, and much like a fish doesn't know it's wet until it's not,
I didn't know I stank until I didn't.

Here in Montana, the Big Sky sun has broiled my body's veneer of
sunscreen, sweat, river water, and mud into a funk that could run a pig off
a manure wagon. Even Mom and Uncle Smokey would raise a brow at
this achievement. But no one in the fly shop complains. They, too, are fly
anglers, and like me, they just want to hang out with like-minded people

and buy some things they may or may not need. I settle on a half-dozen flies and a retractor gadget to keep my other gadgets and gizmos from getting away. When I pay the kid behind the counter, I submit to the stench and ask for directions to the nearest truck stop with a shower.

The kid's answer is Montana's version of New England's "You can't get there from here." So I drive south to Helena and then west toward Missoula. At a travel plaza a few miles before Missoula, I give ten dollars to a lady with tangerine hair, a missing tooth, and a distinctive scar under her left eye. In return, she hands me two avocado-colored towels, a matching washcloth, and a key to room number two. It's a practical room with a sink, a toilet, and a shower, all clean enough to ease my worries about not wearing the cheap flip-flops Roxanne said would keep my feet from becoming athletic. Fifteen minutes later, I'm back at the truck, and—like the label on the body-wash bottle promised—I smell like a Caribbean island vacation. But the inside of the Suburban does not. The once-sweet smell of adhesive, fabric, and plastic that saturated the cab when I first drove off the Chevrolet lot is gone. In its place is a remnant of the crud I just scrubbed from my body, plus something I might blame on my dog if he were here. But despite all that, I smell the books.

I have a box of books on the floorboard behind the driver's console, next to the place I lay my head at night to sleep. Anyone on a trip like this should have one of these boxes. In mine, I have *The Longest Silence* by Tom McGuane, *Angling Days* by Bob DeMott, *Trout Madness* and *Trout Magic* by John Voelker, *A Place on the Water* and *The River Home* by Jerry Dennis, and every book Jerry Kustich wrote about his life in Montana.

I first read Tom McGuane's book nearly twenty years ago on a backwoods Upper Peninsula fishing trip. Huddled in the back of my truck with a battery-powered light flooding the pages, I learned that McGuane's voice was everything but silent:

> I'm afraid the best angling is always a respite from burden. Good anglers should lead useful lives, and useful lives are marked by struggle, and difficulty, and even pain. Perhaps the agony of simple mortality should be enough. But probably it is not. As they say in South America, everyone knows that they are going to die; yet nobody believes it.

Human lapses of this kind enable us to fish, fornicate, overeat, and bet on horses.

I had never bet on horses—and still haven't—but I had varying degrees of familiarity with the other pastimes. I felt like McGuane knew me or, at least, knew who I wanted to be. His fishing stories were the kind I'd come to prefer: fishing stories that weren't really about fishing.

When I reread that book now, the deckle-edged pages and powerful prose remind me of a time when I hoped—as it had for McGuane—fly fishing could become my way of looking at the world. I was at a stage somewhere between neophyte and whatever place I'm in now. I could tell the difference between a mayfly and a caddis, I knew 6X tippet was finer than 4X, and I had caught several fish on a dry fly I had tied on my own. But every large trout I would catch and every memorable cast I would make were still in front of me then. Like most of us, I hope and believe many more notable fish and casts will come. But those fly-fishing *firsts*—much like a first date, a first kiss, and a first love—only come once, and we need to keep reminders of that *pre-first* excitement in our box.

Bob DeMott's invitation—and Roxanne's insistence that I accept it—are the primary reasons I'm in Montana. Of course, like hydrogen and oxygen need help to make water, other things had to happen. But you don't make water without two H's and one O, and I don't make it to Montana without Bob's invitation and Roxanne's encouragement. Bob is not a Montanan; instead, he is a self-described *regular tourist*, and for a summer month each year, he adheres to the Thoreauvian model. It's a calling he says compels him to *travel deeply in one place or region rather than widely and see what results*. It's worked well for him, and in a few days, Bob and I will fish, eat, drink, and laugh together. And after a predictable evening storm passes through the valley, we'll sit on a log beside the Madison River and wait for a nice fish to rise. But until then, when it's late at night and I want to feel what Bob describes as *the unimpeded flow of a contextual story that binds together experience, gives it emphasis and vitality, and creates a running thread of participatory, immersive knowledge*, his honest memoir about discovering and mastering all things trout is—as Bob describes the trouting experience in general—*a movable feast that travels well.*

I've read John Voelker's books more times than Yogi Berra is said to have said something he didn't say. I've internalized the yarns to the point I often tell the stories as though they've happened to me. And in some manner, I suppose they have. I might not read from either book during this trip, but both are first editions, and they are most responsible for the sweet smell of vanilla emanating from the box. *Testament of a Fisherman*—the prelude in *Trout Magic*—is the type of prose a person might have chiseled onto their gravestone. With 207 words that start with *I fish because I love to*, and end with *I suspect that so many of the concerns of men are equally unimportant—and not nearly so much fun*, Voelker made answering the "Why do we fish?" question as difficult for any writer who came after him as Patsy Cline made singing "Crazy" for any singer who came after her.

I bought Jerry Dennis's book, *A Place on the Water*, on May 9, 1995, at Snowbound Books in Marquette, Michigan. Four days before that, I attended a dinner for the honor-society students in our electrical engineering department at Michigan Tech. George Swenson Jr.—a University of Illinois professor whose father founded our department—spoke to our group. At seventy-two years of age and largely overlooked by the balding gene, Professor Swenson stood at the podium with the slight bend of a man who had ducked through doorways for most of his life. He repeatedly ran one hand through his thick white hair as he told us about building an impromptu antenna to record the first transmissions from the Soviet satellite Sputnik. I remember details of that night partly because of those recordings' historical significance and partly because of the flair with which Professor Swenson told his story. But mostly, I remember that night because of the phone call.

Roxanne and our children were at a Cinco de Mayo party with friends in Houghton's twin city of Hancock, where I would be if I were not our speaker's host at the dinner. So when the server interrupted Professor Swenson to announce a call for me, I expected to hear Roxanne tell me one of our kids had sprained a joint or broken a bone at the party. Instead, an unexpected voice said I should come to the hospital. Something was wrong with Roxanne.

I returned to the presentation room, apologized to Professor Swenson, and told him I needed to go to the hospital. My colleague and good friend Warren—who must have noticed my face was the color of Professor Swenson's hair—insisted on driving. When we got to the hospital, the doctor said Roxanne had had a stroke, and they needed to move her to the regional center in Marquette. A man named Roxy told me he would drive the ambulance fast, and under no circumstance should I try to keep up with him. Warren said he'd make sure I got there safely.

We stopped once for gas and coffee and to take a pee. A guy in the store smelled just like Uncle Smokey, and when he bought a pint of Wild Turkey and two packs of Marlboros, I got mad. Why wasn't this guy in an ambulance instead of Roxanne? When I got outside the store, I screamed with all the strength my diaphragm could supply. Warren let me finish, then grabbed my arm and said, "Come on, we have to go." The drive to Marquette takes a little under two hours, and I suppose that's how long it took that night, but I don't remember much about it. Warren was in the middle of a personal and painful divorce, and I was at the beginning of something neither of us understood. He drove, and I watched the trees appear and disappear in the tunnel of light before us.

In the candid and sometimes circular way doctors talk, the neurologist said there wasn't much he could say. Roxanne could have a near-perfect recovery, or she could have another stroke that night and die. There was no way to know. A seemingly endless stream of people in white jackets came into the room, shining lights in her eyes and poking her left foot and hand with dull needles. I watched it all from a small chair in the corner. And as believers and nonbelievers do in times like these—I told God I was ready to make any deal it would take to fix whatever was wrong. An hour or two later, a nurse took me to another room to sleep on a cot. Warren was already there.

Warren stayed for two days but then needed to get back to Houghton. I went with him to get my truck, or someone brought it to me. I just don't remember. On Tuesday, I went to a local bookstore to find something to read. *A Place on the Water* was on the "of local interest" rack. On the back of the book, people like Nick Lyons and John Gierach said it was an excellent book by a superb writer. That sounded good and would have meant a lot more if I had known who those guys were at that time. The author's biography said Jerry Dennis lived in northern Michigan with his wife and two sons. In the table of contents, I saw that one of the essays was called "A Big Two-Hearted Pilgrimage," in reference to the only story about fishing in the Upper Peninsula I had read at that time.

I sat beside Roxanne's bed and read Jerry's book. *Amazing, the way the world grows smaller as we grow older*, he began the first sentence. *I clench my eyes tightly and row*, he ended the last. In between, he told me about fathers and sons, boys and fish, kindness and empathy, love and desire, hope and strength, search and discovery. He showed me a young man's love for the outdoors, his family, and the beautiful, kind woman he adored. He described a life of wonder in Michigan's Upper Peninsula. A life that Roxanne and I had moved here three years before to build for ourselves. A life I now desperately hoped we could still have.

Leonardo da Vinci said, "A painter should begin every canvas with a wash of black because all things in nature are dark except where exposed by the light." In normal times, I approach life the way I approach fishing. After one hundred unanswered casts, my next loop unrolls with all the promise of the first. In abnormal times, though, the empty casts are too much. The pleasure is not worth the pain, and a string of pointless casts and empty retrieves easily defeats me. Hope gets lost in a wash of black, and I can't find a light. But Jerry's words brought light to my shadows, especially this passage from "The Hand of the Earth":

> There had been times in the past when Gail questioned my reasons for fishing. She understood the urge to be near water, to go out early in the morning and see the mist rising above it, to stand and feel the current against your legs and hear the murmuring and chuckling sounds around you. But she never comprehended why I could get so excited about hooking a fish on a tiny lure and pulling it in. Now she knew.
>
> "It felt," she said, "like the hand of the earth reached up and grabbed my line."

Roxanne is a small and quiet woman of the still waters run deep sort. She's the first to pick up a shovel when dirt needs to be moved. She's the last to put it down. She sees through fake people the way Superman sees through walls, and if she can't leap a tall building in a single bound, she usually gets it on her second or third try. She doesn't like the sight of blood, but she runs straight to your side with a towel when you're bleeding. And in those times when I stare at the tiled floor, hoping I won't hear what the doctors have to say if I can't see them, Roxanne looks straight into and through their eyes. She is an oak in all the ways I am a willow.

So if the neurologist had known who he was talking about that first night, he would have simply said Roxanne would recover, and he would have said it with all the confidence of a falcon in flight. Sure, sometimes the wheels on the little engine wouldn't turn, and the doctors and nurses said she wouldn't get all those cars up the hill. But every word of doubt was another scoop of coal in the little engine's firebox. She didn't think she could get up that hill. She knew it.

Now, over twenty years later, a long-since recovered Roxanne is in Michigan looking after our fourteen-year-old dog, and I'm in the back of the Suburban on a ridge beside Rock Creek. I'm sheltering from a thunderstorm that will boom long into the night, so I reach into the box and pull out Jerry Kustich's book, *At the River's Edge*.

If you were an Israelite hoping to cross the Gulf of Suez about three thousand years ago, no one could give you better advice than Moses. Sure, you could take a chance and just show up at the Red Sea, but you'd be much better off following the guidance of a guy who knows all the good places to cross. And if you are a fly fisherman in southwestern Montana today, Jerry Kustich is your Moses.

Nick Lyons once wrote that Jerry is "quietly but fiercely independent, free from the commercialization that cloaks the fly fishing world like a fungus, and full of a dozen key skills." Indeed. Jerry writes the truth. Not in the sense that he doesn't exaggerate the size of a fish, although I doubt he does that either. But in the sense that he tells you who, what, and why he loves.

Psychologists say every person has a baker's dozen of secrets they don't tell anyone. Of course, that's an average, and fly anglers make up for all the Catholics who tell everything to their priests. Montana's famous rivers have few secrets left, but if you're willing to walk and get off the well-trampled paths, you might sometimes feel you've found one. Jerry's advice has guided me to a few of those places. And although Rock Creek is not a secret, for Jerry, it is sacred, and sacred is much more significant than secret for anglers like him and me.

On the bed in the back of the Suburban—between blasts of thunder—I listen to Rock Creek rhythmically whittle the western Montana stones into sand. I think about something Norman Maclean famously wrote about another Montana river: "Under the rocks are the words, and some of the words are theirs." Jerry's words are in his books, but they're under the rocks, too, reminding us about precious things like true love:

> Opportunity doesn't always knock, sometimes it whispers. Vision is the result of not closing your mind and heart to all the possibilities.

About treasured things, like ancient Martin guitars:

> Although it was unlikely that my talent would ever be a worthy match, I was convinced of one thing: such a fine instrument would have the power to make a significant statement in a life searching for purpose.

And about "Tipping Points" in life, when fly fishing is how we pass the time between funerals. How happy endings are the exception, not the rule, and when people get sick and don't get better, a good fishing story can help get us through:

> It is the fishing story that creates a desire to seek a spiritual depth in the quiet places where one can be alone, unabashed by the din of modern civilization. In touch with waters that flow from the heart of the Earth, it just may be that an angler is as close to true inspiration as possible in today's world.

Legend says that when asked about his most famous sculpture, Michelangelo said, "It's easy. You just chip away everything that doesn't look like David." It's an exaggerated analogy, but the best fishing writers sculpt their stories that way. The artist starts with a river and some fish, then chips away everything that isn't about life. When you find stories like that, put them in your box.

CHAPTER 9

Just in Time

If you don't know how to manage time,
time can rule you like a tyrant.

—FRANK PARTNOY

NORMAN MACLEAN'S ACCLAIMED STORY ABOUT FAMILY AND FISH TAKES place on the Big Blackfoot River. But when Brad Pitt's stunt double—Jason Borger—stands atop a Volkswagen-sized boulder to cast forward a revolution in fly fishing, the Gallatin, not the Blackfoot, is the river running through it. I wake up this morning about two hundred miles from that boulder. Yet when I climb from my truck and slide down the bank to Rock Creek, I feel like I've stepped onto the stage where Robert Redford filmed *the movie*.

Names can be misleading. Near my home in Michigan, you can fish Perch Creek all summer without catching a single perch—with a similar story for the Carp River. And any name that involves mosquitos, snakes, or bears is probably verbal chaff deployed by selfish anglers to deceive their rivals. But like Honest Abe, the Invisible Man, and Death Valley, some people and places are named for their most notable features. So it is with Rock Creek, at least where I stand this morning.

The river here bounces from boulder to boulder the way a pinball ricochets off bumpers. Resolute but unhurried. Trusting gravity the way a shaman trusts intuition. The water's as cold as a witch's kiss—the air even more so. On my third cast, a cutthroat trout with a goldenrod body and brilliant blood-red slash along its throat engulfs a purple mayfly I bought at the shop in Craig—reminding me again that purple is the new gray. When my hands get wet, my fingers compete with the water and air to see which can be the coldest. At the first hint of numbness, I return to my truck and eat a bowl of oatmeal.

In his book *Wait*, Frank Partnoy tells us to procrastinate with a purpose. We should make important decisions at the latest possible moment, but no later. Unlike the little sycophant in the front row waving his hand before the teacher completes her next question, we should wait until we need to make a decision and settle on an answer. Having *an answer* before we need it is not as important as having *the answer* just in time. Even in a high-noon duel with Bat Masterson or Curly Bill Brocius, it's okay—even good—to hold your fire until you've had a chance to aim.

This just-in-time approach to decision-making has served me well. I make a pancake on the bank of the Beaverhead when the sun rises in the morning. I cast my fly to a shoal of whitefish on the Big Hole when it goes down. My next destination is like pornography was for good old Justice Stewart. I can't explain how or when I've known where to go next—I can only say I've known it when I've seen it. It's in that spirit that I now drive south from the campground.

The dirt road to the confluence with the West Fork is about thirty-five miles. It would take just ten extra minutes to drive the eighty-five-mile loop north and east on the paved highways. Of course, that route wouldn't follow Rock Creek, and—like a spawning redd for a salmon—Rock Creek is why I'm here. I want to see this place that has meant so much to my friend Jerry Kustich. Beyond that, I don't know where or when I plan to stop to fish again. There's a mixture of private and public land around the river, and small pull-offs along the narrow road provide places to park. But some are occupied, so as I crawl steadily to the south, I confront the *access problem*.

Mathematicians call this the *secretary problem*. Or, sometimes, the *sultan's dowry*, the *fussy suitor*, or the *marriage problem*. Regardless of what they call it, they use it to explain *optimal stopping* theory. To illustrate the puzzle, they ask you to imagine evaluating ten candidates for a job as your secretary. If you interview all the candidates before deciding, you can rank them from most to least qualified and hire the best person for the job. But because mathematicians enjoy complicating simple tasks, they change the rules. After interviewing a candidate, you must hire them or remove them from the pool and move on to the next. According to the mathematicians, there is an optimal decision rule, but even if you use it, you only have about a 40 percent chance of finding the best candidate for the job.

One more twist winds this problem into a nice, tight mess. Suppose someone might hire one or more of your candidates before you have a chance to meet them. Today is Saturday, and the cars and trucks parked in the pull-offs are signs that other people—anglers who have paid better attention to childhood lessons about early birds and worms—have already interviewed and hired most of the spots. Someone familiar with this river would likely know how to fish between the well-marked sites, but I'm not that someone, so I continue to drive south. Because my phone's GPS doesn't receive enough signal, I resort to a primitive book with illustrations that resemble the maps I'm used to seeing on my phone. The concept seems vaguely familiar.

Confucius said, "Roads were made for journeys, not destinations." He also told us to remember, "No matter where you go, there you are." Living in my truck for a week has given thoughts like these a home in my head—circular logic and clever quips that mean nothing and everything at the same time. The ideas agitate, and when Confucius takes the wheel, I stop looking for places to fish. The journey becomes my destination.

The scenery shines like a page from a *Visit Montana* guidebook. The road is well-traveled, but the forest is a wild place. Signs warn me to look out for bears, telling me to neither approach nor feed them. Like the labels advising me to take off my shirt before ironing or to empty my stroller before folding, these are unnecessary warnings. A great astronomer once said, "Two things are infinite, as far as we know—the universe and human stupidity." Albert Einstein proved the universe is not. The guy with ironing scars on his arm trying to feed a bear while his baby cries in a folded stroller makes a compelling case that our stupidity might be.

It's a relaxing drive, although every corner holds the possibility for a Rock Creek Road impasse. A predicament involving an informal negotiation to resolve who will drive in reverse until the road widens enough for the other vehicle to get by. But not all impasses are equal. When one happens on a hairpin turn on a hogback high above the valley floor, my palms glisten with sweat. I keep my eyes on the horizon and rejoice when the young lady in the Ford F-250 smiles and drives backward. I don't know the proper etiquette for this sort of thing, but I suspect the experienced locals prefer to go backward rather than watch an out-of-state greenhorn tumble down the side of the mountain. When I reach the Skalkaho Highway, I look for places to access the West Fork of Rock Creek.

Jerry told me to be sure to fish around the confluence with the West Fork, but every place I try to get in has a sign inviting me to stay the hell out. So I find a place to park, set out some bread and cheese, and cut up a tomato and cucumber for a sandwich. For the first week of this trip, I have planned not to have a plan. But my son, Daniel, will be here in less than two weeks, and I need a plan for that. We'll fish with a guide on the Madison River south of Ennis. And because the Suburban is cramped quarters for even one person, I need a different place for Daniel and me to sleep. With each bite of my sandwich, I worry more about not having a place to stay. My just-in-time approach to planning has worked fine for me, but I'm afraid it won't work for the two of us. So, after lunch, I take an unplanned drive through Anaconda, Butte, and Cardwell, then head south to the Madison River valley. For neither the first nor the last time in Montana, indecision may or may not be my problem.

⚬⚬

Some of my hockey buddies say we have a drinking team with a hockey problem. In the same spirit, people in Ennis say they have a drinking town with a fishing problem. The problem is so severe that some people consider Ennis the fly-fishing capital of the world, which, I suppose, is the sort of problem that doesn't need to be solved. There are several motels and lodges in and around the town and most have clever names to lure in anglers like me. One is actually called Lure Me Inn. The town has everything we'd need, including a bigger-than-life bronze statue of a fly fisherman fighting a trout. But, although the river flows through the town, I want to stay somewhere upstream, closer to its more famous sections.

Relying on the just-in-time approach to learning about Montana, I didn't do much homework. Because of that, the horizontal land formations called benches that flank the Madison River south of Ennis surprise me. At first glance, they appear to be agricultural artifacts. But much like the Mississippi River bluffs that border my childhood town, these benches are reminders that—on a geological clock—mighty rivers are like fidgety kids who can't sit still. They might let you contain them, but you can't control them.

Forty miles south of Ennis, I pull into the parking lot at Galloup's Slide Inn. Inside, Kelly Galloup stands near his extensive bins of flies, surrounded by several middle-aged men in crisply pressed pastel-colored shirts. Like seagulls circling a kid eating a bag of French fries, these guys hope Kelly will toss something tasty in their direction. But if you have a computer, tablet, or phone with access to the internet, you can get all the advice Kelly is willing to share, and you can get it at any time you'd like. These gentlemen seem to believe he retains a few secrets for his special friends—especially those who portend to buy a half dozen flies from his bins.

I go straight to the counter and ask a tall kid with remarkable tan lines around his eyes if it's possible to rent a room for a few nights in two weeks. When he says yes, I wish him blessings from God, pay the deposit, and ask about fishing and camping for the night. He tells me I'll catch fish anywhere, especially if I'm willing to stay out past dark, then mentions a few camping sites at the Raynolds Pass access, along with a campground at the upper end of Quake Lake.

After driving about a mile and a half south of the Slide Inn, I get my most spectacular just-in-time learning experience of the day. My first clue that something's amiss is a tree in the middle of the Madison River. Not an island with a tree on it. Just a lone tree rising from the river. Then I see a mountain without a face—the result of a 7.5 magnitude earthquake in 1959. This is the place where eighty million tons of rock slid at roughly one hundred miles per hour across the Madison River below Hebgen Dam. The disaster trapped hundreds of people and killed twenty-eight campers. A lake immediately formed between the dam and the slide, and—in less than a month—the US Army Corps of Engineers constructed an emergency spillway that still relieves pressure from the natural barrier. Once again, I'm reminded how we can contain, but not control.

I'm obsessing about what happened. Sixty years ago, at a campsite that's now at the bottom of Quake Lake, someone ate their last hot dog, poured a pan of water on the campfire, and went to sleep forever. I know life is fragile, but seeing a mountain's face scattered across a vale sobers me. The planet lets out a burp. Someone's mother gets battered by boulders and buried under two hundred feet of water. It's too much for me to handle, so I drive back to the Raynolds Pass access.

There's a small campground here, but tents and campers hold every site. I'm not sure what to do, so I send a text message to Justin Edge—the guide Daniel and I will fish with in a couple weeks. I know Justin because he's a close friend of a friend, and he invited me to send him a note anytime I had a question. "I'd fish $3 if you can," he texts back. And like the kid in the shop, Justin suggests I stay on the river well past dark. For sleeping, he recommends a rest area at Lyons Bridge or any out-of-the-way place I find to park.

Three Dollar Bridge was built over the Jefferson River in 1930, then moved to the Madison in 2001. It's one of the most famous trout-fishing access points in the country—something I did not learn just in time. Initially, the landowner asked anglers to pay three dollars per day to park and access the river. But in 2006, the Trust for Public Land ensured that the Three Dollar Bridge would provide permanent, public access for the Madison. You can still donate if you'd like, though.

A battalion of vehicles crowds the large parking areas on both sides of the bridge. It's the kind of thing that gives me the mental yips. *Where should I fish? How should I do it?* I park on the bridge's east side and walk down a trail to look at the river. Riffles sparkle like gemstones as far as I can see, both upstream and down. Fifty miles of riffles, I've read. I look back at the lot that holds my vehicle, then at the other across the river. It is the most crowded place I've ever parked to fish.

Back at my truck, I chat with two friendly men who've been here before. I tell them it's my first time on the Madison, and I'm not sure where or how to fish this water. They tell me the water's just water, the fish are just fish, and I shouldn't let the river intimidate me. I should take a small section of the river, work all the seams and pockets, and fish it like a small stream. One of the guys compliments my ragged waxed-cotton hat, and—for the sake of small talk—I say something about how it's the perfect hat for Michigan's Upper Peninsula. "We're from Michigan, too," one of the guys says.

I give them a copy of *The Habits of Trout*. "Maybe you guys will like some of these stories about fishing and living in the Upper Peninsula," I tell them. They invite me to follow them to the river along a trail that curves in the downstream direction along a ridge. After walking about a quarter of a mile, I stop near a couple of islands that divide the river into two smaller streams and ask the guys if this would be a good place to fish. One of them grins and says, "This is a spot on the Madison River. Of course it's a good place to fish." I introduce myself to this famous place by stepping into the water, sitting on a rock, putting my rod across my lap, letting both arms dangle to my side, and asking this fabled river to baptize me in the name of the cast, the drift, and the rainbow trout.

I have a remarkable view of the iconic bridge and the mountains that frame it. From my limited understanding of this region's geography, some peaks are in Montana and some are in Idaho. The bridge's steel trusses light up in the late-afternoon sun like a glimmering monument, providing rich contrast with the dark mountains in the background. Looking upstream toward the bridge, I count more than a dozen boulders, each big enough to support two or more anglers. I've tucked myself between the island and the river's east bank. On the other side, the Madison growls through a seemingly endless flow of riffles. On my side, smooth slicks and gentle eddies make it feel like a completely different river. It's the perfect place for our introduction.

The first sign of a fish is subtle. A nose pokes from a soft-water pocket between a boulder and the grassy bank. At first, I think I have imagined it. But when I see a fidgety caddis disappear at the exact time and place where the nose appears, I tie on my favorite emerger pattern. My first cast is a mess and, fortunately, so far off target that the trout has no clue it happened. I shuffle out into the river and put my next cast two feet above where I saw the nose. The fly vanishes, and I set the hook.

When Lewis and Clark christened this river in honor of their Secretary of State, James Madison, their men would have caught whitefish, grayling, and cutthroat trout in these waters. But in the late 1800s and early 1900s, the newly formed State of Montana stocked the river with rainbow and brown trout. By the time they stopped stocking browns in 1951 and rainbows in 1973, these fish had planted deep roots in the riffles. So although the fish on the end of my line is not a native, the blood in its veins comes from over seven generations of ancestors who knew no other home.

It's a big fish for me, but not for this river. It careens around the boulders, seeming to expect a rock to grab my line and release the hook from its mouth. That doesn't happen, and I net the rainbow at my knees, placing the net's handle between my legs so the rubber basket makes an underwater corral. I look down on the hundreds of oddly shaped and irregularly arranged freckles on its back—a pattern as familiar as the night sky but as unique as a fingerprint. Then, with the trout still in the water, I carefully do the deed the fish and the rocks could not. As the last tinges of emerald, crimson, and pink fade into the water and horizon, I see a swarm of caddis dancing just inches above the river's surface. Then a rainbow leaps high into the air as though attempting to free itself from an angler's hook. Then another. And another. I squeeze my fly to dry it, then shake it in some powder to make it new again. The fish ignore my casts, so I add some tippet to the bend of the hook and tie on a small sinking caddis emerger. I connect on my second cast. The fish leaps twice and takes advantage of a boulder in a way the other fish could not. The light is gone now, and—although both Justin and the kid at Kelly's shop said I should fish well past dusk—I retrieve the flyless line and walk the trail back to the truck.

I drive to the Raynolds Pass campground, hoping a spot might be open now, but none are. Some guys with a drift boat appear to be sleeping in the back of their truck in the parking area. So I park as far from them as possible and crawl into the back of the Suburban for the night. My phone picks up enough signal to download a message. It's from the guide Justin Edge:

> *I know it's late, but I just got canceled for tomorrow. Do you want to get together and fish?*

It's around 10 p.m. now, and my call makes it through. Justin and I plan to meet at Ennis in the morning. I apologize for calling so late, but he says it's not a problem. He was going to bed soon, and I had called him just in time.

CHAPTER 10

Guide's Day Off

How we spend our days is, of course, how we spend our lives.
—ANNIE DILLARD

I PULL INTO THE LOT AT THE LION'S CLUB PARK BESIDE THE MADISON River in Ennis a little before 8 a.m. The temperature is around sixty degrees but will pass ninety by the time we are off the water. I move my gear to Justin's truck, and he drives us to a downstream ramp where we can launch his boat. I offer to help, but he's a guide, and most guides demand to be both captain and crew of their ship. Extra hands have a way of making the guide's job more like putting an octopus to bed than the streamlined process they're used to.

We float away from his truck and trailer, knowing—or at least believing—they'll be waiting for us at our downstream destination. Back in Michigan, I call this magical feat *spotting*. Here in Montana, they call it *shuttling*. Either way, you invest both money and trust when you rely on a third party to move your vehicle from the put-in to the take-out. The cliché says a bad day of fishing beats a good day of working every time. But if after a long day of rowing you find nothing but the damp evening air in the spot where your truck and trailer are supposed to be, your day of fishing will be downright shitty.

Justin says we can't fish from the boat in this part of the river, so he'll row us to the sections he wants to wade. Here above Ennis Lake, we're in a series of braided channels that provide what must be four times the fishable water you'd see in a more traditional section of a river. The braids spread like arteries and veins, bringing life to the beating heart that is Ennis Lake. When we get within sight of the first place Justin wants to fish, a guy sprints into the water from the east bank. His legs move like paddle wheels on a steamship, and a splashy rooster tail rises from his wake. He seems to want us to know that the smooth seam on the other side of the river belongs to him. When he gets into position, he turns his back toward us and scans the water near the far bank, as though he's looking for rising fish. The whole thing would be more believable if he didn't forget to bring the rod his buddy holds for him back on the bank.

Neither Justin nor I am upset with this guy. Instead, we understand him. We're in a boat with plenty of water waiting for us downstream. He certainly knows that. What his comical behavior reveals is that he doesn't seem to know that if we had gotten to the gentle bend before he made it down from the lodge, Justin would have seen his predicament, told me to get back in the boat, and we'd have wished him luck as we floated on. And if the guy would take them, Justin would have given him some flies that would catch fish here. As Justin rows us away, I tell him a story about a similar incident on Michigan's Au Sable River.

Years ago, I sometimes fished with a retired chemistry professor from Michigan Tech on my trips to the lower peninsula. Terry Warrington was his name, and he had that "old man of the river" status a guy gets from doing things like catching eighteen-inch trout on zero-weight rods with size twenty-four flies. When he was younger, he had that "young man of the river" status, but when I first met him, time had already stolen the hip from his hop and a few feet from his cast. On our last trip to the river together, we sat on a log to let another guy fish a run before we waded downstream to where Terry wanted to take me.

"How have you been lately?" I asked.

"Every sphincter in my body is failing, Tim, but other than that, I can't complain."

Terry was taking me to a place we'd find a pod of trout gorging on blue-winged olives at dark. The excitement wouldn't begin for another hour or two, so we sat on the log and talked about how time takes things that even trout can't replace. We didn't want to disturb this guy's water, and Terry was too old to climb through the downfalls in the woods, so we were content to sit, watch, and wait.

"You guys can have the river now. I'll get the hell out of here," the guy yelled at us.

"You're fine. Take your time," Terry answered.

"No, I can see you guys want to fish this run. It's yours, take it. But as a guide, you should know better than to hound me out of my spot."

Terry wisely held his words as the guy waded by us. He would have given the guy a box of flies along with expert instruction on how to fish them in that run before he would ever hound him out of the spot. When the guy was out of earshot, I told Terry that our little section of the world would be a lot better if people didn't assume other people were assholes.

"Yeah, but assholes have a hard time doing that," he said.

With each powerful and precise stroke of the oars, Justin reveals his skill with the sticks. Those of us who row occasionally don't do it like the gals and guys who do it daily for a living. For them, each push or pull makes the boat move just like it's supposed to move, with little or no wasted energy. I once played hockey with a guy who skated as a professional for several years. Watching him move, I thought, "Ah, I'm trying to skate too fast. I need to go slower and use less energy." He probably did exert less energy, but unlike mine, all of his power went where it needed to go, and unlike me, he wasn't slow. Half of the energy I employ gets wasted when my right leg counters what my left leg wants to do. Unlike us amateurs, the pros make their legs and oars work with—not against—each other.

Justin drops anchor to hold the boat in shallow water near a long bend in the river. "Let's catch some trout," he says. We wade out and stand about sixty feet from each other, and Justin waits for me to catch the first fish. Like a robin waiting for its chicks to show they can fly before abandoning the nest, the guide inside won't let him roam until he's sure I'm okay on my own. When I land a small rainbow and release it, Justin reels in his line and slides away toward another channel, ringing the figurative bell that signals the beginning of the guide's day off.

Guiding is hard work. As clients, we only see what goes on between pick-up and drop-off. They instruct us, entertain us, feed us, and laugh at our jokes. Tie the knots we need—untangle the ones we don't. Make us feel like we're the only client they've ever had, which, for that day, we are. They are Alfred Pennyworth; we are Bruce Wayne. But expert guidance doesn't just happen. Our guide is on the clock long before and after our trip, gassing their vehicle, icing their coolers, stocking up on food and drink, cleaning out their boat, refurnishing their fly boxes, and sorting through any messes the last clients left behind. Then, after they drop us off, they do it all over again. And if they can find the time, they might even sleep.

There are many reasons young women and men become fly-fishing guides. One I've never heard, though, is, "I don't like to fly fish." Of course they like to fly fish. Pilots like to fly, chefs like to eat, writers like to read, and guides like to fish. For the next several hours, then, *Justin the guide* is *Justin the fly fisherman*, and this version of Justin is not interested in using any minute of those hours for anything other than fishing.

If you needed to script a compelling character for your great Montana novel, you might embrace the stereotypes and make him a fly-fishing guide and expert skier. Perhaps you'd have him grow up in the South, take a summer job in Yellowstone, meet a young woman from the Midwest, fall in love, and go with her to Michigan so she can finish medical school. While there, he could guide in the Upper Peninsula, finish a graduate degree in wildlife biology, and then the two of them could move to Ennis, where she'd be a successful physician, and he'd be a local guide. If you did that, your character would be Justin Edge. And on this particular Sunday, he'd gallop through the channels of the Madison River like a pronghorn antelope while his new friend from Michigan plods around like a three-toed sloth.

I used to think I could fish with more focus and endurance than anyone. Perhaps during Bill Clinton's presidency, I could. But now during a presidency no one could have predicted back then, I'm more prone to sneak along the shoulder than I am to burn rubber in the fast lane. After Justin disappears around the bend, I'm standing in the bright Montana sun with a ragged tin-cloth hat as my only source of shade for the day. Slivers of snow still mark some of the peaks in the surrounding landscape, but I've been in Montana so long I almost take these mountains for granted. Almost. Tiny caddisflies flutter and flit on and above the river's surface, and several trout frolic a short cast from where I stand. One of my favorite flies is at the end of my line.

Many people mistakenly believe the X-Caddis is a pattern invented by Craig Mathews and John Juracek. Instead, Craig's wife, Jackie, devised the idea and tied the first pattern for Craig and John while working on something to imitate an emerging and impaired caddisfly stuck in its pupal shuck. "Why not tie one like your sparkle dun for imitating emerging mayflies using a trailing shuck?" she asked. The guys used the fly with great success for the hard-to-catch rainbows in the Henry's Fork. As Craig put it, the fly was "killing that day," and the rest—as they say—is history. Since then, it's proven effective anywhere mayflies or caddis emerge from the water, and, like so many excellent patterns, it's deceptively simple. It has a trailing Zelon shuck, a dubbed abdomen, and a deer-hair wing tied in the Elk Hair Caddis style. My variation on this pattern is slight. I tie the fly on a bent hook, commonly sold as the Klinkhammer style. The bend ensures that the shuck and body ride below the surface film. Then I add a few wraps of peacock herl at the thorax to separate the dubbed body from the wing. If someone told me I had to choose between having no flies with peacock herl or all my flies with peacock herl, I'd pack my boxes with Prince Nymphs, Zug Bugs, Royal Wulffs, Griffith's Gnats, and many others, including this fly. Sometimes, when a tier slightly changes a pattern, they give their fly a new name. I suppose a revolutionary change is worthy of that, but evolutionary changes like mine aren't. So when a friend once asked what name I use for my pattern, I told him I call it the X-Caddis.

Without moving my feet, I take three more rainbows from the place where Justin left me. None of them are bruisers—the largest is maybe a foot long—but they aren't pushovers. If I hit a fish in the head with my cast, they stop rising. The same thing happens if my fly drags instead of drifts. Between soft gurgles from the river, I hear the lowing of cattle in the distance. Closer by, grasshoppers chirp. Because of the braided channels, I'm standing in or near three or four different rivers. One is broad with a strong flow in the middle. Another is narrow enough to jump across but deep enough to hold fish. The others have features in between, but they all share the common characteristic of two banks lined with tall grass. I wade toward one of the medium-sized channels.

When my mom bought live crickets from a bait shop when I was a kid, she pinned them on my hook because I couldn't do it without instantly killing the bug. But despite my assassin-like tendencies when it came to impaling, she always let me pull the cricket out of the container. I was good at that part, and I don't remember ever losing one. We used grasshoppers too, and when they flooded our yard in late summer, I'd scour the ground like a squirrel gathering nuts, filling up a jar with bait for our morning trips. I was good at that, too. But now, if a grasshopper lands on my arm, I swat it away immediately and shake off an acute case of the heebie-jeebies. I don't know when I lost my nerve, but I did.

Unlike Nick Adams in Ernest Hemingway's "Big Two-Hearted River," I don't have a bottle full of soot-stained grasshoppers for bait—just a box of imitations made of hair, fur, rubber, and foam. I haven't seen one of the live hoppers yet, and I'm sure as hell not going to walk into the grass to find one. So the one I pick from the box is medium in size and neutral in color. A line of stooping grass shades an undercut bank at the entrance to one of the braids, making it the perfect spot. But I can't get into position for the cast I want to deliver because of a small island just above the braid. Instead, I stand directly upstream, just like Nick:

> *Holding the rod in his right hand he let out line against the pull of the grasshopper in the current. He stripped off line from the reel with his left hand and let it run free. He could see the hopper in the little waves of the current. It went out of sight.*
>
> *There was a tug on the line.*

84

The trout rolls and flops like a Brahman bull then dives deep under the bank. When the connection takes on a dull tightness, I worry the fish has tangled the leader in a root. But when the line moves toward the center of the small channel, I coax the fish into the open water. It's a spectacular brown trout, about a foot and a half long. Roxanne once asked which trout I think is the prettiest: brown, brook, or rainbow. The answer isn't simple. In a one-on-one comparison of two individual fish, either could win. A particular brookie might be prettier than a specific brown, but it could go the other way too. I'm a freckle guy, so the fish with the most flamboyant freckles usually wins, with extra credit going to a brown with a copper-colored head and burnt orange flank, a rainbow with a bold pink stripe and rosy cheek, or a brook trout with deep orange fins and pumpkin-stained belly. At 11:23 a.m. on this particular Sunday, though, "brown trout" is my answer.

After catching a few smaller trout, I wade to the boat for a quick nap. The people at RO Driftboats design their boats to be light, spacious, low-draft, fish-catching machines, but they need to put more thought into how well these vessels accommodate a napping angler. Still, I make it work by pivoting the seat and positioning the cooler just right. In the ninja-like way he disappeared into one of the braids, Justin reappears from another just after I wake up. "I've had some good days in here, but this might be the best I've ever had," he says. Justin covers this type of water the way a beagle weaves in and out of the brush looking for rabbits. He uses a hopper pattern to flush a fish from each likely riffle, run, or undercut bank, then hurries on to the next if nothing jumps out.

We break for lunch, and Justin eats with the same focus he'd fished. We have a pleasant conversation, but a guide's day off isn't the time for tall tales and jokes—Justin is here to fish. When our sandwiches and energy bars are gone, he pulls up anchor and rows us downstream to another base. Beyond the two guys we saw early in the morning, we haven't seen another person all day. But we aren't alone, and we anchor next to a herd of two to three dozen cattle, which I take to be Black Angus. Justin slips off and disappears into a channel, and I wade toward a long run of soft water on the west bank of the main part of the river. A few cows stand in the water, just behind a wire fence that pushes out over a small cove.

White ear tags sparkle like sun glints against the ebony clay silhouettes. A bull whose head is twice the size of the cows' stares me down from a semi-prone position on the higher ground to my left. I convince myself the wire protects me from the bull, and I fish for trout.

I remember Ted Leeson's story about his encounter with a large Angus bull in his book *Inventing Montana*:

> . . . *an enormous and forbidding animal with vast cumulonimbus swells of muscle on its neck and forequarters and a torso as big as a steam boiler abutting the great meaty pistons of its rear haunches, between which hung a scrotum the size of a regulation speed bag and farther along the undercarriage, in an image I will carry to the grave, a prodigious erection.*

My bull's position hides his unmentionables from view, but if he gets up and shows them to me, my legs will steamboat paddle downstream in a way that will make the guy we saw this morning look like a tortoise with a sore toe.

The best water is halfway between me and the bull. Hoping my bull's memory contains no scenes of a cowboy striking him with a whip resembling a six-weight bamboo fly rod, I cast my hopper tight to the grass. I give it a slight tug when it hooks on an overhanging blade, and a swirling vortex forms precisely when and where the fly lands. I have a short-lived, unsuccessful fight with the largest, strongest, and angriest trout I've hooked today.

I decide to wade downstream and away from the bull, but the current in this main channel nearly carries me to Ennis Lake. I never float, but I moon-hop on my toes for more than fifty yards. When I make it out of the swift current, I hear Justin fighting a fish in a small braid on the other side of some tall grass. I tell him I almost got swept downstream, and he says, "Yeah, you don't want to do that." Then he directs me toward a channel he hasn't fished, and, in it, I land two of the three largest trout of my day.

We finish about two hundred yards downstream from the boat. Justin tells me to stay put while he wades upstream and then rows back down to me. A smooth lane of deep water cuts along the western bank, and Justin says he'd like to get a few drifts through it before we call it a day. On his third cast, a giant rainbow sucks down the fly, and before his rod bends from the weight of the fish, Justin yells for me to bring the net. The fish takes a swift run downstream, and Justin gives a splashy, adrenaline-fueled chase. He pulls hard against the trout with the stout tippet until it changes direction, and when it leaps high from the river, I see why Justin called for the net so quickly.

In Justin's hand, the fish shimmers like a piece of stained glass an artist might sell at an Ennis gift shop. We don't measure its length, but based on the landing net's opening, it must be nearly twenty inches. Justin releases the fish, then uses a small electric motor to propel us across Ennis Lake, where the only blemishes on the mirrorlike surface are rings from sporadic rises.

"Damn, that was a great day," Justin says.

"Beautiful."

"I'd like to stay out here longer," he tells me, "but I have to get home and put things in order. Tomorrow's a work day."

CHAPTER 11

Coincidence

What a delightful thing a coincidence is!

—MARK TWAIN

SAMUEL CLEMENS WAS BORN AND THEN DIED UNDER THE GLOW OF Halley's Comet. Some people call this a fantastic coincidence. But the comet is visible for about five months every seventy-five or seventy-six years, and dying at seventy-five wasn't unusual in Mr. Clemens's time if you made it through birth. I don't suggest this isn't a good story; I just don't think it's as impressive a coincidence as me parking next to two guys from Michigan yesterday at the Three Dollar Bridge.

In the strictest sense of the word, much of what happens in our lives is a coincidence. Automobile accidents are at one extreme, love at first sight at another. Fishing is laden with them. You can't catch a trout unless the time and place it decides to eat coincide with the time and place you cast your fly. Sure, your intuition might tell you where and when these coincidences are most likely to happen, but they are coincidences, nevertheless. There is a good reason that "You should have been here yesterday" is a worn-out cliché among anglers.

Describing how we can fool ourselves about coincidences, Nobel laureate Richard Feynman once said:

You know, the most amazing thing happened to me tonight. I was coming here, on the way to the lecture, and I came in through the parking lot. And you won't believe what happened. I saw a car with the license plate ARW 357. Can you imagine? Of all the millions of license plates in the state, what was the chance that I would see that particular one tonight? Amazing!

Feynman was more sophisticated than my mom. She would simply say, "Everybody's gotta be somewhere," and then move on. From her perspective, my new friends from Michigan and I happened to pick the same somewhere to be last night.

Scott and Jim are part of a group from the Michigan Fly Fishing Club, and when they got back to their cabin, they told some of their friends they had met a writer from Michigan who gave them a copy of his book. Two of those friends, Joyce and Al Haxton, were at the "Celebrate Michigan Rivers" event a year ago when Jerry Dennis, Bob DeMott, and I amazed the audience with our variations of half-truths and gorilla dust. When she learned I was in Montana, Joyce sent a text message that arrived last night shortly after Justin and I confirmed our trip:

Hi Tim. Funny, I just heard from our friend who was at $3 bridge tonight. He said you gave him a book. We are staying at Driftwaters Resort until the end of August. Stop by at 6 for a drink if you'd like. We have an extra bed if you need it this week. Tonight is burger night. This is our treat, Joyce and Al!

I've eaten dinner alone and slept in my truck every night for over a week, so the opportunity to share dinner with like-minded people and sleep on a bed in a cabin sounded pretty darn good to me. At about noon during my trip with Justin today, I told Joyce I'd love to join them, but for the sake of everyone else in the restaurant, I'd need a shower before dinner. I'm as ripe as a three-day-old carp carcass on the Fourth of July, and even by Montana fishing lodge standards, that's bad.

I call home and talk to Roxanne on my way from Ennis to the Driftwaters Resort. I do this every time I'm on a drive that lasts more than a half-hour, provided, of course, the American Telephone and Telegraph company has one of their towers in a convenient location. When I tell her I'm on my way to have dinner with Joyce and Al, she tells me to have fun but warns me to beware of one of my notable traits.

"When was the last time you had a social conversation with people?" she asks.

"I just spent all day fishing with Justin Edge."

"Did you guys talk much, or did you mostly fish?"

"We mostly fished."

"Look, you haven't been talking with people for a week, so don't go crazy and talk their ears off."

She makes a good point. I crane my head toward the rearview mirror and realize I've barely seen my own face during this trip, let alone other peoples.' I haven't been silent like Mahatma Gandhi on a Monday, but I haven't said many words either. Roxanne knows I can talk a lot when I get going, so I promise to keep my chatter somewhere between Gandhi and a livestock auctioneer.

When Roxanne and I vacation, she insists we have a well-planned itinerary, which strictly prohibits leaving a night's lodging to chance. She needs to know some modern version of Tom Bodett will leave the light on for us. When I'm on my own, I like to spin the wheel and roll the dice. I woke up beside Rock Creek yesterday, not knowing I would sleep beside the Madison River last night and fish with Justin Edge this morning. And it wasn't until about noon today that I knew I'd dine with Joyce and Al this evening, then spend the night at the Driftwaters Resort. Just-in-time sweepstakes like these are my kind of lotteries. They might seem like timely coincidences, but I think of it as calling the bet and drawing the last card for an inside straight.

The resort is a small bar and restaurant with about two dozen full hook-up campsites and a half-dozen cabins. When I pull into the parking area, Joyce and Al are standing on the porch in front of one of the rooms. I worry my visit is an imposition, but they wash all that away with the sort of handshakes and hugs we usually reserve for lifelong friends. Fishing in general—but fly fishing in particular—has a way of forging these connections. It's nothing like being in a foxhole during a downpour of cannon fire, but you do share something many people don't understand. To paraphrase John Voelker, it isn't that you see fly fishing as being so important; instead, you see many of our other concerns as equally unimportant and not nearly so much fun. And it's nice to be in the company of people who don't think you're lazy or irresponsible for feeling this way.

It's not that you won't find scoundrels in fly fishing the way you find them in politics or other dens of iniquity. They're out there. But often, with enough time, the fishing changes them. In the preface to his book, *Trout Madness*, the same John Voelker suggests we drive the trout fishers into diplomacy or drive the diplomats to trout fishing. "Either way," he says, "we'd be more apt to have more peace: the fishermen-turned-diplomats would hurriedly resolve their differences on the trout stream so that they might return to their fishing, while the diplomats-turned-fishermen would shortly become so absorbed in their new passion they'd never again find time for war."

After I shower, I walk to the lodge's restaurant for dinner. It's a rectangular building fronted by a large rustic porch spacious enough for outdoor dining. Inside the bar, several Moscow Mule–style copper mugs hang from the wall, and the tap line has a bevy of craft beers from local breweries. I order the Gallatin Pale Ale. When the owner, Rachel, comes into the dining area, Joyce gives her a giant hug and brings her to the table to meet me. Rachel wants to make sure I feel at home. In this setting, there isn't any other way to feel.

My mom owned a place like this when I was a kid. Of course, her bar wasn't alongside a world-famous trout river. Instead, it was across the highway from one of the largest railroad-switching yards in the country. Missouri Pacific engineers and brakemen—not Madison River trout anglers—populated her stools and chairs. Rugged men in Dickie coveralls, washing down Slim Jims, pork rinds, and pickled eggs with Falstaff beer while teaching me card tricks and bank shots. If I had grown up here, I might have learned roll casts and clinch knots. But either way, I always feel at home in a place like this.

The burger is a great break from the dinners I've been assembling in the Suburban, and the conversation is much livelier than the ones I've been having with myself. I do my best to ration my words, but I'm the new guy, and everyone at the table wants to know my story. Roxanne said

I should take a big swig of beer whenever I feel the words, "That reminds me of a story," staging in my chest. I'm on my second pint and thinking about ordering my third.

When we finish dinner, some of the people in the group gather up their gear and head to the river. I fished all day with Justin, and I've never enjoyed fishing after more than one beer. So when Joyce and Al say they're not planning to fish this evening, I ask Rachel if I can buy a couple of bottles of wine. After dinner, a small group of us go to one of the cabins and do the second-best thing besides fishing. We talk about fishing.

Joyce and Al are the fishiest pair you could ever meet outside of Emily and Dave Whitlock. Al proposed to Joyce on the bank of the Yellowstone River in Montana, and they married alongside the Au Sable in Michigan. The nuptial was at Gates Lodge, where Joyce entered the riverside shrine in an Au Sable River Boat. She and Al substituted brightly colored, oversized flies for their corsage and boutonnière. After they exchanged vows, they exited the open-air altar through an archway of fly rods hoisted by their angling friends. Some of us talk the talk of the fishing life. On the day they married, Joyce and Al walked the walk in the most literal sense of the phrase.

Al has organized and hosted the Michigan Fly Fishing Club's Montana trip for nearly twenty years. His love of fishing is as infectious as his grin, as is his love of people. And after all this time, he still enjoys watching the first-timers in his group adjust to Montana frosts in August. But if possible, Joyce cherishes Montana more than Al, although her fear of grizzlies almost surpasses her affection for the rivers, mountains, and wildlife. To be fair, it's respect more than fear that Joyce has for the bears, and it's a respect that has worked to her advantage. On one of their first trips to Montana, Joyce insisted on fishing close to the car, just in case she needed to make a speedy exit with or without Al. While driving along the West Fork of the Madison River, Al parked near an outhouse so he could do the thing we sometimes need to do in outhouses. Confident that a bear would see Al as the easier target, Joyce got out her two-weight rod and casually caught a sixteen-inch brown trout. "Casually" is the way Joyce describes it, not Al.

"They've seen it all" is an overused expression. But when you embrace adventures like Joyce and Al, you certainly experience a lot. When I ask them about the craziest thing they've seen on these trips, they tell me about the time one of their group fished with his son in Yellowstone Park. After he'd strung up his rod and attached a fly, but before securing the hook to one of the rod's guides, a hulking bison trudged beside the car. Whereas most people fear grizzlies, bison account for twice as many attacks in Yellowstone each year, although most of those "attacks" result from people putting themselves or their children on a bison's back. This guy was brighter than that, but somehow his fly got embedded into the bison's Congo-brown muscular rump. No manufacturer—not Rio, Scientific Anglers, Orvis, or TroutHunter—makes a tippet capable of holding a bison, so the break-off was uneventful. Of course, back at the lodge, the guy insisted on getting the nod for the day's biggest catch.

A shared love of fly fishing makes people instant friends. But a shared love of bamboo fly rods makes them extended family. When our conversation turns to cane rods, I retrieve mine from the truck. For the group, the most notable is the eight-foot, six-inch rod built by Ron Barch. One of the tips makes it a five weight—the other makes it a six. Ron designed the rod to replicate a wand that made John Voelker feel like the famous ballet dancer Nijinsky, and "Voelker's Nijinsky" is the inscription on the butt of the rod. I have a Winston built by Jerry Kustich and several Sweetgrass rods designed by Glenn Brackett. Al and Joyce admire them the way godparents admire godchildren. They don't need to be your kids for you to love them. They only need to be your friends' kids.

I suppose there's an argument that bamboo rods should go the way of the hourglass, sundial, icebox, phonograph, telegraph, carbon paper, carburetor, spear, and sword. Graphite rods can do things bamboo can't, and a creative builder can come close to making them do anything bamboo can. Graphite comes from carbon, which is the crucial element in organic matter. Because most of Earth's carbon has biological origins, graphite—like bamboo—was once alive, but it doesn't look and feel that way. Two graphite rods with the same model from the same manufacturer are nearly indistinguishable, like a pair of new pennies stamped at the mint. Bamboo rods of the same model are more like identical twins. Looking closely, you'll notice a freckle or mole in a different place. A group of anglers won't often ask to see all your graphite rods, but they might if your rods are bamboo.

When Scott and Jim return from the river, Joyce and Al retire to their room. Those guys fished past dark, and judging by the stories, the rewards were well worth their efforts. When I bring my sleeping bag in from the truck, they uncork a bottle to celebrate their fishing and help them sleep. I listen to them summarize this day and make plans for the next with all the enthusiasm of third-graders on the first day of summer break.

What about fishing makes grown men and women feel and act like kids again? The answer is common in nearly all unfading writing about fly fishing. All our lives, someone tells us growing old means growing up. As John Hartford sang, they sell us a suit, cut off our hair, and send us to work in tall buildings. But then we find a book where a wordsmith embeds poetry into their prose and permits us to say hello to the sunshine, the dew, and the flowers. I have a framed print with artwork by Glenn Wolff and prose by Jerry Dennis in my office at home. Physically, it's on the wall there, but I carry it with me wherever I go.

WHY FISH?
It teaches us to perform small acts with care.
It humbles us. It enriches our friendships.
It cultivates reverence for wild things and beautiful places.
It reminds us that time needs occasionally to be squandered.
It offers relief from endless chores and appalling world events.
It makes us participants in nature instead of spectators,
a crucial distinction because participants tend to
become passionate and protective and
spectators tend to become indifferent.

I lay my sleeping bag on the cabin's loft bed and then crawl inside. It's my ninth night on the road and my eighth in Montana. I'm here for two more weeks, but that wonderful feeling that my time in this state is as endless as the sky above has slipped away. My first casts on the Big Hole, the Beaverhead, Poindexter Slough, the Missouri, Rock Creek, and the

Madison are all in the mirror now. I know I can go back to any of those rivers. But I also know I can't see them for the first time again.

This bed is more comfortable than the air mattress in the back of the Suburban, and although I've had a long and full day, sleep does not come immediately. Unlike Hemingway's Nick Adams, I've never been blown up at night, at least not literally—but like him, I have a lot of practice at being awake. I don't think about trout streams to occupy myself when this happens. Instead, I think about tying flies. I start with a bare hook, then wrap the thread back to where it hangs over the place where the barb should be. Then I tie in an Antron husk and wind dubbing up to the thorax. Sometimes I get distracted and have to start over again. On rough nights, I can finish dozens of flies. I don't complete even one on good nights like this one.

The morning at the resort is chaotic but controlled. The cabin I slept in is the breakfast center—the kitchen is stocked with Raisin Bran, Quaker Oats, blueberry muffins, and whatever else people have requested or brought. Some anglers bag lunch for the day, and there's plenty of conversation around the table, but not as casual as last night. Today is a road trip for most, so they pack their cars and double-check their plans. A friendly couple named Boyd and Shirley ask me to donate some books and photos for their Trout Unlimited banquet. I agree, and—with that— pick up another place to stay the next time I'm a trout bum in lower Michigan.

As the cars and trucks pull from the parking lot, I realize I'm in the middle of a massive goodbye pageant. Joyce gives me two containers of bear spray and makes me promise to wear them when I'm in bear country. She and Al give me a couple of big hugs and then leave me alone in the lot. Bear spray is supposed to make a bear cry, and even though I'm not a bear and haven't discharged a canister, it seems to be working on me. I'm not supposed to meet Bob and Kate until around noon, so I walk to the restaurant to see if I can get breakfast. A Mexican couple sitting on the porch welcomes me in, and when I sit at a table, one of them walks into the kitchen, and the other asks what I'd like to eat. I order a burrito with diced onions, red peppers, scrambled eggs, chorizo, and black beans. I top it with both rojo and verde sauce from two large plastic squeeze bottles.

Without a doubt, it's the best meal I've had so far on this trip. "What are the chances," I think, "that a couple from Mexico are sitting here waiting to cook someone a delicious breakfast at the exact time I walk onto this porch?" What a delightful coincidence.

CHAPTER 12

People of Letters

Not all fishing is done in water.

—Bob DeMott

BOB AND KATE'S SUMMER PLACE IS ABOUT THREE MILES NORTH OF Driftwaters Resort, in the closest thing to a residential area I've seen on the east side of the river between Galloup's Slide Inn and Ennis. It's a humble riverside hamlet with about a dozen homes and some rental cabins sandwiched between the Grizzly Bar and Madison River. A cell tower disguised as a pine tree at the entrance to the neighborhood keeps the residents connected with the outside world—a contradictory reminder that even secluded fishing communities need mechanisms for arguing with strangers and sharing pictures of cats. When I pull beside their cabin, Bob is outside talking with a neighbor about the river's fish and the flies that will catch them. What else would he be doing?

Bob DeMott is every pound the fisherman that he is the scholar, and he's a heavyweight scholar. For over forty years, he was a professor of American literature at Ohio University, the state's oldest public university. He is exceptionally deft at connecting angling with writing—something some call *Anglish* to emphasize the melding of angling with English— and he has had rich relationships with the celebrated *Anglish* writers Jim

Harrison and Nick Lyons. Most of all, he knows what he writes. Jim Harrison said Bob and Tom McGuane were the two best trout fishermen he'd ever met. High praise from a man whose fishing partners could fill five chapters of a *Who's Who* volume on the sport. Bob also edited and contributed to a festschrift of sorts for Nick Lyons—something he jokingly called a *fishshrift* entitled *Astream: American Writers on Fly Fishing*.

Bob is one of the world's foremost experts on John Steinbeck, having written numerous books, articles, and essays about the celebrated writer. Naturally, the title for one of those is "Of Fish and Men." In it, Bob writes:

> *Fishing, like writing, thrives on memory, because as soon as a writer records his or her fishing experiences (or any experiences for that matter), they are already past, already part of mythic angling memory, and therefore given to selection, enlargement, exaggeration, embroidery, distortion, and even fantasy—all the elements that complicate representation.*

We remember most events in our lives the way we want to. When asked about his writing, John Voelker said his harshest critics claimed his fishing stories were some of his best fiction. I've had a few people suggest some of my fishing stories might have a fractured relationship with reality, too. All I know for sure, though, is that I tell them how I remember them. For sentimental romantics like me, the road connecting our telling to our remembering can be a busy two-way street. We should always look both ways before crossing.

Like Bob, his partner Kate Fox is a poet with a doctorate in American literature. Unlike Bob, the blood of an angling addict doesn't flow through her veins. But she has a vest and waders hanging on the cabin's porch, and though she shrugs off the compliment, Bob says she's an excellent caster. Their history together is like a boomerang that took twenty years to return after being thrown afar. Once together, then apart, a mutual love of literature brought them together again, and Kate's acceptance of fly fishing has kept them there. "The only question more intriguing than why men take up fly fishing is why women take up with men who take up fly fishing," Kate wrote in 2009. She's spent the decade since refining her answers.

Kate and Bob show me to a small room with a bunk bed and barely enough space to walk around one side and one end of the frame. In other words, it's the ideal room for a fly-fishing vagabond like me. The rest of the cabin has two main spaces—a more spacious bedroom for Kate and Bob and an open area that serves as the living room, dining room, and kitchen. There are also two bathrooms and a storage room with a washer and dryer. They say hands build houses, and hearts build homes. In the same sense, memories make cabins, and a fishing cabin like this one is a souvenir shop for your soul.

After chatting, I put some clothes in the washer, and then Bob and I drive off for Blue Ribbon Flies in West Yellowstone. Once there, we'll pay for tomorrow's trip with guide Patrick Daigle and add some flies to our already overcrowded boxes. Bob tells me Patrick is patient and knowledgeable, with a sharp eye for spotting fish, an instinct for knowing how to fool them, and a relaxed humor to get us through the rough spots, should they happen. The road to West Yellowstone is about thirty-five miles and takes us past the Slide Inn and Quake Lake. After we wind beyond those, I see Hebgen Lake for the first time. The highway follows the lake's shore for about ten miles up from the dam, and it's here, Bob says, where we'll fish for gulpers with Patrick in the morning.

"Do you know about gulpers?" Bob asks.

"I've heard of them," I say.

"They're big trout that gulp flies from the lake's surface. If we hit it right, it can be incredible," Bob says. His eyes are wide, his smile broad. It's the look of an addict who just realized this is where he'll get his next big fix.

Founded in the early 1900s, West Yellowstone is the west entrance to the national park with the famous name. It's the most popular of the park's five gateways—providing the closest access to Old Faithful and accounting for more than 40 percent of the roughly four million annual visitors. The town's population is about twelve hundred people, so, over the year, it gets more than a thousand visitors for every resident. It's the perfect setting for hotels, gift shops, and, of course, fly shops.

Craig Mathews founded Blue Ribbon Flies in 1980 while working full-time as the town's chief of police. Two years later, he and his wife,

Jackie, went all in and didn't look back until they turned the shop over to Cam Coffin a year or two ago. When we walk in the door, the guy behind the counter throws a hearty hello at Bob. His name is Bucky McCormick, and the two of them launch into conversation like brothers who just returned from a foreign war. Like most of Bob's conversations in a shop like this, this one eventually finds its way to the fly bins.

I ask Bucky what he thinks about these purple flies I've encountered in every fly shop I've visited.

"A good fly, catches both fish and fishermen."

"Do the fish really like that color?"

"I think the reason purple works so well," Bucky says, "is that the fish see it the same way they see gray. In that case, why not use gray?"

Then Bucky tells us how he's been tying and fishing classic patterns almost exclusively lately. "They are beautiful, timeless, and they work," he says. According to Bucky, we make too many flies for the anglers instead of the fish. Just when I decide Bucky and I are brothers of a different mother, he says he won't use a parachute pattern anymore. I suppose brothers don't have to agree on everything, especially when they have different mothers.

Bob fills one of those little plastic ketchup cups with flies. "You'll need this emerger for the Madison tonight," he says, so I put some in my cup too. Then I ask Bucky if they have any Henryville Specials—the flies I used up on the Missouri River and don't want to be without on the Madison. He points to their home in the bins, and I take several. When we pay for our flies and tomorrow's trip, Bucky tells Bob how much fun he had the last time they were together when he and Kate played guitar and sang songs.

Back in the Suburban, I tell Bob I've brought a guitar with me, and I'd be happy to leave it with Kate for two weeks until I'm back in this area with my son. It has a carbon fiber body, so the heat and cold haven't been an issue, but I've hardly played it on this trip, and she's welcome to use it. At the cabin, Kate says she appreciates the offer but will only keep it if I play songs with her later that night. I say I will, but then Bob says he and I need to fish. His addict blood is making him shake a little bit, and, frankly, so is mine.

In all the ways that matter, it's easy to be Bob's fishing partner. His knowledge of the sport is remarkable, his enthusiasm is contagious, and he's a gentleman in every dimension. Still, this man has fished with Nick Lyons and Jim Harrison, and not just casually. So—like a freshman quarterback for the Alabama Crimson Tide—I worry about living up to expectations. But Nick Saban didn't become one of the greatest coaches of all time by making his quarterbacks so nervous they couldn't perform. Outstanding leaders like Saban have a calming influence, as do benevolent anglers like Bob. We park on the west side of Three Dollar Bridge, a short distance from a spot Bob says has the perfect log for us to sit on. "Let's go catch some fish," he says to me.

Being a Madison River amateur, I left my raincoat at Bob and Kate's cabin. It's raining when we arrive, so Bob loans me a Patagonia jacket that's as bright and red as a matador's cape. I worry I'll look out of place alongside the river but then realize the only person I care about here is Bob, and this is his jacket. Plus, the lore about red capes angering bulls with scrotums the size of regulation speed bags turns out to be a rural legend.

Bob says many anglers fish the Madison River as though they're being paid by the cast and want to make enough money to retire early. He and his friend Craig Mathews like to sit on a log—just like the one he and I are on—and wait for a fish to make the first move. In an interview with Jerry Dennis, Jim Harrison reflected on sitting on a stump back in Michigan: "When you live in a place a long time you have your secret places, a stump you like to sit on and so on. I told a guy once there's a beer bottle beside the stump, and he asked why I didn't pick it up, and I said because the beer bottle conceals the beauty of the stump." Although there aren't secret places in this stretch of the Madison River, I think some people let the chase conceal the beauty of a sturdy log on its bank. But Bob sees it, and so do I.

The rain comes, goes, comes again, and finally leaves for the night. Bob spots the trout first.

"Did you see that?"

He points about fifteen feet upstream from me.

"I didn't, but I see it now."

The river's surface is too rough for a rise form to stay in the shape of a ring. The telltale sign of this fish is an extra spatter from the surface, with an emerald nose in its center. "Go catch it," he says. I shuffle on my knees to a place I can present a fly to the fish. The brush at my back stands in the way of an easy cast. I need to push my backcast high and gently drop my forward stroke to avoid plopping my fly into the river like an acorn. Despite his disarming lack of pretension, I know Bob's a certified casting instructor, and I suspect he's watching with an instructor's eye. But all he says is, "That's a good cast. Put another out there just like it." I'm using a small caddis pattern, but the fish ignores even the good drifts, keeping its focus on whatever it's eating. So I switch to a small flying ant because, well, I don't know what else to do. On my second cast with the ant, the fish takes it.

"You got it," Bob says. I stand up from my knees and wind the loose line onto the reel. I'm at the upstream limit of a bank-side clearing that extends about seventy feet downstream. Bob stands fifteen feet below me, and when I finally direct the fish to swim in front of him, he scoops it up with his long-handled wooden net. The rainbow trout is two inches shorter than the net's opening, which I guess is eighteen inches. Bob takes some pictures, and when he shows them to me on the camera screen, I'm delighted by how the red jacket accents the rainbow's crimson stripe.

Bob moves upstream, and I slide down. I switch to the small mayfly emerger Bob recommended I use when it starts to get dark, and with it, I hook a nice fish that pulls me forty yards downstream before I can land it. Sometimes, a brown trout's skin displays a sparse array of well-defined freckles, each standing distinct and outlined in white. Other times—like this one—the spots are densely packed, with none standing out from the crowd. Both patterns are beautiful in their own way. My favorite is the one that happens to be cradled in my hand when I push the hook from the fish's jaw.

We return to the cabin just after dark to find Kate playing folk songs on the guitar. When Bob goes to work in the kitchen, she tells me he does all the cooking in their household, most of the cleaning, and the bulk of the yard work. I tell her I cook, clean, and do some work in the yard too, but probably not as much as Bob. "No one does," she says. Bob pours a beer for me and asks if I like elk meatloaf. "Sure, that sounds great," I say, even though I don't really know if I like elk, and I can't remember the last time I had meatloaf. But an hour later, after I eat the final speck off my plate, elk meatloaf is shoulder-to-shoulder with fried walleye and blackened catfish near the top of the list of things I like to eat.

Kate says her father was a musician who played the bass and Piedmont-blues guitar. He taught her to cast a rod, shoot a gun, and generally be comfortable in the company of men. Not so far as to cuss like them, though. Only to tolerate their cussing. Her father's influence is evident in a poem she shares with me called "That Evening Sun."

> *Let me end this song on a not-so-minor note,*
> *rest my head on the Gibson L-1, sing goodbye*
>
> *to every lyric I have ever learned: the one about the boat*
> *that can carry two and the lonesome picker, the one*
>
> *about how Louise rode home on the mail train*
> *and how walking is most too slow. And, of course,*
>
> *the one about riding down the canyon that, even after*
> *forty years, conjures my father on a Saturday night*
>
> *wrapping the fingers of his left hand with adhesive tape,*
> *swaying and slapping an upright bass in some small-town*
>
> *dance hall while my mother glides across a floor strewn*
> *with corn meal, and my brother and I fall asleep among coats*
>
> *piled high on folding chairs against the wall. He once*
> *told me that music was the one thing he could count on,*
>
> *married, as he was, in 1929, his first child, a girl, born*
> *and buried a year later, a life of lung trouble that finally*

sent him out West to either die or get well. At thirty,
I took him at his word, picked up the guitar he gave me

the one around whose neck he wrapped my fingers
and taught me songs that survive on breath alone:

how the water is wide, how I won't be worried long,
how I hate to see that evening sun go down.

As the novelist Alice Walker wrote, "A writer's heart, a poet's heart, an artist's heart, a musician's heart is always breaking. It is through that broken window that we see the world; more mysterious, beloved, insane, and precious for the sparkling and jagged edges of the smaller enclosure we have escaped."

—◦—

The Hungarian mathematician Paul Erdős published more than fifteen hundred articles with over five hundred co-authors. Because of his prolific collaborations, mathematicians created the concept of an Erdős number. If you wrote a paper with Professor Erdős, your Erdős number is one. If you wrote an article with one of those co-authors, your number is two. It is a way to measure degrees of separation. Because of my secret life outside fishing, my Erdős number is four. This number doesn't make me a famous mathematician, though. For instance, Germany's former chancellor Angela Merkel has an Erdős number of five, but few people think of her for her math prowess.

Today is the second time I've fished with Bob. That makes my DeMott number one and my Lyons and Harrison numbers two. I don't want to come off like a teenage groupie, so I don't ask Bob to name his or Nick's or Jim's other notable fishing partners. Without asking, though, I know I have only three degrees of separation from people like Jimmy Buffett, Tom McGuane, Richard Brautigan, and Russell Chatham. I don't think Chancellor Merkel has fished with any of these folks—she might be next to me in math, but she's not close in fishing.

I don't mean to imply that I see this as a celebrity contest. Among all the qualities that make a good fishing partner, fame is not one. A good fishing partner could be famous, of course, but I suspect they'd be so despite—not because of—their fame. You pick them much like you do a life partner—except for the chocolate, roses, harps, and orchestra strings. One day, you realize you're finishing their sentences, and they're completing yours. Like a nine-year-old spaniel, their presence enhances, not diminishes, your solitude. You enjoy watching them catch a fish; they enjoy watching you. Their memories are short enough to forget which stories you've told them but long enough to remember the ones they've told you. There is no eHarmony or Match.com to determine if someone will be a good fishing partner. But if you want a simple yet accurate test for compatibility, you can ask yourself one question. Is this a person you'd gladly give the front position in a drift boat, and would they gladly give it to you? If so, you have likely found a good fishing partner.

I'm convinced Nick Lyons and Jim Harrison were good fishing partners with Bob. I say "were" because Nick has retired from rivers and Jim has retired from life. Bob's bond with both men was born from their scholarly kinships and nurtured and raised by their mutual love of fishing. Recalling a day on *the* spring creek with Nick, Bob wrote in *The American Fly Fisher,*

> *Fly fishing is a collector's art. We gather, collect, scrutinize, evaluate, and organize many things—flies, rods, reels, books, so why not other valuables as well in the form of rivers, impressions, spots of time, and memories? Later, I netted a nice brown for Nick, so fishingwise, anyway, there was some success to be had.*

Regarding Jim—who Kate says was as different from Nick as a freestone stream is from a spring creek—Bob wrote in *Anglers Journal,*

> *For many of us, the gorgeous 20-plus-inch brown trout Jim caught on a monstrosity of a rubber-legged girdle bug (he was not a small-fly adherent) would have been the prize of the trip. But for him, I suspect the greatest pleasures were a single 14-line poem and the sweet smiles and salty byplay of knockout beauty Nicole, his favorite fantasy barmaid at the Hitchin' Post.*

To some degree, I'd rearrange my life to have fished with either Nick or Jim. Nick for his self-deprecating humor and childlike enthusiasm. Jim for his love of large doses, be they fish, food, fun, or frolic. Tomorrow, I'll fish all day with Bob. I won't recognize it when it happens, but at some point, I suspect he'll say something Nick would have said or point out something Jim would have. Much like they warn the kids in sex-education class, when you fish with someone, you fish with everyone who's ever fished with them. By that, I don't mean to imply fishing with Bob connects me to Nick Lyons and Jim Harrison in some meaningful way. That would be like equating reading a great book with writing one. But damn it, I love to read great books.

CHAPTER 13

Everything After That Is a Bonus

My expectations were reduced to zero when I was twenty-one.
Everything since then has been a bonus.

—STEPHEN HAWKING

AT DINNER LAST NIGHT, BOB TOLD ME WE'D FISH ON HEBGEN LAKE
this morning, followed by a more traditional trip down the Madison
River in the afternoon. I said that sounded good, and I meant it. But I've
mainly fished on rivers for the last few decades, and I was most excited
about the Madison. Moving water sings to me, both figuratively and
literally. I love how a river pushes me around—even shoves me—when I
wade. Or how it delivers me downstream like royalty in a rickshaw when
I float. Rivers are alive, and when I pay attention, I hear them breathe.
But despite all my admiration of waters that move, I first learned to love
fishing on a lake.

I did most of my childhood fishing on foot, roaming around a pair of
soggy-banked pay-to-fish lakes with my mom close to our home. But
when the company my stepfather worked for hired Biebel Brothers
Roofing, we got permission to fish on the Biebel family lake in nearby

Freeburg, Illinois. Some guys in gray flannel suits ordered their second Bombay Sapphire martini, signed a contract, and, just like that, my mom and I were mariners. The Biebels had a hundred-acre farm for cows, chickens, and crops, and in its middle, they dug a twenty-acre amoeba-shaped pond and stocked it with sunfish, bass, and channel catfish. We could fish from one of their aluminum johnboats any time we wanted, provided we closed the gates behind us and returned any boat we borrowed to its original upside-down position on the bank.

At first, we rowed for short distances with oars that came with the boats. After my mom bought a used Minn Kota electric motor, we powered into all the amoeba coves like Bill Dance or Roland Martin. We used the same fishing methods that worked from the bank: a worm impaled on a bait hook, a split shot squeezed onto the line above that, and a plastic or balsa bobber to float the rig and signal the strikes. These were harvesting trips, and we filled our cheap Styrofoam cooler—distinguished by its duct-tape reinforced corners—with some of the fattest redear sunfish my mom had ever seen. "Bigger than shit," she'd say, assessing both the size of our fish and the scale of our accomplishment. We cast toward the commotion when the fish were on their spawning beds in the spring. Most of the time, though, we threw our bait at promising spots in the shade or around logs. "Look at us, sitting on our asses catching fish," she'd say while using the fading butt of her Winston to fire up another.

Our guide Patrick says the forecast calls for an overcast sky with little wind, and if the breeze stays mild, we might want to stay on the lake in the afternoon. The lake is a twelve-thousand-acre reservoir held back by an eighty-five-foot-high dam. Its sixty-five miles of shoreline outline the irregular shape of an asymmetric inkblot with a body and three extended arms. The Madison and Grayling arms project to the east—the pathway to the dam spreads to the northwest. Montana Power Company built the dam in 1914, but not to generate hydroelectric power. Instead, the dam's job is to store water and regulate the river's flow to the power plants and other reservoirs farther downstream. One of those is the smaller lake caused by the earthquake in 1959, just a couple of river miles below the dam.

Patrick grew up on the Salmon River in Connecticut, where he found a job in the fly-fishing department of an outdoor specialty store, learned to tie flies, and caught the unique virus that causes young men and women from all social and economic backgrounds to shun traditional careers in favor of long hours and financial uncertainty. Fifteen years ago, he migrated west to Montana, running—as many young people do—away from an old way of life and toward a new one. In his words, he was spinning in circles like a compass with a broken needle and going nowhere fast.

He found his first job in Montana at a fly shop in Twin Bridges. Later, when he applied for a position with Blue Ribbon Flies in West Yellowstone, Craig Mathews didn't ask him to submit a résumé. Instead, he asked him to write a short essay explaining why he wanted the job. Traditional résumés tell employers *what* a prospective employee has done and *where* they've done it. Craig didn't want to know those things. Instead of where Patrick worked, Craig wanted to know *why* Patrick worked. Rather than how many clients he had guided, Craig wanted to know how Patrick felt when he guided them. Craig Mathews wanted to know *who*—not *what*—Patrick Daigle was.

"Was there a particular thing you wrote in that essay that caught Craig's attention?" I ask.

"I can't remember what I wrote, but I remember being honest and convincing. I had to be convincing. I don't like being told no when it comes to applying for a job."

We put Patrick's boat in the lake at a public ramp that looks and feels like private property. No signs mark the place, so I suspect locals do most of the launches here. It isn't exactly a secret spot, but visitors would have had trouble finding it in the days before satellite maps. To be clear, *we put Patrick's boat in the lake* is another way to say Bob and I relieved ourselves in the bushes and pretended to do something useful while Patrick launched his boat. Both Bob and I are experienced clients. We're good at staying out of the way without looking like our only job is to stay out of the way.

Patrick rows away from the ramp and lays out the plan. For trout, a river is much like a full-service restaurant with an attentive staff. The fish find a nice seat, and the current brings all the food straight to their table. A lake is more like a buffet, with a sideboard drifting around the room. When the trout wants another crumpet, they have to chase it down themselves. At first, most of the action is out of sight, but when a fish takes its next bite at or just below the surface, we see a familiar rise form. But, unlike in a river, the next time the fish eats a bug, it's in a different spot.

Patrick says to look carefully at the ring when we see a rise. If the dorsal fin and tail breach the surface, the direction the fish is swimming should be obvious. As long as the flies don't have hooks in them, the trout rarely go tail over teakettle when they eat one. He tells us that even when we don't see fins, we should be able to see a leading and trailing edge to the ring. In his essay "Re-Reading the Rise," John Juraceck stresses, "The high side of the rise always indicates the direction the fish was facing at the time he rose." Patrick quizzes us when we see our first. "That one's going to our left," Bob says. Patrick asks what I think. "Yeah, uh, what Bob said."

A ceiling of white clouds with gray splotches covers the sky as far as we can see. A floor as calm as a worn-out puppy spreads around us. Outside of the occasional rise forms, another drift boat with two anglers is the only disturbance on the lake. "These are perfect conditions," Patrick says. We're in a classic drift boat, complete with braces to stabilize our legs if we stand. But Patrick tells us we'll do much better if we can stay seated when we cast.

"I have no problem with that," Bob says.

"How about you, Tim? Will that work?" Patrick asks.

"Yeah, uh, what Bob said."

The next item on the docket is a discussion about terminal tackle. Bob and I both hope to catch some fish on the surface, but Patrick says our best chance in the morning will be below it. We'll have a much better chance to take them up top later in the day when we see some steady risers. This is our court, though, so he tells us he'll defer to our judgment.

"Let's start below the surface now, and move to dry flies later," Bob says.

"How about you, Tim? Will that work?" Patrick asks.

"Yeah, uh, what Bob said."

Even though it might sound that way, I'm not parroting Bob. Perhaps regarding the direction of that riser, but I'm agnostic about how we cast and fish. As a kid, my experience with lake fishing involved aluminum johnboats, tin cans filled with worms, and duct-taped Styrofoam coolers. We're in a fiberglass drift boat with plastic boxes full of tiny flies and a pressure-injected polyurethane cooler strong enough to withstand an attack by a bear. We aren't in my district. Jimmy Buffett says clichés are a good way to say what we mean and mean what we say. In that spirit, I'm a fish out of water and happy to give Bob full power of attorney.

Patrick sets us up with two flies and a bobber, or an "indicator" as he calls it. He makes the indicators himself out of foam with an adhesive backing. Below the float, we have two flies: a nymph and an emerger. After Patrick rigs our rods, a fish shows itself about one hundred feet to the port-bow side of the boat. Patrick sculls into position, then tells Bob to cast. Bob puts the cast exactly where it needs to be, and when the tiny indicator trembles like a flickering flame, he sets the hook, and Patrick yells, "Hell yes!" It's a gorgeous fish—about a foot and a half long with an explosive peach rouge on its cheek. We've been on the lake for twenty minutes.

"Bogey at nine o'clock," Patrick announces, then quietly crab strokes the boat into a position for me to cast.

"There, now cast to the left of that ring."

Casting over your opposite shoulder is a vital skill in fly fishing, and it's one of the few special techniques I do well. I learned to do this for wade fishing in streams, but it pays off in a boat too. Your guide is generally delighted when your hooks hurtle over the bow or stern instead of buzzing their skull like a stable fly. Some guides even declare the region above their head a no-fly zone, especially when the hooks have numbers with single digits. I get the flies where they need to be, or at least close enough for Patrick to say, "Leave it there." When the tiny orange dot twitches, I'm on to my first Hebgen rainbow—an energetic fish that jumps three times before Patrick gets it into the net. It's a couple of inches shorter than the one Bob caught and noticeably thinner, but the two fish appear to use the same rouge on their cheeks. We've been on the lake for less than half an hour.

After Bob and I alternate through a few more fish—each apparently siblings to the first ones we caught—Patrick asks if we want to switch to dry flies and catch some fish on the surface.

"You guys are casting well. You'll do fine with dries," he says.

"That sounds great to me," Bob answers.

"What do you think, Tim?"

"Yeah, uh, what Bob said."

Patrick removes the indicators and flies, lengthens our leaders, and sets us up with a sparse poly-wing spinner he ties just for these fish. Then he asks me to swap seats so he can use the motor to propel us to a place he expects to have more surface-feeding fish.

"Don't accidentally hit that cleat with your foot and drop the anchor while we're motoring," he tells me.

"Is it okay if I do it on purpose?"

A smart-ass client is right behind bananas on the list of things guides love to have in their boat. Luckily for me, it's poor business practice for a guide to throw a sport overboard in the middle of a lake, and I'm pretty sure Patrick laughed. When we get as close to shore as we can without our wake alerting the fish, Patrick turns off the motor, and we swap spots again. I see some riffles where a small stream enters the lake and assume this is where Patrick plans to take us. I'm right about our destination but wrong about the riffles. The broken water is a pod of trout—some over two feet long—gorging on flies like they're auditioning for the role of the shark in Spielberg's next *Jaws* movie.

"There are several fish in there, but you'll be lucky to catch two each before we put them down. Pick a particular fish, study its feeding pattern, then make your cast count."

I feel my heart pounding in my chest, and I suspect Bob feels his too. We've both caught big trout on dry flies before, but there's something special about this moment. If bright sunshine caused our line to draw sharp shadows across the surface, or a steady wind made our boat and casts hard to control, we could blame our failure on harsh conditions. But today is cloudy and calm. Every dollar we leave on the table is our failing and our failing alone. I know it, Patrick knows it, and I think Bob knows it too.

Bob picks a fish and makes a perfect cast. The rainbow takes the fly and launches into the air. After Patrick nets it, I take my turn. My cast isn't as good as Bob's, but it's good enough for the fish. Like the ones we caught with nymphs, my fish is a little smaller than Bob's. The first time, I thought this was just a coincidence, but now I wonder what's happening. I don't know if it's mojo or juju, but Bob has something I don't. After Bob and I each catch another fish, the orgy is over, just like Patrick said it would be. "We'll head over to another spot and let these fish rest. They'll start eating again in a bit," he tells us.

A plane flies low overhead while we eat lunch. Besides being a ski instructor in the winter, Patrick is a volunteer firefighter, and he tells us this plane is carrying local smoke jumpers on a weekly training mission. In *Spring Creek*, Nick Lyons describes how heavy winds once blew a friend in a float tube across one arm of this lake, depositing him in some brush on the opposite shore from his car. Just as the fellow resolved to shuffle his way around the arm, he saw a helicopter and mistook it for firefighters on a training mission. Hoping for a leisurely ride back, his friend waved and called out, then stopped when he saw they were "depositing something from a scrotum-like net" beneath the copter. It turns out they were relocating a grizzly, so his friend hid in the bushes until the wind died down enough for him to kick his way back to the other side of the lake—another reason to be thankful for today's calm conditions.

After lunch, we fish over a dense field of underwater vegetation. Patrick warns that if a hooked fish burrows into the foliage, we'll have little chance of getting them out. I provide compelling proof of Patrick's point first, then—to leave no doubt—Bob corroborates with a fish that appears to be a couple of inches longer than mine. While Patrick replaces Bob's fly, I hook a fish about thirty feet from the boat's port side. Not wanting to leave another of Patrick's flies in the weeds, I violate the "no stand" rule and hold my rod high over my head to keep the fish near the surface. The trout flips, flops, and rolls, but the tippet doesn't break. Bob puts the net in the water, I direct the commotion toward it, and we miraculously land the fish. "Damn, Tim, you rodeoed that trout like Jimmy Houston," Patrick says.

Patrick's spinner works whenever Bob or I put it near an active fish for much of the afternoon. Around 2 p.m., though, the fish get picky, and we experiment with different flies. After a few failures, I ask Patrick if I can try a size 18 parachute Borcher's Drake, a fly that shows up in the bins of very few fly shops outside of Michigan. It's worked for me on the Big Hole and Missouri rivers, so maybe it will work here. He looks over the fly and says, "Sure, try it." I tie it on, make two false casts out of the fish's view, then drop the fly right where Patrick tells me to drop it. The little white tuft of hair disappears into a gulp, then snaps off when I set the hook too hard. "Just for the record, I didn't tie that knot," Patrick reminds me, getting even, I suppose, for my anchor-cleat remark.

A pelican walks slowly and deliberately along the shallow water off the shore. At first glance, it doesn't seem to move. But when I stare at it, I see its right leg lift slowly from the water, move forward, then drop back in. Then the left leg follows the same process. "Watch this," Patrick says when the pelican stops moving. First, the bird bends its neck back so that its head sits flat on top of its body. Next, it moves its head forward as slowly as the shadow on a sundial. When everything aligns, the bird thrusts its beak into the water, flaps its wings to stabilize its body, then lifts its head with what Patrick says is the largest trout he's ever seen a pelican catch. The bird has the fish in a T-bone position at first, but with three shakes of its head, the trout's nose points toward the pelican's throat, and the bird clamps its huge beak shut. The trout shakes and shudders in the pouch, much like it would in Patrick's net. Then the pelican points its head upward, extends its neck, and we watch one of the largest fish we've seen today slide down the bird's esophagus and into its stomach. It is one of the most incredible acts of nature I've ever seen.

"Look at us, sitting on our asses catching fish. Bigger than shit," I imagine my mom saying. So I say it myself. A little after 5 p.m., Patrick motors us back to shore. "Astonishing to see the size and number of these fish—all the hype and stories are true about gulper fishing," Bob will later write in his journal. Patrick says it was a great day too, but I know he's seen many. He floats famous rivers—hikes, rides, and camps in the Yellowstone backcountry. Patrick would be it if there were such a thing as a typical Yellowstone guide. Like onions, guides often look the same from a distance. But when you peel off the layers, they are all unique. On our drive back to Cameron, I ask Patrick if he found what he was looking for in Montana after spinning out of control in Connecticut.

"I try my best to keep life in perspective. Having been fortunate to have rowed a drift boat for fifteen years now, I have been blessed with many priceless life lessons. I've had many people with health struggles in my boat or on my horse trips, and they've shared insights about life being taken out from under them like a rug. Those moments tend to leave an impression. It's not about quantity for me anymore—it's more about quality and being grateful for just being healthy enough to be on the water. Everything after that is a bonus."

CHAPTER 14

Sunshine and Rainbows

If there are no dogs in Heaven,
then when I die I want to go where they went.

—WILL ROGERS

LIKE OBJECTS IN THE SIDEVIEW MIRROR, THE DAYS WE DREAD ARE sometimes closer than they appear. Our mind distorts reality the way a convex looking glass distorts light. Psychologists call this optimism bias, and it's one reason states sell billions of dollars in lottery tickets each year. Evolution trains us to believe we'll beat the odds for both the good and the bad. Forty percent of marriages end in divorce, but few couples exchange rings expecting to flip them at the Gold & Silver Pawn Shop. Optimists are stubborn, you see. You can't explain probability to someone certain they'll win at Powerball. I've tried. Likewise, you can't explain canine mortality to someone who loves dogs, especially when that someone is you. I've tried that too.

They say a year for a dog is like seven for a human. If we are monogamous with our pets, then, we're lucky to raise a baker's half-dozen of them. They only get one of us, though, or, perhaps, one family of us, and those soft, innocent eyes see Mother Teresa, King Solomon, and Hercules all bundled into one adorable body. We all strive—or at least we should—to be the person our dogs see. But I'm in Montana now, and my shoulders ache from the weight of an anvil of guilt. I feel neither kind, wise, nor strong knowing that today, tomorrow, or any day after might be Sunny's last back in Michigan.

Those eyes watched from the sidelight window as I rolled down the driveway a week and a half ago. Since then, apologia has bounced around my head: it's a once-in-a-lifetime trip; my son has tickets to fly from San Francisco to Bozeman; I have commitments with friends and guides. The optimist in me knows it's possible—even likely—for Sunny to be there when I get back. But I know he might not, too. I want to have done the right thing, whatever that is, but I'm afraid I haven't. I know I'm not perfect, but my dog shouldn't have to know that too.

Bob and Kate are in Bozeman today, shopping, dining, and taking care of the business that doesn't take care of itself when you hole up in Cameron, Montana, for a month. Later this evening, Bob will talk with an audience about his book, *Conversations with Jim Harrison*, so I'm on my own for the day. I wake to an empty house in the morning, have breakfast on the cabin's deck, catch up on laundry, and walk to the river. Kate told me I could fish here, but the trail seems to end between two houses on the bank. I'm afraid someone will yell at me and later chastise Bob and Kate for bringing a vulgar vagrant into the community if I walk between the houses, so I drive to an upstream stretch of the Madison River.

I stop at Galloup's Slide Inn to buy some flies, get advice, and maybe talk with Kelly. I first learned about Kelly Galloup from my friend Jerry Dennis's book, *The River Home*. "Of all the guys I fish with, none has his priorities straighter than Kelly Galloup," Jerry wrote back then. Today, Kelly is one of the most influential and notable personalities in fly fishing. I'm wearing a hat I bought in 2001 at The Troutsman, Kelly's old place in Traverse City. It's a cotton baseball cap soaked with enough bug spray and sunscreen to make it look and feel like old-time tin cloth. I wear it partly for Kelly to see, but mainly because the bill's left corner is ripped and frayed, the way so many hats come off the rack these days. But unlike those, this one was tattered by the teeth of a young Labrador retriever in 2005.

When I introduce myself, Kelly says Jerry told him I'd be stopping by. We talk about Michigan, and Kelly recounts the days when he fished alone on the rivers that attract anglers today the way shit attracts pigs. His exact words, or something like that. Kelly has a mesmerizing presence. A master of common sense; a hyper-sensitive bullshit detector; an innovator who figures out new ways to do things because he never takes the time to learn what we can't do in the first place. Had he been a mathematician, he would have devised a method for dividing by zero. I'm sure of that.

"I see you have a Troutsman hat," Kelly says to me.

"Yeah, I thought you might like that. The fray on the bill is from my dog when he was a puppy."

I tell him that puppy is fourteen years old and might not make it until I get back to Michigan. But a quarter of the way into those words, I lock up. Kelly looks me in the eye and says, "Losing a dog is tough." A phone rings, and the kid with reverse raccoon suntan lines tells Kelly the call is for him. "Stop by later. I'd love to talk more about Michigan," he says.

I drive north from the Slide Inn and park beside a historical marker for Raynolds Pass, one of several passes that cross the Continental Divide. A sign says Captain W. F. Raynolds—leading a group including Jim Bridger among other explorers—deemed it one of the most remarkable features of the Rocky Mountains. In "USFS 1919: The Ranger, the Cook, and a Hole in the Sky," Norman Maclean writes about hiking to the divide along the Idaho-Montana border and making "a small section of it real by pissing on it." Though we didn't piss on it, I remember how my mom made a big deal about the Continental Divide on our trips to Colorado. As a kid, I thought it was the only divide. But I also thought Wonder was the only bread and Kleenex was the only tissue. I sometimes miss my naive world of one-and-onlies.

I swap my cap for a wide-brimmed packer hat, walk about a quarter-mile down a trail, and stop on a ridge above the river. An island divides the flow into two channels, with several homes close to the far bank of the far channel. I worry I'm trespassing, but a woman fishing with a small kid waves instead of yells. I see two ways to get to the river, but I don't want to push my luck and crowd the woman, so I watch them fish until I worry they might worry about me. I look more like John Gierach than John Wayne Gacy with my waxed cotton hat and bamboo fly rod, but I don't want to test this. More than two out of three residents of Montana own a gun. It's not a good place for a stranger to make someone uncomfortable.

Back at the Suburban, I see a message from Roxanne on my phone. I should call her, she says. Before doing that, I check for email messages. John Voelker said we should love fishing because "mercifully there are no telephones on trout waters." A billow of blasphemy clouds the tiny screen, but the judge lived in a time when you could be away from work and family for three weeks without sometimes checking in. I don't live in that time. I have nineteen email messages, but one, in particular, seizes my attention: *All Dogs Go to Heaven.*

> *I am so sorry to have to report this news. I said goodbye to our sweet, stubborn, regal, annoying, face-licking, stick-chewing, cowardly, cheese-loving, thunder-hating creature of habit, Sunny, yesterday afternoon. He was 14 years and one month old. We had an unordinary walk in the a.m. He wanted to go down the road toward the trail parking lot, opposite our usual trek. We passed Don Weiss and his faithful German shepherd on the way—it seemed fitting. From there, we went around the Ring Loop through the trails like we used to and wound back on the Hobbit Loop to home. I brought him in and cleaned him all up, his ears and eyes. Then we went outside to brush him up. Because of his back legs, he wasn't able to let me wash his feet, which I suppose was okay. I knew it was time, and that confirmed it for me. He got some cheese and bacon, and I drove him over to the vet's office.*
>
> *He knew you loved him. I gathered all my recent photos; that's the way we remember him anyway, and I put them in a slide show. You might not want to watch around people.*
>
> *He wouldn't want you to be sad, though.*
> *Love you guys,*
> *Mom*

She sent this message to the kids and me because things like this are sometimes easier to write than to say, although easier is not the same as easy. I start the truck and drive north toward the rest area at Lyons Bridge where I'll have enough signal for a call. I can't say anything for the first few minutes after she answers. "It's alright," she says. "It was time. He was fine. I was fine." She tells me the kids took it hard too, and talking to them was more difficult than talking to me.

"Was he afraid?" I ask.

"Not at all. He was ready. Of course, he got excited when he smelled the other dogs at the vet. He never stopped being a Lab, you know."

I sit in the rest area, and Roxanne listens to me say nothing for a few more minutes. Then I tell her I love her, loved Sunny, and am so sorry to be thirteen hundred miles from home. She tells me she knows it, Sunny knew it, and there isn't anything I could have done differently. Then she says I should go fishing.

I turn off the highway toward the Three Dollar Bridge and park at the first sharp bend, well before the crowded parking areas. I don't want to see or talk with anyone. I walk a little more than a quarter of a mile to the place I fished two nights ago and find a spot downstream on a broad, slow stretch of water. It's early, and I'm alone. The famous bridge frames the mountains just like when I was last here. The water is gorgeous in a fishy sort of way, but I sit on the bank and think about my dog.

"Happiness is a warm puppy," Lucy Van Pelt—the crabbiest character in the Peanuts gang—was the first to say. Of course, she said that Puppies are happiness wrapped in a bow of delight, trusting you with their life, never doubting your loyalty. The night we brought him home, Sunny was tiny, fragile, and defiantly unaware of either condition. He claimed the spring-loaded door stops as his toys and, to the kids' horror, the electrical outlets too. "We can't leave him alone!" they declared in shock. "We'll teach him to obey our rules," I assured them. Then I stayed up all night while Sunny taught me his.

I've never been good at training dogs. I tell myself I don't have the heart for it, but my problem is patience. So I contained Sunny but never controlled him. Except for a few sleepless nights, it worked well for us. Sure, we had to wash the skunk off a couple of times and absorb ridicule and stares when he pooped in the water next to a family swimming in

Lake Superior. But he never pooped on the beach, and that has to be worth something.

He would have given his life to protect us, at least in those times when there were no thunderstorms within fifty miles. He shivered and shook as though he heard the voice of God in those blasts. The only things that would take him out of his element more than thunder were harsh words between Roxanne and me. We'd hear his enormous heart break anytime either of us slightly raised our voice at the other, and though I liked to think Sunny was my dog, in those rare moments when he felt he needed to choose between Roxanne and me, his allegiance was clear. I never faulted him for that.

Afternoon storms are as prevalent in the Madison River valley as parades and beads on Bourbon Street, and sometimes just as colorful. Sunlight striking water droplets causes it to bend—or refract—according to its wavelength. There's a well-founded physical theory for this, but most people simply call it a rainbow. Today, two brilliant bows paint parallel arcs high above the bridge. Rainbows have a way of brightening dark days, and on the day I say goodbye to a dog named Sunny, the sky reminds me how he could brighten my darkest days—even this one. He wasn't perfect, but, for me, his only substantial fault was that he couldn't live forever.

When the rainbows dissolve from the sky, several rise in the river, scatter throughout the pool, and eat with the unwary abandon of a pod of hatchery fish. But they are wild, and they feast on caddisflies, not Purina Fish Chow. I stay on the bank for at least half an hour, sitting with my rod still unstrung. I have driven thousands of miles to be at one of the world's most famous trout rivers, and though a dozen wild trout feast on every bug on the water, I just sit and watch and think about how I've betrayed my dog.

As a part-time guide, I've watched a pool churn with rising trout while a client struggles to put a fly in a place where a fish would eat it. But that's different. In that situation, I'm not supposed to fish. My job is to instruct, encourage, and provide a little tension-easing humor. The pool and all the fish belong to my client. Here on the Madison, I have the water to myself, and the decision about which fish to catch is mine and mine alone. I finally pick one out—one of the larger ones—and watch it eat. At first glance, it's playing the way a small puppy might, but with closer inspection, I see it is practicing the art of survival.

Trout eat bugs for the life-sustaining calories they provide. In the process, though, every movement of a tail or fin burns some away. Accounting for this is both brutal and straightforward. All the calories they consume go in one column; all they expend go in another. If consumed calories sum to more than those burned, they live and even grow. If the relationship flips, they die. As I watch this trout, I'm amazed at how efficiently it carries out this task, as though it does this for a living.

I pull some fly line off the reel, fold it near the end, and push the bent part into and out of each eye. I continue until I draw the line and leader through the final eyelet at the rod's tip. I tie a traditional X-Caddis in size sixteen to the 4X tippet. Sunny never fished with me when he was alive. He'd have banished every fish from this pool if he were here in body, along with every fish in every other pool within sight. Anglers generally love Labrador retrievers, but it's usually the docile ones who sleep on fly shop floors or the obedient ones who sit at heel beside the river. Frolicking through a trout stream and leaving the occasional excrement floating in the water is generally frowned upon. But he's here only in mind now, and I tell him to watch this cast.

I hook and land eight fish over the next two hours without leaving the pool. Another guy watches most of the show from his position upstream, and about a half-hour before dark, I cut off my fly, rewind the line onto the reel, and sit down on the bank. I don't smoke cigars, but—if I did—this would be the time and place to choke one down. The guy from upstream walks along the trail and stops to chat.

"Man, it looks like you had a great day today," he says.

"Actually, one of my worst."

"You normally do better than that?" he asks incredulously.

"No, it's just that my dog died today."

"Oh, I'm so sorry, buddy. I know how much that hurts."

"There are still some fish feeding in this pool. You're welcome to try for them," I say.

"No. This is your spot tonight. Take care."

After the man walks away, I finally cry. Fourteen years is a long life for a Labrador retriever, and Sunny's was a life well lived. He was the smallest of his litter, so, technically, he was the runt, but I liked to call him a miniature Lab. His shoulders were sturdy and broad for his body, his smile wide and contagious. "That's the happiest dog I've ever seen," was the most common reaction we'd get from strangers. Oh, how I miss that smile.

I know it won't hurt like this forever. Roxanne's words bounce around in my head now, pushing out some of the guilt that's made a home in there since I left Michigan:

"It was time. He was fine. I was fine."

I'll turn fifty-eight in November, so my life expectancy is about two more dogs. It's dark now, but there's enough light to see some trout still feeding heavily. I could catch more fish here tonight, but I don't want to. I take out a flashlight and walk the trail to my truck.

Bob and Kate should be back at the cabin soon if they're not there already. I'm not sure I'll tell them about Sunny, or—to be honest—I'm not sure I can. But Roxanne said Sunny wouldn't want me to be sad. He'd like me to be that Mother Teresa—King Solomon—Hercules hero he always saw in me. Half of a continent away, all I can do is try my best. To paraphrase Charles Schulz, I have tried all my life to be a good person, but I know I have failed many times. I am a human, after all. I'm not a dog.

CHAPTER 15

The Troutsman

It's the most incredible thing you'll ever do.
It's way better than sex.

—KELLY GALLOUP

MANY YEARS AGO, MY FRIEND CAM AND I SPENT A FEW NIGHTS AT ABE'S
Motel in Navaho Dam, New Mexico, fishing for big rainbow trout on the
San Juan River. Two doctors from Los Angeles stayed in the room next
to us, and the more talkative one garnished nearly all his sentences with
F-bombs. Usually, I am neither offended nor surprised when someone
blows up a sentence, and Cam is an expert powder man himself. But this
guy's sentences didn't ignite properly. Cam and I knew something was
wrong, but we couldn't pinpoint the flaw, even with Jim Beam moder-
ating a lively evening debate. But it hit us like a charging bull when we
walked down the *forking* trail to the river the next day. As *The Chicago
Manual of Style* dictates, the proper use of an F-bomb is as an adjective.
The doctor from Los Angeles used his as adverbs. Instead of walking
down the *forking* trail to the *forking* river and catching a big *forking* fish,
as an experienced powder man should do, this guy *forking* walked down
the trail to the river and *forking* caught a big fish. I understand it's okay to
break or bend the standards of style, but at some point, you have to show

your audience you know the rules and are breaking them on purpose. This *forking* guy didn't know the *forking* rules.

My friend Bo—whose name is short for Bozena—emigrated from Poland to the United States with her husband, Jarek. She grew up Catholic, and the nuns told her she'd go to hell if she blew up sentences with F-bombs. But Bo believes God speaks Polish, so F-bombs in English are just gibberish words that don't count. She's exploited this loophole so much that the navy has offered her a part-time job teaching sailors to cuss. She flings her bombs with a conscience as clear as the high mountain air, and if you—like I once did—doubt her logic on this, then notice the complete lack of emotion you feel when you say the word *pierdolić*. Unless, of course, you speak Polish.

Most people's aptitude for this craft lies somewhere between Bo's and the Los Angeles doctor's. Some people are outliers, though, and Kelly Galloup is the best cusser I've ever met. Four-letter words come as naturally to his mouth as sunlight comes to the sea. When he uses one as a noun, verb, adjective, or even as an adverb, you can't imagine another word that would work better in that specific sentence at that particular time. Compared with his, Al Swearengen's dialogue in *Deadwood* is pedestrian and unoriginal.

If you fly fish with streamers—and are serious about it—then you've heard of Kelly. In his book *Outliers*, Malcolm Gladwell explains that all great innovators share two traits: they are born in the right place and at the right time, and by the time you hear about them, they will have spent over ten thousand hours mastering their trade. For Kelly, the right place was Northern Michigan, and the right time was when no one imagined flies the size of hamsters with names like *Sex Dungeon, Butt Monkey, Stacked Blonde,* and *Smoke Wagon,* forever changing the way people viewed streamer fishing for trout. No one that is, except for Kelly and a few of his friends.

The thought of catching freakishly large brown trout in the middle of the day by stripping what looks like a two-pound sculpin perpendicular to the current must have seemed as unhinged to traditional trout anglers as the idea of flopping backward over the high-jump bar did to Dick Fosbury's competitors in the 1968 Olympics. Showing how the line between pioneer and madman can be as thin as 8X tippet, their methods not only proved to work, but they also transformed their respective sports. The *Fosbury Flop* has been used to break every high-jump world record since 1978, and I suspect an army of anglers has used Galloup's *jerk-strip* retrieve to attain equally impressive feats.

Kelly's father was one of the first guides on the Pere Marquette River in Michigan in the 1940s, but that was an era when most fishing guides were men with full-time factory jobs. Making a career out of taking people on fishing trips was as unheard of as carrying a phone in your pocket or having a robot voice tell you where to make your next turn on the highway. As Kelly might say, the idea of becoming a famous guide was the shit you dreamed about if you liked to dream about shit that could never happen. Steelhead have been in Lake Michigan longer than brown trout have been in North America, and Kelly likes to tell a story about asking his father why he and his friends didn't spend more time fishing for Lake Michigan's steelhead. "Well, dumb ass, we had this thing called a job," his dad told him. The blunt, dry-humor peach didn't fall far from the tree.

Kelly's mom built a fly-tying table for his room when he was young, and his dad put a fly angler's spin on Tom Sawyer's old trick to help him get the first few hundred of his ten thousand hours:

"Wow, Kelly, that's the best version of that fly I've ever seen."

"Really?"

"Oh, yeah. I've never seen one better."

"I can make some more for you."

"That would be great!"

Other than a boutique Orvis shop in Grand Rapids and Rusty Gates's part-time shop on the Au Sable River, Michigan didn't have fly shops in those days. So when Kelly quit his full-time job with Shell Oil to start a shop, his boss gave him that dumbfounded look you'd likely give someone if you thought they were abandoning their steady job to raise flies in their basement, which is the way he must have interpreted "fly shop" the first time he heard it. The fly-shop gig worked out for the young Galloup boy, and the rest is, as they say, history—or *forking* history, as Kelly might say. He ran his shop, The Troutsman, in Traverse City,

Michigan, for about twenty years, and he's had the Slide Inn in Montana for nearly twenty more.

If you want two paragraphs to summarize Kelly's enthusiasm for fishing, read Jerry Dennis's story "Fishing Buddies" in his book *The River Home*. In it, Jerry gives a censored recount of a conversation he and Kelly had while driving to the Manistee River in Michigan:

Of all the guys I fish with, none has his priorities straighter than Kelly Galloup. Besides being a fly-shop owner, fishing guide, fly tier, taxidermist, bodybuilder, kick-boxer, champion downhill skier, former seminary student, and dedicated family man, he's an inspired and inspiring angler and one of the few people I've ever met who fishes with more passion than me. He's also one of the most opinionated, outspoken, direct, foulmouthed, quick-witted, clearheaded, honest, funny, infuriating, and altogether delightful people I know. Count on it: He always speaks his mind. Once I asked him what it was like to fish for steelhead in British Columbia. For the sake of the kids, here's the PG-13 version of what he said:

"It's the most incredible thing you'll ever do. It's way better than sex. You watch a beeping twenty-pound steelhead eat the beeping dry fly you're skating across the beeping Camp Pool on the Dean, and I guarantee you'll never be the same. I swear to God. People talk about the way having children changes their lives, but that's nothing. A steelhead comes blasting out of the water from five or six feet deep to chase the fly, and it's coming so hard it can't stop, its momentum launches it right into the air like it's been catapulted out of the water, and you realize this son of a bitch is pissed, there's no other word for it, and you don't know what it is you've done exactly, but somehow you have really pissed him off. You can see him coming from fifteen feet away, and you think there's no way he's going to miss that fly streaking by on the current at twenty miles per hour—after all, when's the last time you missed your face with a cheeseburger?—and you get a whole beeping body rush. There's nothing like it in the world.

"But he's so stoked up he overshoots the fly, vaults right over the top of it, and crashes into the river. It's like hand grenades going off. I watched one steelhead rise like that to my buddy Mike's fly eleven times in a row before it was finally hooked and landed. It came to the beeping fly three times on the same beeping cast, each time Mike going, 'Whoa! Beep! Did you see that?' and turning to see if I had seen it, and at that moment having the fish rise,

boom! beep! and take it again, yanking line out in a screaming, ripping run, ten or twenty yards gone in a heartbeat, only to get off again. Three times on one cast! Listen: It changes your whole beeping life."

The first time Kelly and I have a lengthy chat in his shop, I tell him about the pelican I saw catch the trout on Hebgen Lake.

"I've had some great fishing on this trip, but one of the coolest things I've seen is a pelican stalking, catching, and eating a big rainbow on Hebgen Lake."

"Those *forkers* will beat the shit out of a fishery."

"How's that?"

"Well, a friend and I sat on his deck overlooking a pool in the Big Hole River one evening, and we watched a dozen of those son of a bitches dive in and eat more *forking* trout than most people will catch in a season, even if they fish on the river every day. I know they have to eat, but for God's sake, could they leave of few *forking* fish for the rest of us?"

"Does anything eat pelicans?"

"Have you ever seen eagles cartwheeling in the air?" he asks.

"No, what's that about?"

"It's a mating ritual where they lock their *forking* talons and spiral downward, letting go just before smashing their goddamn asses into the ground. I saw a pair spinning once while I was driving, but then one flew away, and the other falls to the ground like a bag full of horse shit. I stopped the truck and walked out there, and it was a goddamn pelican with its *forking* neck slit. The eagle had taken the *forking* fish right out of its gullet."

"Wow! That happens?"

"I've only seen it live once. But I found another pelican while hunting, and that *forker's* neck was slit just like the other one. There's some goddamn Godfather shit happening out there."

We talk more about Michigan and how the concept of a secret place seems more prevalent there than here in Montana, especially on a river like the Madison.

"Well, I used to work as a taxidermist in Michigan, and I had a guy bring in a brook trout he wanted me to mount. I asked him where he caught it, and he said, 'I can't tell you that.' I said, 'Yeah, we wouldn't want people to know there are big brook trout in Stanton Pond, would we?' He looked at me like I was a *forking* ghost. I'd caught that same trout three times already that season. There aren't as many secrets as people think."

Kelly is widely known in fly-fishing circles for his educational videos on fly tying. The studio for his episodes is to my right, in the room with all the shop's fly-tying materials. One of Kelly's videos usually lasts thirty to sixty minutes, loaded with personal anecdotes and detailed descriptions of subtle techniques. In contrast, if you search for videos about tying a wooly bugger, parachute Adams, or hare's ear nymph, most will be between five and ten minutes long. But not Kelly's. I tell him how much I appreciate his instruction—so much so, I try to mimic a few of his pedagogical techniques when I teach electrical engineering.

"People won't watch unless I complete a specific pattern," he says.

"But if you want to learn to tie good flies, you need to master all the basic techniques. Take a hundred hooks and just learn to set a tail. I don't mean wrap some *forking* thread around some material at the bend of the hook. You have to get it down, so it doesn't slip or rotate or extend at some half-assed angle off the hook. Then take another hundred hooks and learn to dub a body. Everybody wants to tie the entire fly when they get started, and because of that, they never move beyond being a shitty tier."

"I once heard someone complain that your videos are too long," I tell him, "but I don't get that at all."

"Yeah, some people send me emails complaining about the length of my videos, as though I'm making them watch. It's *forking* amazing. These people just want to complain about something, and I'm a good target, I guess."

A sign on the wall behind the counter has a clever—perhaps off-color—saying about whitefish. I tell Kelly about the evening I caught those whitefish on the Big Hole and apologetically say that doing so was on my to-do list.

"Don't apologize for catching whities. This is their home state. Hell, all of us anglers and most of the other fish should be apologizing to them for being here. I love those guys."

"Speaking of the Big Hole, do you fish there?"

"Sure. I have a place on that river."

"Do you get there often?"

"I floated it two days ago and didn't get anything until I switched to a little ant pattern. Then I rolled a few good ones."

He invites me to park on his property and get in the river there if I'd like.

"Thanks. I'm heading back in a few days, and I might take you up on that."

"There's a rattlesnake under my deck, so watch out for that."

"Oh no, I've been worrying about those things most of this trip."

"I don't like those bastards, either, and everyone knows that about me. We were filming a video about fishing the Big Hole up in Maiden Rock canyon a few years ago. A big brown was feeding on the surface, and the guys shooting the video said they wanted to film me catching it. So we walk down the tracks to get behind the fish, and I start climbing down the rocks to get into the river. One of those son of a bitches pulls a little plastic box with split shot from his pocket and starts shaking it behind me like a goddamn rattler. I jumped into the river, and all those *forkers* up on the tracks were laughing their asses off."

"Did they film it?"

"The camera guy laughed so hard he dropped his *forking* camera on the rocks."

A guy walks in the front door and looks lost, as though he's never been in a fly shop before.

"Can I help you?" Kelly asks.

"Yeah, I need to buy a fishing license."

"Hang on, I gotta help this guy," Kelly tells me.

After Kelly sells the guy a license, I ask him why the State of Montana needs to know someone's occupation when they buy a fishing license.

"I don't know," he says. "And I'll bet the bureaucrats who put that on the *forking* form can't tell you either. I once had a woman wearing thousands of dollars of jewelry ask me to sell her a fishing license. When I asked for her occupation, she said 'porn star' without blinking a goddamn eye. I knew right away we were going to get along."

"Another time, one of my favorite clients comes in wearing a pink feather boa and tells me he needs to buy a license. He always bought his license online before that, so I knew something was up. He's a short gay guy, looks like Nathan Lane, and always fishes with his brother, who looks like a defensive end for the Jets. When I get to the part where I ask for his occupation, he flings one end of the boa around his neck, raises both arms in the air, throws his head back, and shouts, 'Luuuuumberrrr-jack!' His brother rolls his eyes and says, 'You should feel honored, Kelly. He's been waiting all year to do this.'" I laughed my *forking* ass off.

Kelly has taken heat for the double entendres associated with the names of some of his streamers. Some say they promulgate a misogynist culture and make it more difficult for women to be comfortable in the male-dominated world of fly fishing. That's undoubtedly a downside. From what I know about Kelly, though, associating him with those things is like trying to make a two-hundred-foot cast with ninety feet of line on your reel. You're aiming way beyond your reach.

On my previous visit to the Slide Inn, I left a signed copy of *The Habits of Trout* for Kelly. Today, he tells me he's been reading it, and he really likes the introduction to a chapter called "Marginal Water for Trout":

> *Where can I catch a big trout? I sometimes field this query from fishing friends who seemingly mistake me for a person who is smart enough to know and dumb enough to tell. Our subsequent dialogue generally transpires like a scene from* All the President's Men:
> *"Follow the money."*
> *"What do you mean? Where?"*
> *"Oh, I can't tell you that."*
> *"But you could tell me that."*
> *"No, I have to do this my way. You tell me what you know, and I'll confirm. I'll keep you in the right direction if I can, but that's all. Just . . . follow the money."*
> *Whereas Deep Throat instructed Bob Woodward to follow the money, I direct my angling investigators to follow the oxygen. Trout, you see, consume oxygen like politicians devour money. Find one and you will surely find the other.*

"What resonated with you from that?" I ask.

"Oh, shit, I *forking* love the way you put Deep Throat in a story about fly fishing. That's something I would do."

Why did I bother to *forking* ask?

CHAPTER 16

Spring Creek

It was a truly remarkable river,
but on a given day you could catch nothing.
—Nick Lyons, Spring Creek

Before I left Michigan for Montana, Bob asked me to sign a
copy of my book, *The Habits of Trout*, for his friend Jim Wellington. I
recognized Jim's name from Bob's book, *Angling Days*, but I was neither
smart enough nor curious enough to associate him with his late father,
Herb, the sage-like character in Nick Lyons's book *Spring Creek*. Bob
asked if I wanted to fish in O'Dell Creek with him today, and in a parallel
fog of ignorance, I said "sure" the way I'd say "sure" if he asked me to fish
in a ditch. I'd go just about anywhere Bob asked me to go, but when he
invited me to Mecca today, I yawned my acceptance like a fool.

In an original blurb for *Spring Creek*, Harry Middleton said, "Nick
Lyons is a national treasure . . . a writer of literature who fishes, and one
of the best we have." Indeed. His writing is honest, wise, and entertaining, but devoid of overreaching cliché. Writing about his own writing,
Nick said:

I'd like the stew to be rich enough to catch some of the stillness, complexity, joy, fierce intensity, frustration, practicality, hilarity, fascination, satisfaction that I find in fly fishing. I'd like it to be fun, because fly fishing is fun—not ever so serious and self-conscious that I take it to be either a religion or a way of life, or a source of salvation. I like it passionately but I try to remember what Cezanne once said after a happy day of fishing: he'd had lots of fun, but it "doesn't lead far."

Like Sigmund Freud, Nick Lyons has always had the good sense to realize that sometimes—perhaps most times—a cigar is just a cigar.

I don't remember when I first read *Spring Creek*, but it would have been when the thought of fishing the creek was as foreign to me as the notion of playing guitar at Ryman Auditorium is today. Yet when Bob introduces me to Jim at his new home near Ennis, I'm one mile from the house where Nick stayed with Jim's father, Herb, and about four miles from where the East Branch meets the West Branch. I'm like a Civil War buff strolling along East Battery Street in Charleston, South Carolina, oblivious that Fort Sumter is the tiny island in the distance. *Learning the creek was a metaphor for all the learning I have ever done,* Nick wrote in his celebrated book—a powerful statement from a man who learned enough about writing and fishing to transform much of fly-fishing writing into fly-fishing literature.

"You're in for a tough day," Jim tells us. "Give it a try if you want, though." A storm rages to the south, and even here, we smell the rain. Scientists have a complex name for everything. *Paresthesia* is the tingling in your foot when it falls asleep; *rhumba* is a group of rattlesnakes; a *logophile* is a lover of words; and *petrichor* is the smell of rain. Generally, I love petrichor, but today the smell of rain makes me as restless as a poet searching for the right words to describe a man with a petrified foot trying to run from a rattlesnake.

Bob and I take the same two-track Nick and Herb rattled along every morning for thirty-one days over thirty-one years ago. Nick was roughly my age back then; Herb was roughly Bob's. Herb—a man whose opinions Nick described as *sharp, often raw, always telling, even when they made me smart*—studied English at Princeton, fought Nazis in Normandy, and chaired a firm on Wall Street. Just the sort of person who, as Nick described him, would *read with a shrewd and independent mind, guffawing at pretenders and second-handers.* Bob isn't a Spring Creek expert like Herb was—no one could be—but he's caught fish here twice as long as a foot-long sandwich, so he's Herb-like from my perspective.

We descend the bluff on the last bench and roll toward the wondrous place where the rutted lane crosses a shallow stretch of the East Branch. Twenty miles to the south, lightning burns the sky like alcohol, and a sheer curtain of rain enriches the distant mountains—including the one named Sphinx—with the spiritual feel of a Russell Chatham painting. We turn right toward the East Branch's confluence with the West Branch, where, just after the two branches combine, a narrow arm splits off toward the west, leaving us to continue alongside a broad and shallow main channel. Bob parks near what I ought to know are the Farrago and Paranoid Pools, but I don't. If ignorance is bliss, I'm drowning in a pool of delight alongside a stretch of the holiest water in Montana.

Field and Stream published Nick Lyons's first fishing stories, "Mecca" and "First Trout, First Lie," in the late 1960s. After that, he wrote stories for *Fly Fisherman Magazine,* where his column, *The Seasonable Angler,* ultimately became a regular feature for over twenty years. Though he was neither bumbler nor fool, he portrayed himself as both with witty tales and self-deprecating humor. Whether unknowingly singeing his fly from the end of his line with a cigar or catching a three-foot snake on a #18 dry fly, Nick Lyons was the fisherman most of us wanted to be. Knowledgeable, skillful, efficient, but self-aware and humble about his shortcomings. A student of the sport, but not the teacher's pet. When Nick first arrived at Spring Creek, his weapons of choice were flimsy bamboo rods and gaudy attractor flies, like Humpies and Royal Wulffs. By the time he left, he was matching the hatch with an eight-foot graphite rod and a custom braided leader protected by a Shockgum absorber in its middle. A seasonable angler flew from New York to Montana in June; a seasoned angler returned in July. *Spring Creek* is Nick's gift to all of us who want to believe that fishing in general, and fly fishing in particular, can play a small part in our journey.

I don't have a month to learn all Spring Creek taught Nick about stalking paranoid fish in gin-clear water. The South Bend Pool won't light up with spurts and splashes during a Green Drake hatch. I won't glow with a false sense of accomplishment after fooling a throng of overzealous fish in the Nursery Pool. Today, the temperature and barometer will drop, the wind will squawk, and Spring Creek's superintendent will close the schools. An evil wind will burn my cheek, numb my neck, steal my hat, and beat my self-esteem. I'd be smothered by anxiety if I'd had the foresight to reread *Spring Creek* before coming to Montana. But so far, I've only connected a few of the easy pieces around the border of this puzzle, and for me, *Spring Creek* is still just one of Nick Lyons's books I read many years ago. What I don't know won't hurt me. At least not today.

Bob and I begin fishing while the conditions are *bad*—about an hour before they become *wretched, bleak, desolate, depressing, miserable,* and *godforsaken*. Despite all the obstacles in our path, Bob will catch fish because—from all I know about him—Bob always catches fish. He possesses the vital characteristics all great anglers share: talent and tenacity. You can be a good angler with either, but you can't be great without both. Not knowing—or at least not remembering—how challenging this creek can be, even when the weather is ideal, I rig up planning to impress Bob by catching one of the rising fish he ignored when he moved on to the narrow channel. These fish, the ones I expect to easily catch, rise sporadically in nearly stagnant water where the main flow of the creek splits around an island. I stalk with the poise and self-assurance of a mountain lion shadowing a rabbit, but when I cross through calf-deep water to get to the island, the fish stop rising.

The river was never kind to anyone who fished poorly, to bumblers, or to those who just didn't know enough of its secrets . . .

I wait ten minutes for the fish to reappear, but they don't. Unimpressed by this sluggish flow, I look upstream and see two fish rising in relatively shallow water, just above the place where the narrow channel splits from the main flow. The little rings appear and disappear with a musical cadence, signaling that these fish will not be difficult to catch. So I move upstream into a comfortable position to cast. I don't know what they're eating, but Spring Creek is on private—and impenetrable—property, so they shouldn't be picky about the pattern. Any fly that looks like a bug should work. I wish I could tell you that my fly drags in an uneven current, my leader is too heavy, or something else that implies my cast is skillful enough to get the fly to the water before alerting the fish. But the rise forms transform into tsunamis precisely when the forward motion of my first false cast extends the fly line over the creek.

> *I called this the Paranoid Pool and, from the beginning, I never expected to catch a fish in it, though Herb said there were times, when there was a slight chop on the water perhaps, when the fish could be caught, when you might gain entrance to the Castle.*

The lightning flashes are so far away that I don't hear the thunder, giving me a false—and potentially life-threatening—sense of security. Life is plentiful with paradoxes. The more we fear, the less we enjoy. The more we learn, the less we know. The more we argue, the less we persuade. And the biggest reason we get struck by lightning is that we rarely get struck by lightning. Of course, the "rarely" part depends on the choices we make about our professions and hobbies. The Guinness World Records claims lightning struck a Virginia park ranger named Roy Sullivan seven times, the last of which set his hair on fire while he used a stick to fend off a bear stealing a trout from his fishing line. The golfer Lee Trevino was hit three times, once making his heart stop on the thirteenth green during a tournament in Illinois, but otherwise leaving his humor intact. "If you are caught on a golf course during a storm and are afraid of lightning," he advised afterward, "hold up a 1-iron. Not even God can hit a 1-iron."

Unlike steel golf clubs or graphite fly rods, bamboo is a poor conductor of electrical current, and because of that, God's lightning bolts won't find me as readily as they will someone waving a graphite rod, like Bob, for instance. So I'll keep fishing as long as Bob does, and if the little bit of hair left on my head gets set ablaze by a fiery bolt of lightning, Bob can tell Roxanne I went out happy.

Now there was nothing to think about but the fishing. It was a truly remark-
able river, but on a given day you could catch nothing; during the weeks I
was there, three people—all fine fishermen—got skunked. Once I got none;
Herb always got fish.

I've always preferred games that mix luck with skill in a way that gives
both nearly the same importance. Because of this, I love to play cribbage,
but I barely know the rules of chess. Cribbage—like fishing—is a game
of chance, but much like the guy who taught us to pasteurize our milk
advised us, chance tends to favor the prepared mind. If we are skilled at
cribbage, we'll beat a lesser player more times than not, but we won't win
if we consistently get cards that smell like the inside of a guide's waders
in October. So we play the cards we're dealt the best we can and start
anew with the next hand. Somedays, we dance between the raindrops,
dry as a cactus. On others, the ravens kill every ladybug in our house
while we spill salt, break mirrors, and pound nails after sundown. And
even though I'm blessed to be fishing on Spring Creek today, it is one of
those other days.

Bob says the fishing has slowed—the fish have "lockjaw," as he puts
it—so we return to his car, eat our sandwiches, and regroup. As long as it's
safely digestible, anything and everything tastes like a $25 sandwich from
Katz's Delicatessen when you tuck it between two pieces of bread, wrap
it in aluminum foil, pack it in a small cooler with ice, drinks, and cook-
ies, and eat it beside a river with a friend. When he was dying of cancer,
Warren Zevon told David Letterman we should enjoy every sandwich.
But out here, surrounded by mountains and magpies, neither Bob nor I
need the excitable boy to remind us.

Bob tells me about Nick's last visit to Spring Creek and how Nick
missed a large trout that rose to his black cricket while he was distracted,
telling a story about fishing in the Keys. Another hint that should alert
me to the significance of this day. I ask Bob to describe the fly pattern,
and then I search my box for something similar. Chance tends to favor
the prepared fly, you know. But being favored doesn't guarantee a win.
Harry Truman beat Thomas Dewey in 1948, the US hockey team beat
the Soviets in 1980, Buster Douglas beat Mike Tyson in 1990, and

though you won't see it on the front page of the *New York Times*, Spring Creek will beat me in 2019, even though I—like those more renowned losers—consider myself prepared and favored to win.

But how, really, does a river beat us? I tell people—as, perhaps, you do too—that I don't need to catch fish to have a good time fishing. "A bad day of fishing beats a good day of working," I say when I'm comfortable casting clichés. Again, what exactly is a bad day of fishing? I once found myself ass-deep in quicksand about an hour before dusk with no bars on my cell phone. I didn't think I would die, but I wasn't sure I wouldn't. Assuredly, that had the potential for a bad day of fishing. But if we measure these things by the enthusiasm with which we later tell the story, it turned out to be one of my best.

So, here I am, thirteen hundred miles from home, casting a black cricket tight against one of Spring Creek's countless undercut bends, nearly oblivious to the history surrounding me. One of my casts attracts the attention of a nice fish, but it's the "Excuse me, could you tell me what time it is?" sort of attention, not the "Hey sexy, do you come here often?" type I'm chasing. The wind has whipped up small whitecaps on the water, obscuring my view of the bottom of the creek, which is probably a good thing for my sanity.

> When the wind did not ruffle the surface of the river too harshly—giving it a slate, opaque cover—the water was so translucent that you could see distinctly to the bottom of the deepest pools. What I could see in some of them, five to eight feet down, wavering like living shadows near the bottom, sent shock waves through me.

I won't catch a fish here today, and the truth is, I won't feel the intense magic of this place until I've left it. On my long drive back to Michigan, the audio version of *Spring Creek* will bake a cake layered with sadness and joy in the hollow oven of my stomach. Like Bob Seger running against the wind, I'll find myself wishing I didn't know then what I don't know now. I'll reread *Spring Creek* many times back in Michigan, hoping to understand this day better. On cold winter nights, I'll see the lightning, feel the wind, and hear the creek cut away a little more soil from underneath these mysterious oxbow bends. And it will all make me desperately want to return and find the truth of this day.

Ernest Hemingway said every writer should strive to write one true sentence, and Harlan Howard famously described good country music as three chords and the truth. But what is this thing we call "truth?" By its definition, fiction is a lie, though some of the greatest truths ever told are accounts of things that never happened. Nick Lyons fished Spring Creek over several summers. That's as true as a mother's love. But the truth in his writing has little to do with the factual accounts of his time at Farago, Second Bend, or the Nursery. The truth is what he thought and felt in those places. We readers will tolerate—perhaps even encourage—a writer who stretches the size or number of fish they catch. If they want us to believe something deeper and more spiritual, they better be like Nick:

> I would as well be here, beside this pool, right now, as anywhere in the universe. I have thought about such a place without knowing it existed. At times I have wished life as simple as this riverbank—the world a logical structure of bend, current, riffle, and pool, the drama already unfolding on the glassy surface, and me, here on the bank, my ass wet, armed with some simple lovely balanced tools and some knowledge, prepared to become part of it for a few moments.

I want to become part of this place again, if only for a few moments.

CHAPTER 17

The Richest Hill on Earth

It's a mining town in lotus land.

—F. SCOTT FITZGERALD

I SAY GOODBYE TO KATE AND BOB, DRIVE NORTH TO ENNIS, THEN WEST on MT 287 toward Alder Gulch. The highway twists through the narrow tourist towns of Virginia City and Nevada City—artifacts of an era when every self-respecting gulch-goer owned a gold pan, sluice box, and at least one of Samuel Colt's revolvers. The need for heat was acute—in a single year in the mid-1800s, bandits killed nearly one hundred people on the road between here and Bannack, causing counter-gangs of *Montana Vigilantes* to round up and hang suspected marauders, including the Bannack sheriff and his gang of *Innocents*. In a script as old as civilization, gold begot greed, greed begot guile, and good and evil stamped their seals on opposite sides of the same calamitous coin.

The nefarious activities of those days were byproducts of one of the richest placer gold strikes the Rocky Mountains would ever yield. In its basic form, placer mining was a simple operation: European immigrants with walrus mustaches, flat-crowned hats, leather boots, button-up gaiters, and moleskin pants shook and swirled shallow metal pans, betting their lives on the minuscule—but non-zero—chance that all that glitters would be gold. Good old Sven Bergman might wake up too broke to pay attention in the morning, find a nugget more precious than a baby's smile in the afternoon, and go to bed one of the wealthiest rascals in the gulch that night. Much like people, though, mining towns begin to die the day they are born, and all that shimmers and shines eventually decays to dust.

Some people and places postpone the inevitable by choosing the more promising of Charles Darwin's conflicting paths. William Andrews Clark was one of those. Clark made modest money during the Alder Gulch gold rush, but instead of holding tight to what used to be, his interests evolved into the business of selling food, tools, and other supplies to miners. Through those ventures, he made enough money for an East Coast education at the Columbia School of Mines, then returned to buy some fledgling shafts in the mostly abandoned gold-mining town of Butte.

Because nearly all the easy gold was gone, Butte's population had fallen from around one thousand to about one hundred in less than ten years. Silver ignited a revival, and a half decade after the inventions of the lightbulb and telegraph, another mining operator—Marcus Daly—unearthed copper in the Butte hills, triggering Butte's transformation from a dying town into "The Richest Hill on Earth." As the copper-mining empire grew in Butte, Daly and Clark—along with the newcomer Augustus Heinze—played a seemingly endless game of king of the hill. The stakes for the feud between Daly and Clark were wide-ranging, including a US Senate seat, for which Clark unabashedly boasted about his corrupt campaigns: "I never bought a man who wasn't for sale." Unimpressed by Clark's exploits, Daly's friend Mark Twain wrote that Clark was "as rotten a human being as can be found anywhere under the flag." Clark was doubtless as dirty as a dung beetle, but none of the king's scepters were shiny and clean.

The Copper Kings' narcissistic battles brought both prosperity and pain to Silver Bow County. A notable part of the prosperity was the establishment of the Montana State School of Mines in 1900, which opened with one building, twenty-one students, and the option for two degrees. Today, the university operates as Montana Tech with more than sixty degrees and roughly three thousand students. The chancellor is a man named Les Cook, who, until about a month ago, was a vice president at Michigan Tech—the place I teach electrical engineering to young women and men when I'm not off living my secret life of fishing or writing about fishing. Because of that, I've known Chancellor Cook for a decade and a half, and when I told him about my trip to Montana, he invited me for a university tour, an evening in Butte, and a night's rest in the chancellor's residence.

Much like the Keweenaw Peninsula's Michigan Tech, which began as the Michigan Mining School with twenty-three students in 1885, Montana Tech's reason for being was to serve a booming copper-mining industry at the turn of the century. And this bond through mining in general—and copper mining in particular—makes Montana's Silver Bow County and my home range in Michigan's Copper Country somewhat like fraternal twins reared by different parents.

The first known use of copper—a pendant discovered in Northern Iraq—was over ten thousand years ago, and for the next five thousand years, the patriarch of the penny was the only metal in use. After millennia upon millennia of pounding stones and honing bones, Ancient Sumerians began smelting copper around 3500 BC and alloying it with tin or arsenic to make bronze, prompting a dramatic changing of the Age. Bronze made more durable hammers, halberds, daggers, dirks, swords, and spears than other materials of that time, which afforded significant advantages to the people who used them. And most notable for an angler, bronze made better fishhooks than shells or bones.

The twenty-ninth element on the periodic table also played a prominent role in the anatomical development of modern society. Copper pipes were the arteries; copper wires the nerves; copper-coiled machines the muscles. In its early history, the United States relied on transplants, and most of the copper came from Europe and Latin America. But in 1840, Douglass Houghton—the state geologist of Michigan and the namesake for the town in which I live—wrote that he hoped "to see the day when instead of importing the whole of the immense amount of copper and brass used in our country, we may become exporters of both." His description of the copper deposits in Michigan spurred a copper rush—and as he hoped might happen—Michigan's Copper Country was the world's number one supplier of copper from 1869 until 1876. Here in the United States, the Copper Country was king until 1887, when Butte began its two-decade reign before ceding the crown to Arizona.

The chancellor's residence is a jewel in the navel of Montana Tech's campus, stationed about a block and a half from a statue of Marcus Daly. Past occupants include J. Robert Van Pelt, who piloted Montana Tech in the early 1950s before becoming Michigan Tech's president until 1964, further solidifying the parallel histories of these two regions. "Much like Michigan Tech, Montana Tech is a gem in a beautiful part of the country," the twelfth chancellor tells me. "The history of Butte and the legacy of this region is remarkable."

Les escorts me on a walking tour of campus, around and through the well-worn buildings for mining, geology, science, engineering, and, of course, by a dormitory called Prospector Hall. We stop beside the Museum Building where we look east across Leonard Field—a recreation space for students—with brilliant pine-green grass everywhere except for the sun-burnt blonde and buttermilk patches the sprinklers can't reach. Beyond the field, the city of Butte unrolls to the southeast, held back by the East Ridge of the Continental Divide, where a ninety-foot statue of the Virgin Mary looks down upon the city. Dark clouds hover above the East Ridge, and although miners snatched the pots of gold long ago, a faint rainbow arcs over the multicolored terraces and roadways of the open mine surrounding the Berkely Pit.

The Berkely Pit is a time bomb of sorts, containing over forty billion gallons of water laced with copper, arsenic, cadmium, zinc, and sulfuric acid. The surface level for the pit is about fifty-three hundred feet—only one hundred ten feet below the Environmental Protection Agency's highest permitted level. To keep the gauge height safe, the Atlantic Richfield Company and Montana Resources draw out the contaminated water, extract the venom, and expel what remains into Silver Bow Creek. Beyond the pit, the hill's history reveals a lethal ground for time bombs, and just a half-mile northeast of the pit, a memorial marks the site where one hundred sixty-eight miners died in the 1917 North Butte mining disaster. The culprit was a three-ton electrical cable insulated with oil-soaked cloth that—in a tragic twist of irony—workers had lowered into the mine to provide power for a state-of-the-art fire sprinkler system. When the men lost control of the cable, it plummeted a thousand feet down a shaft, and when a foreman later inspected the wreckage, the flame from his lantern ignited an eight-day disaster.

Les and I leave Montana Tech's campus and drive to Foreman's Park, where the Mountain Con mineshaft displays the self-explanatory slogan, *Mile High, Mile Deep*. Looking out over a mixed residential and commercial section of Butte with mine shafts interspersed between buildings and houses, Les tells me that nearly ten thousand miles of tunnels—roughly the distance from New York City to Sydney—twist beneath this city in a complex arrangement that would impress a town of prairie dogs. To put these burrows into sharper perspective, Earth's diameter is less than eight thousand miles.

Our next stop is the Granite Mountain/Speculator Mine Memorial. Flags for sixteen countries line a wall, representing the diverse nationalities of the men who lost their lives from the initial fire and the ghostly fumes that replaced their air. From the memorial's patio, we see the towering skeleton of the headframe for the Granite Mountain Mine, the mournful remnants of the Speculator Mine, and the terraced, patchwork quilt of colored earth surrounding the Berkeley Pit. One display tells the story of Manus Duggan, a thirty-year-old "nipper" who saved the lives of twenty-five men during the fire. Nippers were men who sharpened drill bits, delivered tools, and ran other errands for the miners, serving as underground delivery boys. Like their above-ground counterparts, an essential part of their job was knowing the best way to get from point A to point B, especially when it wasn't a straight line. That knowledge, along with a calm courage you never know you have until you need it, made Manus a natural leader for the frantic miners trapped in that deadly maze. He knew lethal gas was the primary threat, so he convinced a group of men to build bulkheads in a dead-end tunnel. Because of this unimaginably difficult accomplishment, all but four of the twenty-nine men in his group survived. Sadly, Manus Duggan was one of the four who did not. Sensing the dire situation he and the other men were in while huddling in the damp darkness, the heroic nipper scratched a note on the inside wall of the bulkhead, and these were among his words:

Have not confided my fears to anyone, but have looked and looked for hope only, but if the worst comes I myself have no fears but welcome death with open arms, as it is the last act we all must pass through, and as it is but natural, it is God's will. We should have no objection.—Duggan

Les suggests we move on to the An Ri Ra Montana Irish Festival in the nearby Original Mine Yard to lift our moods. The way this community embraces its history is about as subtle as a shark in a tide pool, and the stage sits beneath the restored headframe for the old mine. When we arrive, ten dancers in black costumes and heavy-healed shoes tap and stomp to the haunting music of what I call bagpipes. "Don't let anyone hear you say that," Les warns. "Those are called uilleann pipes and mistaking the Irish for Scots is like mistaking a cat for a dog. You might get your eyes scratched out."

"Fair enough," I say.

"Speaking of the Irish, do you like Bailey's Irish cream?" Les asks later on our way to dinner.

"Yeah, actually, I do."

"Great, I'm going to ruin that for you now."

We stop at the Headframe Spirits micro distillery in the historic district of Butte. With another tip of the hardhat to the local heritage, the distillers have named their spirits for local mines: High Ore, Anselmo, Neversweat, Kelley, Acquisition, and Orhpan Girl. Les orders two glasses of Orphan Girl bourbon cream liqueur, advertised as "rich and creamy, but not too sweet, finishing with hints of caramel and bourbon." The name comes from a mine Marcus Daly bought in 1879, but the taste comes from heaven.

"Well, you were right. Going back to Bailey's now would be like trading my Sweetgrass rod for one of those $40 Ozark Trail outfits at Walmart."

"I don't know what that means," Les says.

"It means I'll be taking a few bottles back to Houghton. I don't think I'll be able to drink Bailey's again."

"I told you so. How are things back in Houghton?"

Like Butte, the legacy of mining in Houghton and the surrounding towns is one of riches and ruin. Historians credit the region's copper rush with creating more wealth than California's gold rush, but the decades have left more busts than booms. The center of the surge was nearby Calumet, Michigan, whose population today is over seven times smaller than in 1900. The copper mines are closed, but a few headframes and museums remind us of what once was. Strip mining for copper didn't take hold in Michigan, so there are no poisonous groundwater pits to contain and clean. But there is an EPA superfund site at Torch Lake, where local mines routinely dumped tons of polluted mill tailings—or stamp sand as we locals call it—into the lake.

Technically, Michigan's deadliest mining disaster happened in 1926, when a dynamite explosion triggered an underground avalanche and flood that killed fifty-one men. Another tragedy occurred at a Christmas Eve party in 1913—four years before the Butte catastrophe—when seventy-three people, fifty-nine of whom were children, crushed one another in a panicked rush to escape the Italian Hall in Calumet when someone falsely shouted, "Fire!" The party guests—mainly union miners and their families—had gathered in a second-floor room with only one steep stairway to escape. During an investigation a year later, several witnesses claimed the man crying wolf wore an anti-union button on his coat.

The kindred history of the two regions isn't what Les is after, so I briefly respond, "Everything's fine," and order us another round of Orphan Girl.

Later that night, after dinner, I climb the wooden stairway to my Victorian bedroom in the chancellor's house and think about the painful connections between Butte and my home. They say you must crack a few eggs to make an omelet, but these regions have broken enough to put Denny's, Bob Evans, IHOP, and the Waffle House out of business. The Decemberists' song "Rox in the Box" and Nick Spear's "Tap'er Light" are mournful recollections of the mining disaster in Butte, and Woody Guthrie's "1913 Massacre" is a haunting condemnation of the slaughter in Calumet.

Years ago, I saw a brief story about another mine closing in the Copper Country, relegated to the back of the newspaper between the police reports and wedding announcements. Struck by such an uneventful ending to an eventful era, I wrote a song of my own called "They Shut the Last Mine Down":

They sailed 'cross the ocean, with little emotion
The weak, the strong, young and old
And when they came forth, they settled up north
'Cause they weren't afraid of the cold

Their English was broken, so little was spoken
But actions meant much more than words
With backs that were sore, they dug up the ore
Protected from bad air by birds

The iron and copper, they filled in the hopper
Built cities where wealthy folks lived
Time without loved ones, daughters and young sons
Were the hardest things for them to give

And that's what I thought of when I read the news
On the back page of the Mining Gazette
Beside a picture of a young girl in a white wedding gown
It said they shut the last mine down

When they spoke with accents, their words didn't make sense
To people too well-off to care
But the sons of their children, made the well-off a million
By working like they had down there

The times they did change, and their work was to blame
For the stuff that they dug from the ground

Built fancy machines and all sorts of things
That moved all the jobs from their towns

And that's what I thought of when I read the news
On the back page of the Mining Gazette
Beside a picture of a young girl in a white wedding gown
It said they shut the last mine down

The run-down old shacks, that haven't collapsed
Are all that we see of their time
We rarely ask why, as we drive on by
Did they suffer such a decline?

But that's what I thought of when I read the news
On the back page of the Mining Gazette
Beside a picture of a young girl in a white wedding gown
It said they shut the last mine down

They sailed 'cross the ocean, with little emotion
The weak, the strong, young and old
And when they came forth, they settled up north
'Cause they weren't afraid of the cold

Michael Punke ends his excellent book, *Fire and Brimstone: The North Butte Mining Disaster of 1917*, with a poignant tribute to the hardy people of these sometimes cruel and unforgiving towns who gave—and still give—all they had and have so the rest of the nation might grow:

> *The story of the American West is the story of hope. Hope, defiant, in the face of overwhelming proof that it should not exist. Hope, even in Butte, where after every crushing blow, the people stand up again, dust themselves off, and go back to work. Hope so irrational that it can only be understood as faith.*

In Michigan, we use the Finnish word *sisu* for what Punke describes. In English, it's more of a concept than a word, much like New England is a region, not a state. Similar to explaining the scent of memory, the flavor of rain, or the sound of silence, defining this word is an endeavor in art, and no artist has done it as well as my friend Jerry Dennis:

> On cars and trucks throughout the Upper Peninsula you often see bumper stickers printed with the Finnish word sisu. Derived from a cognate meaning "inner" or "interior," it is usually translated into something like stubborn determination, perseverance, or strength of will in the face of adversity, though it suggests more nuanced qualities as well. . . .

> In English it is most closely approximated by "guts," but that familiar slang swaggers with masculine valor and battlefield heroics, whereas sisu transcends gender and ignores momentary courage to honor the more difficult valor of enduring without complaint a lifetime of ordinary hardships.

> It is the Yoopers's humble anthem, adopted by those who have survived a single winter as readily as those whose ancestors immigrated to work in the copper and iron mines.

> It is stoicism stripped of its philosopher's robe and dressed in a Woolrich hunting coat and a Packers cap, with a chainsaw in the back of the pickup and a snowmobile rusting all summer in the yard. It means sticking to a job until it is finished, no matter how difficult it is or how long it takes, and one of those jobs, the one that requires the greatest endurance and the most courage, is life itself. In a harsh climate and inhospitable land, sisu helps a person get by with dignity.

For someone living in Michigan's Copper Country, getting to know Butte is like meeting a cousin you never knew you had. You shake hands at the reunion, notice your noses share identical slopes, your ears have matching lobes, and just like you did before you lost your Southern Illinois accent, they drop the letter "g" from the end of every word that needs it and add the letter "r" to all the ones that don't. You're saturated with curiosity, but tomorrow's a workday, so you shake hands again, vow to keep in touch, then drive away, knowing you'll likely never see each other again. But you got their number, so who knows?

CHAPTER 18

Learning to Look Out

In a life properly lived, you're a river.

—JIM HARRISON

OTHER THAN REVISITING THE BIG HOLE AND BEAVERHEAD RIVERS, I don't have firm plans when I leave Butte. Instead, I hope to cycle between pools and riffles like a carefree kid with a shiny new sky-blue Schwinn Stingray, racing down the streets with the wind in my hair and the sun on my face. But Bob threw a stick into my spokes when he sent a note last night saying there was a *Hoot Owl* restriction on the Big Hole River. At first, I wasn't sure why a restriction on owls would affect my fishing, but when I asked the guy behind the counter at the fly shop in Melrose, he straightened me out.

Hoot Owl is a phrase that goes back to the logging operations of the early 1900s. When the summer sun scorched the forests, the slightest spark from a chainsaw, choker, or truck could ignite an inferno that might spread like a grease fire in a filthy kitchen. But the fire risk was lower in the cool mornings when the dew still clung to the trees and the air was as soft as a whisper. So the loggers worked only in the early hours, often accompanied by a parliament of owls hooting and flitting from pine to fir to larch. Hoot Owl, then, became the moniker for work or other activities in the earliest—and coolest—part of the day.

In the context of fishing, the State of Montana puts a section of a river like the Big Hole under Hoot Owl restrictions when its daily maximum water temperature exceeds 73°F for three consecutive days. When that happens, anglers can fish only between midnight and 2 p.m. When I ask the guy behind the counter at the fly shop in Melrose what this means for the river here, he tells me the restrictions apply only below the Notch Bottom access site, about twelve miles downstream. "The river is fine up here for now, with a water temp of fifty-nine in the morning," he tells me, "and the guides are doing well."

Following six nights of sleeping in beds, I look at the air mattress and sleeping bag in the back of the Suburban with the disdain of a pampered cat who's gotten used to sleeping on satin sheets and goose-down pillows but now has to settle for a worn-out bath towel in a cardboard box. Then I see the Sportsman Motel next to the fly shop and run through the pros and cons: the Suburban lets me use the just-in-time approach to finding a place to sleep for the night; the motel has a bed, refrigerator, freezer, microwave, toilet, sink, and shower. Rugged fellows like me must get soft when they sleep in beds for a week—before the automatic lights on the Suburban have turned off, I'm standing at the counter asking the gentleman behind it if I can pay with cash, as though I'd made up my mind back in Butte, well before I entered the Interstate 15 ramp.

I decide to fish the Big Hole River in Maiden Rock Canyon the following morning, so after I check into my room, I drive thirty miles south to Dillon, park the Suburban, and walk another mile to my favorite spot on the Beaverhead River. It feels good to be alone, even for a guy who hates to say goodbye. I treasured the time with my friends, but now, alongside the hypnotic meter of the Beaverhead River, I find that thing every solitary angler seeks: solitude without loneliness. Other than the day Sunny died, I haven't thought deeply about him. Of course, I've thought of him every day, but I've had enough distractions to keep me living outside my head. Now that I've moved back in for the evening, Sunny's in there with me.

Native American cultures hold a deep respect for the natural world, believing animals possess unique wisdom, spiritual energy, and even an innate ability to communicate with us two-leggeds. Animals, they believe, can be totems, providing insight in our times of confusion and understanding in our times of distress. Bears symbolize strength and wisdom, eagles signify courage, wolves embody loyalty and freedom, and the American buffalo or bison represent abundance and manifestation. Over the next three hours, a duck, deer, muskrat, and porcupine will all come within arm's length, nearly impervious to my presence. It will be up to me to figure out if these creatures are totems or just four happy-go-lucky spirits utterly unafraid of the intruder in a sweat-stained fedora with sunscreen paste on his nose and two days of stubble on his cheek.

As I approach the river from the east, and as I take my last step before entering the water, a mottled brown patch of grass shifts off to the right. "Quack!" it says. The duck doesn't panic or set off a bomb of feathers and foam like they often do. Instead, only that quack, or, to my ears, something more like a low-pitched "murk." They say ducks symbolize emotional balance and adaptability. In this context, the old saying, "Like water off a duck's back," has an appropriate double meaning, reminding us to spread some preen oil over our soul, at least figuratively. Water is a symbol of emotions, and in the water, ducks portray a calmness above the surface, even when those little webbed feet are paddling like mad below. "Murk," this one says again, then sets afloat for a downstream destination.

I cross to the west side of the river, then wade mindfully downstream, searching for a little nose pushing through the water's surface, signaling a hungry—and possibly catchable—brown trout. Enough flies are in the air to warrant my search, but I don't see the precious little dimples that bring eager grins to my face. The chirps and trills of sparrows ring out like a Stevie Wonder song in the key of life. I feel a presence in the thicket behind me—the sound of motion and maybe even breathing. Turning around, I lock eyes with a small doe. Her right ear lights up like a faint beacon with a dark chestnut glow—upright, fully splayed, and backlit by the sun. The deer totem is one of quiet inner strength, innocence, gentleness, grace, and healing. I brace for the deer's exit: a spring-loaded escape as close to flying as an animal can make without wings. Instead, we stand eye-to-eye until I say something stupid like, "Hi there, how are you doing?" As if it's thinking, "Oh no, not another guy who wants to talk about old dogs, children, and watermelon wine," the deer turns away and disappears into the bramble.

After the doe shuffles away, the sun pops from behind a lone low cloud and shines its light on thousands—perhaps millions—of caddisflies bobbing and weaving like tiny prizefighters in a ring. I move upstream and sit in the weeds on the point of one of many oxbows in this section of the river. As a kid, I never found a limit to how long I could sit and watch a bobber. And now that I'm on the AARP mailing list, I can sit alongside a river until darkness pushes me off, provided I have the tiniest belief that a good fish might rise. I'm not overly picky about where I sit. Anything with support for my back is better than something without, and I always check logs, rocks, and boulders for ants and snakes. After today, I'll check soft undercut banks for muskrat burrows too.

From my seat on the bank, I see about a hundred yards of the river. The flow is mostly smooth, with one rock breaking the water's surface into swirls and eddies about ten yards upstream. As the sun sinks behind me, its rays serve as stage lighting for the supporting actors fluttering about in the first scene of this play. The big stars are still below the curtain, patiently waiting for their cues. Something that looks like a peanut-shaped log appears to my right, just above the broken water from the rock. It floats with the current the way a log should until it angles to its left and starts swimming directly toward me.

Muskrats are symbols of resilience and perseverance, reminders of the importance of resourcefulness and hard work. Stubbornness too, I suspect, based on this one's behavior. When it recognizes a two-legged sitting over the entrance to its home, it curls around the current and up into the lee of the rock. Then it turns toward me and starts floating again, occasionally stopping, apparently to size me up. About ten feet away, it holds a position with its nose and eyes barely out of the water, waiting for me to make the next move. I try my "How are you doing?" trick, but the oversized vole doesn't flinch. Neither my fight nor flight instinct kicks in, so I get back to scanning the river for rising trout. At some point—five, ten, or even thirty minutes later—I look to my right, and the muskrat is gone. It's not as scary as seeing Michael Myers no longer lying on the ground behind Jamie Lee Curtis in the penultimate scene of the fifty-seventh sequel of *Halloween*, but it's a little unnerving.

The first fish rises close to where I hooked and lost the enormous brown trout on my first night here. But like a fleeting dream, it never returns. A confetti storm of bugs hovers in the air and drifts on the water now, and I'm in a race with darkness. I have a good flashlight—four of them, actually—but I don't like the idea of walking back to my truck in the dark of night. I want to catch a fish or two and walk out before the blue-gray ceiling turns pitch-black. With all the protein on the water, this should look like a piranha attack in the Amazon, but the fish aren't rising the way they should. Maybe the muskrat ratted me out to the trout. This is the way it works, isn't it? In an interview with Jim Fergus, Jim Harrison said, "In a life properly lived, you're a river. You touch things lightly or deeply; you move along because life herself moves, and you can't stop it; you can't figure out a banal game plan applicable to all situations; you just have to go with the 'beingness' of life." A life properly lived is unpredictable at the margin, and so, too, is a river.

I gather my fly and reach for my clippers to remove it from my line, symbolically ending my fishing for the evening. But just as I do, a trout feeds like a drunk gourmand in the center of the river. I regroup and cast. The trout takes the fly on my first try, boring upstream like a wild mustang stung by spurs. A caddisfly flutters between my right eye and the lens in front of it, and another flies into my left nostril. But I hold tight to the reins, hoping to tame this feisty colt before my self-imposed curfew. When the fish tires—or surrenders—I cradle it between my legs in the basket of my net, remove the hook, and release it into the "beingness" of life.

On my way back to the Suburban, I see a dark clump waddling along the half-hearted trail in the shrubs and brush in front of me. The porcupine is said to be tough on the outside but soft on the inside, sometimes associated with self-defense and caution. It's not as romantic, but these prickly rodents walk like they're carrying a load of bricks on their back. Like the other animals I've encountered tonight, though, this one seems aware of—but completely unconcerned by—my presence. It just waddles along like it's navigating a minefield, and when we get to a fork in the trail, the porcupine takes the low road, and I take the high one.

I walk to the Hitching Post the following morning for a breakfast of scrambled eggs, hash browns, sausage, and toast with enough butter to grease a tractor. I sit alone at the bar next to a pair of antique-style tin signs: one advertises Trixie's Fly Fishing School, where they "teach you to keep your rod up," and the other promotes Mary Lou's Backwater Fishing Excursions, where they "take you deep into the bush." Not surprisingly, Jim Harrison frequently stayed at the Sportsman Motel and often ate and drank his meals here at the Hitching Post, probably sitting on the same bar stool I'm sitting on now. Likely placed there by design, a poster of Harrison hangs high on the wall above the double-edged signs with the quote:

> *Some people hear their own inner voices with great clearness. And they live by what they hear. Such people become crazy . . . or they become legend.*

I dreamt about Sunny last night. But I still haven't figured out what I'm supposed to make of my encounters with the animals on the Beaverhead River. "Death steals everything except our stories," Harrison said. Outside of his fear of thunder, Sunny had admirable emotional balance, and he was wholly and immediately forgiving of all perceived wrongdoings. He was innocent, gentle, and graceful, with a resilience that sometimes bordered on stubbornness. Tough on the outside when he needed to be but always soft as an innocent child on the inside. Death has stolen him, but you'd see all those totem characteristics in any story I could tell about my dog.

I don't have the insight of a great poet like Jim Harrison, but maybe learning to look inside begins with learning to look out. And like it is with so many things, the three essential parts for doing that are location, location, and location. So we'll see what happens today when I drive to Maiden Rock Canyon and immerse myself in the Big Hole River, where hawks weightlessly defy gravity the way stories defiantly defy death. I'll dip my ragged hat into the river and ask the cold, regenerative water to soothe my sweaty scalp and calm my crowded mind. From a seat on an ancient boulder, I'll listen to the noise of nothing and everything at once. And if those things aren't enough, I'll take up chain-smoking American Spirit cigarettes and learn to love lamb tongue, beef cheek, and calf brains.

CHAPTER 19

Skunked

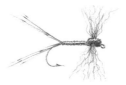

The fishing was good; it was the catching that was bad.

—A. K. BEST

LATE ONE SUMMER NIGHT IN MICHIGAN—IMMEDIATELY AFTER I LET Sunny out for his evening constitutional—the hypersensitive olfactory nerves in his snout sent an urgent signal to the olfactory bulb in his brain, and that triggered his legs to propel his body on a beeline toward a small stand of birch trees in our yard. The siren that drew him wasn't a tree; instead, it was a small, stocky animal with black fur banded by two ivory stripes. My warning was as useless as a tungsten bead on a dry fly, and in the time it takes a sailfish to go from zero to sixty, Sunny was the target of a chemical-warfare attack.

The consequences of losing this battle were immediate and severe. We removed our vehicles from the garage so the yellow dog doused in yellow oil could "shelter in place" for the night. In the morning, Roxanne mixed up a concoction of baking soda, dishwashing detergent, hydrogen peroxide, tomato juice, newt eyes, frog toes, bat wool, and lizard legs. A few rounds of wash-rinse-repeat and Sunny's stench faded from an awful amalgamation of rotten eggs, cabbage, garlic, reefer, and burning rubber into a milder mix of bat wool and tomato juice. But after that, every drop of water that touched Sunny's coat for the next three months awoke the foul-smelling hellhounds squatting in his downy fur.

The word *skunk* originated in the early 1600s as an Algonquian term that loosely translates to *the fox who squirts urine*. Eventually, the Algonquian's *skunk* evolved and branched into the denominal *skunked*. Since then, politicians, athletes, cribbage players, college students, curious dogs, and anglers have come to know the word more intimately as a verb than a noun. For my first two weeks in Montana, I've been most worried about encountering a grizzly bear, rattlesnake, or mountain lion. But on my fourth day in Melrose, I'm chiefly concerned about the proverbial verbal skunk chronicling my days on the water.

Regarding being skunked, I once wrote,

There was a time when I believed I could solve the mysteries of trout in particular and of life in general. But now I think we sometimes need to get skunked. We need to break our line on a good fish every now and again, and sometimes we need to cast all day without a take. We need to be grounded by the humility of failure so we can be lifted by the hope of success.

Like sex in the kitchen, vegetable smoothies, New Year's resolutions, New Coke, stainless steel cars, and balloon loans, some things make perfect sense the first time you hear about them. But in practice, they leave you shouting, "Who in the hell is the marketing genius who came up with this idea?" Thoreau is famously misquoted as warning that many of us go fishing all our lives without knowing it's not the fish we are after. This popular conjecture is more true than false, but you don't find many anglers—including the enlightened ones—casting hookless flies. To paraphrase the old Harvard professor Theodore Levitt, you don't buy a drill because you want a drill. You buy a drill because you want a hole.

A few years after Sunny's encounter, when our yard again betrayed the telltale signs of a resident skunk—dozens of beer-bottle-sized holes in the ground and, well, the frequent presence of a skunk—Roxanne and I asked our friend Jarek if he could use his traps to relocate the intruder. The traps were wire cages with doors on both ends, designed so the skunk would view them as harmless tunnels. Jarek put peanut butter and chicken on the traps' triggers and told us to call him if the doors went down. The first time the doors dropped, the skunk escaped with Jarek's food. "That happens when they are sneaky sometimes," he explained. The next time they fell, Pepé Le Pew spent a long and lonely night in solitary confinement.

Jarek had trapped and released several skunks with these cages. Enough so that in addition to being Michigan Tech's second-best professor and fly fisherman, he is considered one of the Upper Peninsula's master skunk whisperers. Sensing that we were nervous, he explained his process. "Because cage is small, skunk will not have room to lift tail to spray. To be safe, I will put blanket over cage, cage in car, and skunk will be gone." The blanket keeps the skunk from seeing its captor, and, in principle, a skunk that doesn't see its captor stays calm, and a calm skunk is less likely to concede to the urge to spray.

Skunks come in various sizes, and this one caused a problem by being smaller than any skunk Jarek had trapped before. In addition, the blanket that keeps the skunk from seeing the captor also keeps the captor from seeing the skunk. Because of that, Jarek didn't notice the small skunk had raised its tail into the *ready/aim* position inside the cage. When he placed the trap in his vehicle, the blanket slipped to one side, and the undersized skunk carried out the *fire* command.

Jarek stood about fifty yards from our house as he explained the predicament. "They never do this to me before," he yelled. "This was pissy one, for sure." Roxanne asked if he'd like her to mix up some frog toes, bat wool, and tomato juice, but Jarek said he'd prefer a standard shower when he got home—a place where he'd need to tread cautiously to dodge the torrent of F-bombs his wife, Bo, would undoubtedly launch. Jarek kept the traps active for two more nights, and when they didn't apprehend another skunk, he said, "I don't think you have more skunks at this moment. It explains why this bachelor was so pissy." Because Jarek was then and is now proficient at solving skunk problems, I share this story to illustrate the sometimes-severe costs even the best of us pay when we battle a skunk, be it either the noun or verb version.

I once dueled with the verb form on a branch of the Otter River in Michigan, and it, too, was a pissy one, to be sure. Every riffle and run I visited that day was as dead as a dodo, and my pursuit of water that shimmered with hope took me through a labyrinth of deadfalls, gullies, and crags. Pollen, sweat, and mosquitos competed for the prime positions on every square inch of my skin that was not covered by Gore-Tex, cotton, or waxed canvas, and my fly rod's line shook hands with every thorn, sprig, and bramble in the woods. The fly rod was my favorite—an eight-foot, six-weight bamboo Winston I'd bought from Jerry Kustich when he downsized for his move to Mexico. It was a marvel that the rod and I made it back to my truck unharmed, so, pressing my luck, and with about a half hour of light remaining, I walked a short trail to the most accessible stretch of the river for a few more casts.

The surface dimpled with hope, and on my fly's second drift, a sixteen-inch rainbow quashed my skunk. "It was all worth it!" I shouted on the trout's first jump from its world into mine. But when the fish breathed my air for the second time, I heard a loud pop and sensed something horrible had happened. While my right hand held four feet of bamboo, an equal length zip-lined over the river and toward the trout. Parroting my friend Jarek, I mumbled, "They never do this to me before." As miracles go, this one was minor, but I landed the fish and reclaimed both ends of my broken rod.

Tautologies usually signal poor writing, but dramatic occasions sometimes justify trampling the rules of style. "Well, the only way to say this is to say this. I broke the Winston rod I bought from you in 2013," I wrote to Jerry, including details of how I broke it, along with some photographs of several nice fish the rod and I had landed.

"Great story, but a sad one as well. I should be able to rebuild that butt here at my shop. I want to look at it as well to see how it failed. We can always learn something from a break." With that, I shipped the rod to Jerry's new address in Charlestown, Maryland, and waited for the surgeon to bring my friend back to life.

"I have been agonizing over a path to fixing the rod and went the obvious route of reattaching the ferrule, making the rod an inch shorter, but still effectively the same rod," Jerry wrote. "I can't guarantee it won't break again. It looks like the initial break was due to over-baked cane, making the blank slightly brittle."

"Thanks for all your help with this," I wrote back. "As I said, this has been my 'go-to' rod for many years, and I've had some great adventures with that stick at my side. The rod has been an important part of my life, and now it sounds like it's becoming more and more like me: a little bit shorter and more brittle."

Jerry returned the mended rod in April 2018, and now, in August 2019, I'm thigh-deep in the Big Hole River, hoping this magic wand will help me evade the skunk that's followed me for a day and a half.

❧

There was nothing unusual or exceptional about the beginning of this particular skunk. Gale-force winds on the Beaverhead up by the dam two evenings ago made conventional casting impossible. Instead of gracefully sweeping the rod through a single plane by raising and lowering my elbow like John Juracek, I held my rod vertically in the air, fed line through my guides, and let the wind pull the fly, tippet, and leader along a nearly horizontal path upstream and over the river. As you might expect, I didn't catch a fish, but I had a few near misses, and when the wind beats you until you quit beating back, you write that off with the angler's favorite cliché: *that's why they call it fishing, not catching.*

The next day, with the previous evening's troubles out of sight and mind, I caught an unmistakable whiff of the skunk. I was on the Maiden Rock section of the Big Hole, hoping for billowing clouds of Tricos to bounce above and then onto the river. Impervious to my fantasies, the bugs came in wisps, and scarcely any of those made it to the water. A few small trout denounced my presentations, and after twenty-seven attempts to get my fly in front of it, the one nice fish feeding near the far bank broke my tippet on the hook-up, and the sulfury smell of the skunk became too strong to ignore.

I needed to regroup, so I hiked to the truck, spread tuna over a pita, and considered my next move as if I was a chess player trapped in a zugzwang. "You can catch some nice fish in the Ruby," a guy in one of the fly shops had told me, "but you need to look out for those rattlesnakes. Our guides use their landing nets to tap on the rocks in front of them. That lets the snakes know you're coming and gives them a target other than your shin if they decide to strike."

Lyndon Johnson once alleged that Gerald Ford was incapable of farting and chewing gum simultaneously. For a high-profile politician who spent most of his days under public scrutiny, that strikes me as a feature, not a flaw. Slide a slab of Wrigley's Spearmint in your mouth, and never worry that some snoot might pin a stray *braap* or *fraap* on you. "Hey, that wasn't me," you could say. "I'm chewing gum."

Unlike the thirty-eighth president of the United States, I can fart and chew gum at the same time. What I can't synchronize is worrying about rattlesnakes and fishing effectively. And because the vivid vision of guides tapping rocks with their landing nets kept me worrying about rattlesnakes, I fished the Ruby River with an attention to detail somewhere on the spectrum between Bob Dylan combing his hair and Father Time trimming his beard.

Six guys from New Mexico were drinking beer and stowing their gear when I returned to the parking lot. "Any luck?" the guy with the long black beard asked.

"Nothing. I think I spent too much time worrying about rattlesnakes in the rocks. Did you guys see any snakes?"

"Nah, we don't worry about snakes," the bald guy with the Royal Wulff tattoo on the side of his neck told me.

"Did you guys have any luck?" I asked.

"Nada. When the water looks milky, my friend, you might as well sit in the shade and drink a beer. Especially if you're the kinda guy who's afraid of snakes."

As I pulled out of the parking area, the guy with the Sergeant Carter buzz cut shouted, "Take care, brother." Having been summarily reduced to a downcast pantywaist running from snakes and trying to leave a skunk behind the cloud of dust in my rearview mirror, I drove on to Dillon.

I left the Suburban in a parking area near Poindexter Slough and took off on foot for the Beaverhead River. Along the way, I started a conversation with a man returning from a fruitless outing on the slough. In the process of small talk, we discovered we both knew Jerry Kustich, although this guy knew him better and had fished with him several times.

When I reached the Beaverhead, I sat in some weeds on a small peninsula inside a slight bend. Shortly after settling in, I heard voices coming from upstream, and I waded a few feet into the river so I wouldn't startle the guys in the boat.

The heavy-set guy wearing a straw cowboy hat and pulling on the oars started the conversation.

"Why'd you wade out in front of our boat?"

"Sorry about that, but I didn't want to scare you when you got to me," I explained.

"We both have sidearms, so you aren't going to scare us," the shirtless skinny guy in the bow announced. And to erase any doubts I might hold about the integrity of his proclamation, both men showed me their guns. That should have scared me more than it did, but the third passenger in the boat was a yellow Lab that could have served as a stunt double for Sunny.

"How's the fishing been?" the guy on the oars asked, seeming to want to break the tension.

"Nothing yet. I'm just sitting here waiting and hoping some fish will rise. How about you guys?"

"It's been great. We've caught twenty-six big fish on hoppers so far. You should try a hopper."

Twenty-five minutes after the gunmen passed, a good fish poked its nose through the surface on the other side of the river. Sporadic at first, it soon developed the steady cadence about which every dry-fly angler dreams. But just as I slid off the bank, I heard new voices.

A heavily tattooed man in a yellow inner tube led the way. Behind him, a buxom lady in an undersized two-piece swimsuit sat in an inflatable kayak with an oversized cooler.

"Hey, dude, how'd you get in here?" the tattooed man asked.

"I walked in from a parking spot on the other side of the highway."

"Damn, you hoofed it."

"Yeah, I suppose I did."

"Would you like a beer?" the buxom lady asked.

"No, I'm fine, but thanks for asking."

After they floated and splashed directly over the top of my trout, I wished I had taken the beer, for that was the only trout I'd see rise that night. Back at the Suburban, in the faint light of the moon, something growled at me from the surrounding woods. It might have been a coyote, a wolf, a bear, a Bigfoot, or maybe even a serial killer. I didn't want to know, so I kept my waders on and drove to the Safeway in Dillon to remove them. I needed some supplies anyway, and, as the guys I met on the Ruby would gladly corroborate, I'm a pantywaist.

I've been here at the Big Hole River for about an hour this morning, slipping and sliding on rocks near the mouth of Fishtrap Creek. A few fish rise sporadically, but the skunk has followed me from the Ruby and Beaverhead, and all my casts come up empty. A man is fishing about a hundred yards downstream, and from this distance, he looks like John Gierach. His rod curves like a question mark over his head, but rather than net a big brown or rainbow, he wades out a few more steps, bends over, and frees his fly from the river bottom. After that, he walks along the bank back toward me, and when he gets closer, I realize he looks more like Jeff Bridges than John Gierach, which would be great too, but he's neither of those men.

"How's it going?" I ask.

"Caught the bottom a few times, but that's about it. This might be the right place, but I don't think it's the right time. I'm outta here. Take care, partner."

"You do the same."

I pick a flat boulder, sit, and worry that I've become obsessed with the score. Writing about being skunked in *Fly Fishing Through the Midlife Crisis*, Howell Raines warned, "Time is a rider that breaks us all, especially if our only pleasure—in football, fishing or love—comes from keeping score." Indeed, better anglers than I have been skunked. When John Voelker recalled the *Life* photographer, Bob Kelley, shadowing him for photos to accompany a story about his piscatorial skills, the famous fisherman wrote, "There was one other lesson all of us learned: that my

Upper Peninsula of Michigan trout, at least, want no part in appearing on any photographic command performances."

But then it happens. First, a nose pokes above the surface, then a dorsal fin surrounded by the vermiculate patterns Cormac McCarthy described as "maps of the world in its becoming." I've written twice about catching the biggest brook trout of my life, and if all goes well, this will be the third. Fate has thrown me a hittable pitch, and I will not strike out with the bat on my shoulder. I wade effortlessly into position, draw some fly line from the reel, measure the distance with two false casts behind the fish, then hear the sickening sound of a snap.

Orthopedic surgeons call this a *nonunion*—a fracture that doesn't heal and mend properly. Jerry Kustich warned this might happen when he repaired the rod, and now, with the figurative sound of thunder echoing in my ears and half of my favorite bamboo rod floating on the river, I accept the anguish of arriving at rock bottom. Unmoved by my predicament, the trout continues to feed. I return to my seat to watch this fish devour the unsuspecting flies. Somehow, I find peace, knowing I have no means—and no desire—to fool this trout and haul it to my side. Maybe it's not the fish I'm after, after all.

CHAPTER 20

Grayling

A few observers had the foresight to realize the bounty could not last forever.

—JERRY DENNIS

IMAGINE A LAND OF VIRGIN PINES AND UNTAMED RIVERS, WHERE EVERY new bend reveals a scene envisioned by an artist, not an entrepreneur. Below each river's surface, slate-blue fish with olive-green backs and oversized dorsal fins cruise about in the carefree way of their ancestors. The trees are twice as tall and three times as wide as a telephone pole, but they spread about like staggered pillars in a temple, allowing you to see for hundreds of feet in all directions. A web of limbs and branches frames a thatched roof above your head. A lattice of soft needles weaves a spongy carpet below your feet. Some type of bug lands on the water and promptly vanishes, leaving a fading halo as the only marker of its existence.

The nearest city is Crawford, but the town's name will soon change to Grayling to honor the fish with the elaborate fin on its back. To the south, in cities named Detroit and Chicago, each decade sees twice as many people as the last. The demand for new homes, and churches, and schools, and stores far exceeds the supply. These are boomtowns for build-ers, provided they have the timber.

Rugged men with handlebar mustaches—the sort who inspire the wardrobes of twenty-something hipsters in another century—will fell the trees, then skid them, roll them, jam them, and drive them to the mills. And though the drives will scour the rivers and strip them of their shade, the grayling will win the battle and survive. But like Lee after Chancel-lorsville, they won't win the war. And unlike Lee at Appomattox, they won't be asked to surrender.

Crowds will come from the cities built upon the bones of the pines. The town named for the fish will welcome these people, mostly for the money they spend. The visitors won't be great anglers, but it won't matter. Nothing will have prepared them for a battle like this—the grayling will eat anything that looks like a bug. The people will catch them and catch them and catch them until the day when they can't catch them anymore.

What I have asked you to imagine is the story of Michigan's grayling. I often fish the Otter River, where Walter Erickson caught the last of these fish in 1934. There are still more deer than people along this river and more otters than boats. But the white pine and grayling are gone, and we have failed to undo what we have done. We have tried, but like automobiles and reputations, fragile fish populations are much easier to maintain than to repair.

Tomorrow is the last day I will fish the Big Hole River, and I still haven't caught a grayling. Without a guide, I've struggled with one of fly-fishing's golden rules: *Don't leave fish to find fish.* I catch a brown trout, and—though I know I should know better—I think the grayling will be upstream. When I get a brook trout upstream, I guess the grayling must be downstream. And so I jump from spot to spot when I should pick a section and fish it. I worry now that I've run out of jumps.

When I explain my dilemma to the guy working at the fly shop in Dillon, he asks where I'm staying. I say Melrose, and he says, "Ah, hell, just go up to Lake Agnes. You can catch all the grayling you want."

"Where is Lake Agnes?" I ask.

"See if you can find it on your phone's map," he counters.

I show him what I find, and he says, "Yep, that's it."

"You're gonna drive to Brownes Lake on Rock Creek Road. When you get there, you can park and walk a trail for about a mile to Agnes, or, uh, do you mind driving on a rickety road?"

"Well, I live in Michigan's Upper Peninsula. That's the only kind of roads we have."

"Great, then you can drive past Brownes Lake, and the hike will be about half as far. Some people don't like to drive that road, but if you're good with rickety roads, you'll be fine."

"Should I worry about bears?"

"I don't, but I always take my dog with me, and she barks if a bear gets too close. Ain't that right?" he says to his dog, who doesn't wake up to answer.

"What flies should I use?"

"It won't matter much. If you wanna catch a bigger one, you might need to get a nymph down deep. But if you just wanna catch a grayling, anything on the surface will work."

I want to do this in the Big Hole. It's the only river I know of in the lower forty-eight that still has native grayling. So, the next morning, I drive to the Fishtrap section for my last shot at a fluvial grayling. The river here snuggles against a wooded hillside and flows with modest riffles between occasional braided channels. Shafts of sunlight break through the pines from the east. Clouds of tricos appear from nowhere when the breeze blows them from the darkness into the light. Some of these tiny flies are on the water, and several fish have taken seats at the cafe counter.

The fish are neither easy nor hard to catch. When I make a well-placed cast with a drag-free drift, they take my fly. When I screw it up, they don't. They demand a particular order in their world, as we do in ours. We do not want to see weevils mill about in our oats. When we do, we do not eat them. We should expect no less from the fish.

Every fish I catch is a marvelous brook trout. In the small streams near my home in Michigan, these would be the best fish in the river. And they'd behave that way too. Like emperors, they'd force the small trout to sit at the counters in the easy-to-find Main Street cafes while they received their spread at a dimly lit booth in a hard-to-find reservations-only bistro. Perhaps, it occurs to me, that's what's happening here. The fish I'm catching—the ones in the easy lies—are the small ones. The emperors are taking their meals in seclusion.

I stop fishing and scan the river. I see two boulders closer to the far bank, still shaded from the morning sun, with a smaller rock between them causing a little riffle with an irregular cadence. Something doesn't seem right about the scene, though, and when I look closer, I see that the riffle's source is a snout. And more than a foot behind that, I see a tail.

The fish has chosen its venue well. The two boulders block a cross-current presentation from either side. If I'm to do this at all, it will be from upstream or downstream. Because I'm already a bit down, I decide to attack from the stern. This is the place in a fishing story where the fisherman tells you how he extends his tippet to avoid casting the thicker part of his leader over the fish. How he false casts to the side just once to measure the distance, then wiggles his rod three times at the end of his forward progress to place the tiny fly two feet above the fish with just enough slack to avoid drag but still allow for a quick hook set. Often omitted from this story is the part where, upon being hooked, the fish jets forward, then to its left and into the river's main flow. With the fisherman's line wedged into one of the boulder's cracks, the fish swims directly downstream in a manner that breaks the line just as the fisherman sees how large the trout is. "How dangerous emperors are when they go mad," says the fisherman.

Faced with what now appears to be long odds for catching a grayling in the Big Hole, I drive back to Melrose and set my GPS for Brownes Lake. It's a sixteen-mile drive from my motel. The first nine miles on Interstate 15 will take eight minutes—the last seven on Rock Creek Road will take twenty-five. I must climb about twenty-four hundred feet to get from Melrose to Lake Agnes, and I'll do the first fourteen hundred in my truck.

Like Dr. Jekyll, the introduction to Rock Creek Road conceals the ruthless thing it will become. Despite having to slow for the occasional cattle grid, I make good enough time at first to believe I might beat the

GPS forecast. But after the road splits, it occurs to me that if I had had the forethought to put my dirty clothes into a cooler with warm water and detergent, I could agitate a load on my way in and another on my way out. I actually speed up when crossing the cattle grids now. And when the road enters the woods and parallels its namesake, I abandon any notion of arriving at Brownes Lake before the GPS predicted I would.

About a mile from the lake, I feel like I'm driving along the side of a mountain. A scree slope—sparsely dotted with trees—is on my right, and on my left appears to be an abrupt drop into a canyon. I don't worry too much because large trees have somehow taken hold along that side of the road, and even I—with all my tendencies toward doing so—can't envision my demise. This, I mistakenly believe, is the rickety part of the road.

At Brownes Lake, the road turns right for about four hundred feet, then turns left to parallel the shore. For the next four hundred feet, it's just like it had been before—scree to my right, a barrier of trees to my left. I relax and think about the grayling I'm going to catch soon. Then, on the left side of my truck, the trees vanish, and Brownes Lake is below me.

What happens next has happened before. Roxanne and I were walking across the Golden Gate Bridge, and—for the first thousand feet or so—there was a high fence to my right that protected me from falling, jumping, or having someone push me over the edge. But when we passed a large concrete column, the high fence disappeared, and I saw every way a person could fall, jump, or get pushed over the low railing. I locked up tighter than a cross-threaded wing nut. Roxanne escorted me back to safety, convinced me to focus on the simple tasks of breathing in and breathing out, and with her help, we walked across that bridge, drank margaritas in Sausalito, and hailed an Uber to bring us back to the Marina District.

Perched on a road that seems barely wider than my SUV, with a scree slope un-dotted by trees on my right, and a seventy-foot drop into Brownes Lake on my left, I put the transmission in park and count my breaths. Two people in float tubes on the lake egg me on with their thumbs. "You can do it," they yell, but their version of therapy is nothing like Roxanne's, and—without her help—the demons will win this fight.

I put the truck in reverse, slowly back up until I can turn around, and then park. I take off my sweat-drenched shirt and fumble through my duffle to find my cleanest dirty one. A mile isn't that far to walk, especially on a well-marked trail, so my closed-toe sandals—the waterproof ones that stencil the cool tan lines—should be okay, I think. I head out with my fly rod, a water bottle, and a sling pack with two boxes of flies— all the things I should need to catch a grayling. A few steps into the trail, a yellow sign reminds me I should have picked up my bear spray canisters at the motel in Melrose.

I tell myself this is black bear country, and black bears don't attack people. So onward I go. The guy in Dillon who told me the rickety road along Brownes Lake wasn't that bad also told me the trail wasn't too tough. It now occurs that his definitions of "bad" and "tough" differ from mine. It also appears that the people who built this trail were unfamiliar with the concept of a switchback. Either that, or they charged by the foot, and the people responsible for paying wanted to get it done at the lowest possible cost. The trail has an advertised length of 1.4 miles, and the point-to-point distance on a map is 1.2 miles. That's about as straight as you can make a trail up the side of a mountain.

If you want to climb a thousand feet over 1.4 miles, you could set your treadmill at an incline of 14 percent. But if the first quarter-mile is relatively flat—as it is on the trail to Lake Agnes—you'd need to set your treadmill at an incline of 16 percent for the rest of the way. And if sections of the trail are level, you'd need to go even higher for the other parts.

After more than thirty minutes of this heart-pounding hike, I come to a fork in the trail. There are no signs, and I don't have my phone to use for GPS. But I catch a break when a hiker appears on the upward branch of the fork.

"I'm happy to see you," I say. "I'm not sure which way I should go."

"You must be looking for Lake Agnes," he says as he points one of his hiking poles at my rod. "You'll have fun up there. The fish are jumping all over the place."

The guy isn't a fisherman. He has leather hiking boots on his feet, a hiking pole in each hand, and four canisters hanging from his belt. Two of the canisters are vacuum-insulated water bottles. The other two are bear sprays.

"Am I almost there?" I ask.

"Yeah, the hardest part is behind you. You still have some climbing, though."

From there, the treadmill incline increases to 20 percent, even higher for some segments. I put my shoulder to the wheel, as they say, and arrive at the lake unscathed, except for a few bruises on my unprotected ankles and ego.

Lake Agnes covers about one hundred acres, with a circumference of roughly two miles. The trail dumps me on a sandy beach about the size of a hockey rink. I sit on a log and take it all in. A civil engineer can make a career out of this simple rule: *water runs downhill and sits in the relative lows*. Though her surface is about seventy-five hundred feet above the sea, Lake Agnes is in a relative low. Mountaintops rise all around her, and when the wind doesn't blow, she paints their portraits on her surface. The lake is sandy and shallow here in front of the beach, but large boulders line the shore and lake bottom to my right. That, I decide, is where I will catch my grayling.

The hiker said the fish were jumping all over the place, but none rise now. Is it possible? Could it happen? I banish those thoughts, pull the line through the guides, and put on a small fly called the Betty McNault. It has a red tail, a peacock-hurl body with a red floss abdomen, brown hackle, and a calf-tail wing canted backward in the Trude style. This style was "invented" around the beginning of the twentieth century by Carter Harrison during his stay at the Trude Ranch in Idaho. Bill Nault created my pattern for the streams in Michigan's Upper Peninsula and called it the Betty McNault in deference to a similar fly from Colorado called the Betty McNall. In fly tying, as in most fields of scholarly pursuit, every original idea you'd like to claim as your own was likely plagiarized at least once by someone before you.

A fish rises in front of a large boulder that slopes down into the lake. I strip line off the reel, make three false casts over my left shoulder, and then set the Betty in the rise's vicinity. *Pick up and cast again*, says the voice in my head, but I resist. The wind corrugates the lake's surface, and the little fly bounces on the ripples. Just before I give it a twitch to imitate life, a compact oval-shaped mouth claims it for lunch.

It's a small grayling, but the noun—not the adjective—is all that matters. An olive-gray body with tiny heart-shaped freckles arranged in solos, pairs, and trinities, all aligned obediently in rows defined by silver-hued railings. And of course, a flashy fin on its back. I catch and release four more—including one over a foot long—and then cut off my fly, rewind the line on the reel, and start the downhill march to my truck.

When hiking up the mountain, my eyes focused on the place I planned for my next step. If I looked up from the trail, I saw more of the trail. Pretty much the definition of monotony. Hiking down the mountain is a different game. I still keep my eyes mostly on the place I plan for my next step, but I don't see more of the trail when I look up. I see the sky, and below the sky, I see a seemingly endless hill. The kind of incline that—once you got rolling—would lower your altitude by several hundred feet in the time it took to say, "Oh, the humanity!" Unless, of course, a tree brought your body to an abrupt, V-shaped halt.

Mountains are inherently unstable. The bellies of some are literally on fire, always working up their next violent belch of magma and basalt. And for the others, gravity relentlessly pulls them down rock by rock, scarring their sides with scree. When the trail brings me to the crossing for one of these slides, I lock up, just like I did on the road beside Brownes Lake. Standing here, I look out and see the lake and the road below me. The beautiful view and frightful trail have conspired to take most of my breath away. Above the road, a rocky mountain looms over Brownes Lake, flaunting the diagonal markings of its birth. The scree road—the one that scared the hell out of me—is a simultaneous marvel of ingenuity and asininity. The two anglers in their float tubes are tiny white dots beside a shallow shelf in the lake. Facing me down, though, is a faintly marked trail across resting rocks that wait to complete their roll to the bottom of the hill. I find a suitable walking stick, establish a cadence for my breathing, and put one nervous step in front of the other.

By 7 p.m., I'm back for my last evening on the Big Hole, on a section near the Divide bridge. Freed from the need to pursue grayling in the upper part of the river, I'm following a tip two guys in the motel gave me last night. They said the little slick spot I'm sitting beside was thick with rising fish at dark the night before. At about 8 p.m., a raft of seventeen mergansers slowly paddle upstream, then set fire to their trail to get past me. At 8:30 p.m., I see a single fish eat caddisflies in the tail of the pool, and I get a chunky rainbow on my first cast. Another fish rises at 9 p.m. It's been a long, rewarding day, and I tell myself this is the last fish. I hunch to reduce my profile and waddle across the rocks to get close enough for a cast. The fish pulls hard when I hook it, then swims a short arc and flops and rolls like a walleye. On one of the flops, the muscles in its back contract, and then—as if to show they still have some say about the places they choose to live—the oversized dorsal fin flairs to reveal the trademark of Montana's fluvial grayling.

CHAPTER 21

Wait, Watch, and Wonder

The good life is one inspired by love and guided by knowledge.
—BERTRAND RUSSELL

DESPITE THE ADVANCEMENTS IN OUR MODERN WORLD, SOME PEOPLE still listen to music from vinyl disks, fry chicken in cast-iron skillets, learn about the world from newspapers, and scratch unintelligible notes in cursive script with fountain pens. When you encounter these folks, they might be winding their watch, sharpening their razor, or dropping off five quarts of used motor oil at the recycling station. But whether or not they fly fish, you'll never have to explain why you use a bamboo fly rod. It will be as natural to them as the smells of woodsmoke and pine.

I bought my first bamboo rod from Dave Delisi at Sweetgrass in August 2011. It came from their Mantra series, and when assembled, the newborn measured seven feet and nine inches from end to end, with a neatly tapered six-sided driftwood-brown body highlighted by burgundy bands. A marking on its butt said it could handle a four- or five-weight line, depending on my mood. Parenthood suited me, and less than a year later, Dave and I conspired to give my firstborn a seven-foot, three-inch, six-sided sibling with a penchant for propelling three weight lines. With Dave's help, I was hooked on bamboo like a bear on birdseed.

A month later, my next child was Ron Barch's "Voelker's Nijinsky," the most popular of my children during the show-and-tell back at the cabin with Joyce and Al. Like the smallest of my Sweetgrass kids, Nijinsky separated into three pieces, which Ron housed in a handmade six-sided walnut case.

Roxanne hadn't yet figured out what I was up to, and by the time she unraveled the clues, I'd adopted two more bamboo rods from Jerry Kustich. One was a seven-foot, five-sided rod with two tips for a four-weight line, which Jerry made as a prototype during his days at Winston. The other was the eight-foot, six-weight Winston rod that broke mid-cast two days ago on the Big Hole River. I've brought all these rods to Montana, and today I'm driving from Melrose to Butte so the first two can meet their maker, Glenn Brackett.

Mariners extol the importance of a sound and sturdy rudder—that vertical plate or blade on a ship's stern that keeps the vessel on track when the sky turns green and the ocean mean. Without it, high winds and waves might hurl them on an unruly path with no sense of direction and purpose. Ever since Glenn and Tom Morgan moved the Winston Rod Company from San Francisco to Twin Bridges—where the Beaverhead, Ruby, and Big Hole rivers become the Jefferson—Brackett's rudder has been as true as any that has sailed the sea.

The Sweetgrass logo reflects Glenn's calm sense of purpose: two trout swimming in both apposition and concordance; one black, one white; one yin, one yang. In the pre-Sweetgrass days, when Glenn was the heart and soul of Winston's bamboo rods, Russell Chatham wrote—and Charles Kuralt narrated—a documentary on fly fishing in Montana called *Winston Waters: A Philosophy of Flyfishing*. In one scene, when Glenn and Tom McGuane are preparing to fish, McGuane asks Glenn about his gear:

"Why aren't you burdened with a great vest like I am?"
    "That's a good question."
"Where are your flies?"
    "I've never been a big believer in all those accoutrements and condiments and the bells and whistles thing. I keep it simple . . . a box."
    "That's it?"

"You know, with a little leader material and Tao."

"Tao being the fish?"

"Very much that way."

⌒

Building a bamboo fly rod requires a saint's patience, a surgeon's skill, and an inspired artist's eye. The first step is to select a straight and sturdy piece of cane—an oversized wooden straw grown and gathered in the Tonkin region of China. Some builders then use a froe—or cleaver—to split the straw into strips, while others, like Glenn, use a tool resembling a cross between Thor's hammer and a turbine fan. Either way, they aim to split the cane into a half-dozen to a dozen pieces that will be sculpted and later glued back together.

After splitting the cane into strips, the builder dries them in an oven, mills them into triangular shapes, then refines the strips into a precise taper for the rod. After that, they glue four, five, or six of these pieces together to create the rod's blank. Then, like a detective at a crime scene, they hunt for evidence of misdeeds and wrongdoing before further shaping and smoothing the blank to their precise prescription. Next, they fasten the line guides with wraps of thread, and lock the reel seat, ferrules, and cork grip into their positions with glue. When everything is set and secure, they finish off the rod with several coats of varnish. It sounds so simple that even I could do it. Except I can't.

I've heard people who ought to know say it takes less than one hour to learn everything you need to know to remove someone's appendix, but it takes four years of medical school and at least three years in residency to know what to do if anything goes wrong. And so it is with bamboo rod building, although most bamboo artisans skip formal schooling and go directly into residency.

During Glenn's three decades at Winston, three men in particular—Jerry Kustich, Jeff Walker, and Wayne Maca—mastered the craft of bringing cane to life in Glenn's Zen-like residency program, ultimately being anointed the collective title of the *Boo Boys*. Boo being short for bamboo, of course. They were trout-bum rock stars in a trout-bum

Mecca, living a meditative existence of practicing what they preached and preaching what they practiced. Like a Rolex watch or a Mercedes sedan, a Winston rod built by the Boo Boys was crafted with precision and built to last. But their partnership with Winston was not.

For artisans like the Boo Boys, outsourcing any part of building a bamboo rod makes about as much sense as Picasso outsourcing brush-strokes on a canvas or Yo-Yo Ma outsourcing bow pulls on a cello. It simply goes against the core of their craft, which is to create something unique, beautiful, and precise with their own hands and expertise. So when Winston executives suggested moving some of the bamboo rod production work to China, Glenn announced he would leave, and the Boo Boys followed their sensei to his new company, Sweetgrass Rods.

The community of people who care about bamboo rods is tight, and when word spread that Glenn and the Boo Boys were building a new brand of rod, Sweetgrass received hundreds of orders virtually over-night. In April 2006, they set up their shop in a renovated garage and started splitting, sanding, planing, gluing, wrapping, and shipping. They delivered their first rods two years later, and with that, Sweetgrass was a celebrated brand known for making high-quality—yet relatively afford-able—bamboo rods. In 2009, the Sweetgrass crew moved from garages to an honest-to-goodness shop in downtown Twin Bridges, where they stayed until 2015 when Glenn moved the workshop to a modest building in downtown Butte, less than a block from Headframe Spirits and their remarkable Orphan Girl bourbon cream liqueur. A month after Sweet-grass left, an electrical problem in Winston's bamboo shop ignited a fire destroying over one million dollars in property and equipment, including most of their valuable cane supply. By this time, Jerry, Jeff, and Wayne had all moved on to new ventures.

With Winston and Sweetgrass no longer making rods there, Twin Bridges was a figurative bamboo ghost town. But for Jerry Kustich—the most loyal and earnest of Glenn's disciples—the ghosts were literal. Both his mother and wife died in the same week in 2009, amplifying the stress of starting this new business. Jerry fought defiantly throughout but left Sweetgrass in 2013 to move to Mexico with his new partner, Sharon, hoping to shed the demons that lurked on nearly every corner in Twin

Bridges. I bought those two rods from him when he downsized for this move.

~~~

Two days ago, I left a message for Glenn and his newest apprentice, Jamie Kuss, asking if I could visit their shop sometime. Jamie left a message for me yesterday and said I could arrive around 1 p.m. today. I plan to fish the Yellowstone River in Livingston this evening, so Jamie's invitation is perfect. I park across the street from the Sweetgrass shop, then take the short walk to Headframe Spirits, where I stroll up to the long wooden bar, put one foot on the antique brass rail, and pose like Humphrey Bogart in *Casablanca*. The bartender reminds me of Gilda Radner, so naturally, I do my best impression of John Belushi.

"Hey bartender, gimme one, gimme two, gimme three, four bottles of Orphan Girl, please."

"That's cute," she says, "but the sign behind me says two bottles per day."

"Oh, sorry about that."

"No problem. You can go over to Park Street Liquors and buy more if you'd like, but I can only sell you two."

I walk my two bottles back to the Suburban, store them in the cooler, then sit in the front seat and catch up on emails while I wait for Jamie and Glenn to arrive. The Sweetgrass workshop is in a row of half a dozen side-by-side commercial units with front-facing garage doors that suggest they were once small-time automotive repair shops. Most units don't have signs to identify them, but the yin-yang trout logo with the familiar cursive *Sweetgrass Rods* on the sign above the door of the one in the middle makes it easy to figure out where I'm going.

Jamie arrives first, followed a few minutes later by Glenn. I finish deleting thirteen emails that mean nothing to the people who sent them or me, then cross the street to be greeted by Jamie and Glenn. In a 1999 interview, Chris Dombrowski described Glenn as "a kind of cross between your college poetry professor and an old-time train conductor." Although that observation is twenty years old, it's still spot on today. And, weirdly, with his graying beard, thin build, and sharp facial features, it holds equally well for Jamie. If you think about it, the description also applies to Jerry Kustich. There's an old belief that the longer couples are together, the more they look alike. But the modern scientific consensus is that people tend to select partners who look similar to them in the first place. Perhaps that explains it. Maybe there's a force in the universe that sucks bearded renaissance men into the vortex known as bamboo rod building.

The shop is about thirty feet wide and roughly three times that long. Shelves in the back hold piles of unprocessed cane, all vying for the attention of Jamie's or Glenn's trained eye. At first glance, they look like simple wooden tubes, but to the canes, this is the bamboo version of *The Bachelorette*. After traveling thousands of miles to get here from China, they don't want to spend the rest of their lives as fading spinsters on a workshop shelf in Butte. No, they want to be split, sanded, dried, glued, sanded again, wrapped, varnished, and courted by a suitor who will take them on wild adventures in beautiful places.

Between the piles of cane and the front of the shop are some machines and tools and hundreds or thousands of strips of bamboo in various stages of development, ranging from splinters to sticks to rod segments. Initially, I feel I've stumbled onto the set of an avant-garde play about a hoarder's paradise. Bamboo poles in piles, tools strewn about, and twigs and switches scattered everywhere. But when I look closer, I realize I'm witnessing controlled chaos. This workshop is like the love child of Martha Stewart and Albert Einstein—everything is where it's supposed to be, even though it looks like a total mess to my untrained eye. The only thing missing is a plaque commemorating this historical place where entropy and order held their first date.

We return to the front of the store, and Jamie excuses himself to leave for an appointment. The shelves and cases up here hold books, hats, fly boxes, beer glasses, and other fascinating souvenirs that may or may not be for sale. Glenn shows me a realistic fly pattern apparently created to impersonate a ground squirrel, destroying any notion I might have held about bamboo artisans caring only about tiny dry flies and wispy tippets. This fly—and the savage fish it might fool—suggest the only way to attach it to a leader is with a custom steel tippet forged by Brinks or Master Lock.

The four-panel garage door at the front of the shop serves as a permanent wall with a row of windows where the upper two panels used to be. Below the windows, a bamboo bicycle leans against the door next to a retro-style tin sign inviting me to fish naked and show off my rod. Of course, there are photographs, paintings, and carvings of trout throughout the shop. Two of the fish paintings are by Mark Smith in the Japanese gyotaku style—an art-form tradition that makes prints from actual fish. One displays the saltwater grand slam of tarpon, permit, and bonefish, the other a river grand slam of sorts with a rainbow, brook, brown, and cutthroat trout.

Hanging from the wall in the center of the shop's rod displays, Glenn has a painting of a native chief in a brilliant red robe with a yellow-headed blackbird pendant around his neck. Below the chief, there's an old black-and-white photograph of five Winston pioneers: Glenn, Doug Merrick, Tom Morgan, Robert Winther, and Walter "Red" Loskot. Of course, the displays are full of fly rods.

"What's the magic in a fly rod?" I ask.

"It's simple. A fly rod will always lead you to water," Glenn says.

It makes no sense to think a person who builds rods wouldn't like to fish them, but I can see how someone might view Glenn as a builder first and an angler second. But much like a love of music makes a great luthier, the love of angling makes a master rod builder. It's not the other way around.

"Other than them looking like a cross between a college poetry professor and an old-time train conductor, how do you know if someone is worthy of your time as a mentor?"

"I take them fishing. If you want to get to know someone—I mean really get to know them—take them fishing."

I know the clock is ticking on our day, so I ask if I can bring him a few rods from my truck.

"Sure. Of course."

I hand Glenn my first Mantra and sheepishly tell him that the tip rotates out of alignment during a full day of fishing. I expect him to scold me for doing something wrong with my maintenance, but he opens a drawer, pulls out a piece of wax shaped like a little green frog, and tells me to rub the frog's butt on my ferrule every time I put the rod together. If I do that, I shouldn't have any more problems.

"That's it?"

"Yep, that's it."

I don't have any questions about my three-weight Mantra, but I show it to him anyway.

"That's a lovely rod, isn't it?"

"Oh, yes, it is."

Finally, I show him the Winston rod I bought from Jerry that broke two days ago in the middle of a cast on the Big Hole River.

"I don't think I've seen a break like this before."

"This is the second time it broke. Jerry repaired it the first time."

"I can see that, but I'm surprised it happened again. Jerry did a good job on it."

"I love this rod. I have many wonderful memories of it. Can you at least put it back together well enough for me to hang it on the wall in my office?"

"Oh, you'll be able to fish with it."

"Really? Are you sure?"

Glenn dips his chin and looks over the top of his horn-rimmed professor glasses the way Johnny Cash might if some fool had asked him if he was sure he knew how to sing "Folsom Prison Blues."

"Fill this out with your address, and I should be able to ship it to you in a few weeks."

"Wow. Thank you so much. I love that rod for all the stories it's given me."

"It'll give you some more."

I know Glenn has chores to tend to, and I still need to drive to Livingston, so I say goodbye and ask if it would be okay to stop by the next time I'm in town.

"Anytime," he says.

⚊ ⚊

While addressing his first-year physics students at Cal Tech, the brilliant physicist Richard Feynman once asked, "If in a certain cataclysm, where all the scientific knowledge is to be destroyed, but only one sentence is to be passed down to the next generation of creatures, what would be the best thing? The thing that contains the most information in the least number of words?"

As brilliant physicists are wont to do, Feynman answered his own question: "It is the atomic hypothesis or the atomic fact or whatever you want to call it, that all things are made out of atoms, little particles that move around, are in perpetual motion, attract each other when they're some distance apart but repel being squeezed into one another."

In an occasion as uncommon as grayling in Michigan, Glenn Brackett goes against the science on this. Instead, he likes to paraphrase a Muriel Rukeyser quote his father told him many years ago.

"The universe is not made of atoms. It's made of stories."

Ask him where those stories come from, and he'll tell you to go fishing. If you don't know how that works, he'll advise you to sit on a log or boulder alongside a river and wait, watch, and wonder.

CHAPTER 22

Redemption

Do the right thing. It will gratify some people and astonish the rest.
—MARK TWAIN

I LEAVE GLENN'S SHOP A LITTLE AFTER 3 P.M., PUTTING ME IN LIVING-
ston around 5. Physically, I stand more than a half-foot taller than Glenn
Brackett. Figuratively, the man towers above me like an enormous redwood from his native California. His artistry is beyond reproach, but his
humanity and decency make him a giant. Like Glenn's, all our lives are
the sums of everything we do and everything we don't. Occasionally, we
get to undo the things we shouldn't have done but did—and we sometimes get to do a thing we should have done but didn't, as I hope will
happen when I get to Livingston.

The redemption I'm after is nothing like John Newton sought when
he wrote "Amazing Grace," or Oskar Schindler when he saved twelve
hundred Jews, or even my friend Bill who once broke into a rival fra-
ternity house to steal food from their freezer, then biked back later that
night to break in again and return the steelhead because, as he put it,
"Stealing another man's fish is like stealing his soul." No, I only want to
tip the kid who drove a twenty-six-mile round trip to give back my credit
card on my first night in Montana.

As I drive through Three Forks, about halfway between Butte and Livingston, I realize that—except for Rock Creek—all the places I've fished so far are either upstream or downstream of this place. The Big Hole, Beaverhead, and Ruby all flow under the highway as the Jefferson, while Spring Creek and the Madison flow under by the name of, well, the Madison. Then, in the spirit of ZZ Top and Rush, those two form a trio with the Gallatin just north of the road, taking the country by storm as the Missouri River.

Down in Texas, they say there's nothing between Amarillo and the North Pole but a barbed wire fence, and as James McMurtry sings, barbed wire won't stop the wind. I don't know if that's supposed to be an insult to Amarillo or to the rest of the Great Plains States to its north. But I know you see a lot of barbed wire fences when you drive across Montana, and they don't stop the wind.

Driving through Bozeman doesn't feel like I'm skirting an arid prairie of rusty fences. Bozeman is the fastest-growing city of its size in the United States, and of all the spigots showering folks into the Gallatin River Valley, the one with the highest flow has California stamped on its handle. In deference—or, more likely, irreverence—to the herd of Golden State transplants, Bozeman has picked up the nickname Boz Angeles. Evidently, this isn't Norman Rockwell's Bozeman anymore. A little over a decade ago, Bozeman didn't have a single Starbucks. But today, you can't finish your morning's first Iced Brown Sugar Oat Milk Shaken Espresso before driving by another store with that two-tailed mermaid on its window. Real-estate prices are higher than a budtender in a San Francisco weed store, but anyone with the foresight to invest in a shop that sells cowboy shirts, hats, and boots to Stuart, Devin, and Karina is doing just fine.

East of Bozeman, the westbound lanes of I-90 close in on my left, with nothing but a narrow concrete median separating us east-going Zaxs from the west-going ones. Unconcerned with my concern, the Montana Rail Link snakes tightly along my right with the literal weight of a freight train on its tracks. Montana is a state of wide-open spaces everywhere except for the places between the spaces. Those places are called passes, and this one is named for Bozeman. As usually happens in situations like this, my knuckles are as white as the rocky outcroppings rudely intruding on my personal space from both sides of the highway.

After cresting the pass, color flushes back into my knuckles, the road straightens, the east- and west-bound lanes diverge, the landscape flattens, and I feel like Mario Andretti coasting through a victory lap. Soon after that, a sign on the road says *Chain Up Area*, reminding me what goes up must come down, just like Newton's apple or Copernicus's sun. Coming down doesn't seem as bad as going up, and when I pass the *Livingston Next 3 Exits* sign, I put my left elbow on the door rest, my right hand on top of the wheel, and kick back like a rancher coming home from the auction.

Every person I've known with the nickname Slim has been wide; every Curly's been bald. And there's a town in Michigan named Mount Pleasant that is neither a mountain nor, well, you get the idea. As names or slogans go, Paradise Valley shares the stage with White Sands, Grand Canyon, and Crater Lake for the truth in advertising award. When I take the half-loop exit from the interstate, the entrance to paradise beckons to the south. As you would expect when a left turn takes you into Yellowstone Park, the intersection is busy, and, like mine, many of the vehicles have out-of-state plates. The California spigot hasn't gained full pressure in Livingston yet, but the flow is steady, and despite the local resistance, a Starbucks will shine on this Park Street corner in just a few years.

I check into a motel next to the interstate, then drive about two miles south to the Sweetwater Fly Shop. The lady behind the counter greets me as though I'm the one customer she's been waiting to see all day. The kid I'm here to see is talking with some customers about the flies in the bins beside a rack of cinder-, lichen-, and sumac-colored Simms fishing shirts. I've never tipped anyone for bringing my credit card to me on a river, and I didn't pack a volume of *The Gentlemen's Book of Etiquette and Manual of Politeness* to show me the protocol for this, so I have to hope a signed copy of *The Habits of Trout* with some twenty-dollar bookmarks stuffed between the pages will free me from the designation of rogue, rascal, or cad in this kid's mind.

"Can you tell me the name of that kid talking with those customers over there?"

"Kid? He's not a kid."

"Well, they all look like kids to me anymore."

"His name's Evan. What's up?"

"He brought my credit card to me on the river a few weeks ago, and I feel terrible about not tipping him for that. I've got something I'd like to give him."

Evan helps his customers fill one of those plastic pucks with flies, then wishes them good luck on the river.

"I don't know if you remember me," I say, "but I'm the guy you brought the credit card to on the Yellowstone a few weeks ago."

"Yeah, I do, how's the fishing been?"

"It's been a great trip, but I've felt bad about not tipping you for helping me out like you did, and I'd like to give you this."

"That's you? You wrote this?"

"Yeah."

I tell Evan I'm here to fish DePuy Spring Creek tomorrow, and I hope to check out the Yellowstone this evening. He tells me he did really well at the credit-card hole last night, and like he did before, he says I should stay past dark. When I ask about DePuy, he calls over another kid named James who's a frequent guide on the creek.

"You'll need some tiny flies, but don't overlook using one of these," James says, then hands me a foam-bodied fly that looks like a cross between a grasshopper, stonefly, and a purple Tootsie Roll. "Honestly," he says, "if the fishing gets slow, give this thing a try. I got my biggest fish of the year there on one of these two days ago. Those fish are snobs, but they still love protein."

It takes about fifteen minutes to get to the credit-card hole, and when I arrive, my Suburban is the only vehicle in the parking area. This area is heavily used for picnicking and fishing, so the bank has a well-worn trail for several hundred yards in each direction. With the river to myself, I cast a realistic grasshopper pattern with a caddis nymph below it, then walk along the shore to get a drift-boat style drift. When I do it right, I cover over two-hundred yards of the river, which I can also cover if

I do it wrong, and according to the trout, I'm doing it wrong. Still, it's a pleasant way to fish, and I'm logging steps for my cardio health. On about my tenth drift, a bruiser of a brown takes a shot at the hopper but casually calls off the attack right after breaching and revealing the top half of its body. My interest in fishing like this had started to wane, but seeing that trout sent me back to watching the fly like a hawk watching a meadow mouse.

Scattered clouds roll in for the evening, casting a soft, hazy light over the valley. When the sun's rays poke through the cover, the stand of mountains to the east bursts into a brilliant, snow-like glow. The Yellowstone River's surface shimmers like a field of diamonds, diffusing the sunlight into thousands of tiny speckles shimmering across the water. The leaves on the cottonwood trees flutter like mayflies at dusk, and the air mimics Goldilocks's third bowl of porridge—neither too cool nor too warm. I've been in Montana for two and a half weeks, and I've seen countless scenes like this, but every one still takes my breath away. I suppose when you factor in all the microscopic elements that have conspired to make this particular scene—the cloud formations, the position of the sun, the pattern of the wind, and the place I'm standing—I am the only person to see this exactly the way I'm seeing it now. Every moment and every place is unique.

Another vehicle pulls into the parking area around 7:30 p.m. There's a fifty-foot-wide stand of trees separating the parking area from me, and between the sounds of the doors opening and closing, I hear the voices of a young man and woman.

"Are you sure you aren't going to fish?" she asks.

"Naw, I'll get the cooler and stuff. You go ahead."

I'm in the middle of one of my drifts when I look up from the water and see the woman less than a hundred yards below me. My attire is that of your run-of-the-mill fly angler: breathable waders, a chambray fishing shirt, a Filson hat, and a Fishpond sling pack. Besides our fly rods, she doesn't look anything like me. Starting at the top, her long, sandy blonde hair is drawn back into a classic ponytail, with a few strands breaking free to hang alongside her face. She hides her eyes behind oversized tortoise-shell sunglasses, and as far as I can tell, if she has extra flies or tippet or anything else an angler ought to carry, they're in one of the pockets of her form-fitting wine-colored flannel shirt. Rather than waders, she's wearing blue-jean cutoffs in the style of Daisy Duke, and because she stepped into the water before I saw her, I have no idea what she's wearing on her feet. I don't see a single flaw in anything, including her cast, and because this isn't the sort of thing that happens on my home water, I discretely take a picture and text it to some of my buddies. They're all past middle age, but they respond like a clique of seventh graders:

"Does Roxanne know what you're looking at?"

"This is why you went to Montana?"

"You've discovered paradise!"

"Roxanne will not approve this message!"

"You did it you old son-of-a-bitch. You finally caught a mermaid."

I suppose we're just a bunch of overgrown preteens, with cans of Miller Lite where our pouches of CapriSun used to be. I walk back upstream to take another drift, and when I turn around, she's gone. I have a photo, so I know I haven't made her up, but I expected to see something like this about as much as I expected to catch a fish with my bare hands. I hear laughter and the sound of two twist tops coming off their bottles somewhere in the woods behind me, and I'm so preoccupied with the noises I don't notice a guide and his clients floating down the river beside me.

"Hey man," the guide shouts. "You ought to walk up to those riffles. There's a pod of fish taking caddisflies. There might be a few good ones in there."

"Thanks, I appreciate that."

I wouldn't have noticed the rise forms mixed in with those riffles without his advice. But this is that guide's home court, and it's his job to know the angles and play the bad bounces better than the visitors. So I walk upstream and scrutinize the scene for life in the riffles. I don't see it at first, but I focus on this task like a pilot in a thunderstorm, and then, just the way a three-dimensional image appears in a stereogram where nothing used to be, I see a nose, then a fin, then the entire glorious pod of feeding fish.

I clip off the hopper, extend the tippet, and tie on a size sixteen elk-wing caddis. On my second cast, a sixteen-inch rainbow grabs the fly and launches an angry downstream dash. We're in a dance as old as time, and the trout has no way of knowing my intentions, so from its perspective, this fight will decide whether it lives or dies. But I don't intend for either of us to die, which raises the uncomfortable question I've asked many times before: Why do this at all? If I love and respect these trout as much as I claim, then why do I spend so much time scaring the living hell out of them and watching them fight for their lives?

You inevitably face this dilemma when you follow up any question's answer with a new question.

"Why do we like to have sex?"

"Because it feels good."

"Why does it feel good?"

"I don't know. It just does."

Though it might not be convincing for everyone, Darwin's answer is compelling. You like to have sex because the two people who made you did too. The folks who dislike having sex didn't pass that preference on for obvious reasons. And though modern society makes survival easier without an innate desire to hunt, fish, and gather, it wasn't that long ago when a genetic urge to catch a fish meant the difference between life and death. Perhaps it's that simple, after all. Something deep inside compels folks like me to catch fish by telling our subconscious we'll die if we don't. However, I've said this before: I'm an engineer, so what do I know about these things?

After I land the fish, I take a photo and text it to my buddies. Texting photos from the Yellowstone River in the company of the Absaroka Mountains feels crude and unfitting, but for a guy who likes to tell stories, I've picked up some good material with this. Maybe I'll write one called, *A Mermaid Runs Through It*, or perhaps, *A Midsummer Night's Mermaid*. I don't know it yet, but the surreality of this evening will grow by an order of magnitude once the sun dips below the mountain tops on the horizon.

I catch two more rainbow trout before the pod disperses. I don't see any other fish rising in the dim light, so I clip off the caddis and replace it with the more visible silhouette of the hopper. Although there's still some light in the sky, I can't see the other side of the river. But Evan told me to fish after dark, so I'm doing it. I walk the shore to get longer drifts, but not the whole two-hundred yards I walked in the daylight. Now, I do ten or twenty yards, then recast for another float. On about my tenth drift, the water around my fly erupts, and I'm hooked to a brown trout fighting like a cornered lion.

I haven't been paying attention to the couple in the woods behind me, mainly because they weren't making much noise. Evidently, they weren't making much noise because the pre-mating ritual for a young couple is relatively quiet. But now that they've graduated beyond the pre-mating part, I hear the unmistakable moans and groans of youthful lust. Darwin would love this scene: an old fisherman fights a mighty brown trout on the bank of the Yellowstone River while a young couple sexes each other up in the woods behind him. Everyone is an actor in this primordial play, doing what the adenine, cytosine, guanine, and thymine in their genetic code have programmed them to do. The only surprising part in this clip is that the old man in the river believes he is the one having the most fun.

CHAPTER 23

Those Are the Gods I Turn To

Turn me loose, set me free, somewhere in the middle of Montana.
—MERLE HAGGARD, "BIG CITY"

MONTANA HAS MORE MILES OF PUBLIC ACCESS THAN A TROUT HAS scales, but today I'm fishing on private water and paying a *per-rod* fee to do so. Fortunately, private spring creeks like Nelson's, Armstrong's, and DePuy use the word *rod* to mean *angler per day*, so I'll only pay a hundred dollars instead of the thirteen hundred I'd pay if *rod* meant rod. By paying this fee, I've solved several problems I usually face when fishing on unfamiliar turf. First, because people get in line to pay a hundred dollars per rod, I'm probably in an excellent place to fish. Second, because the landowners allow only sixteen rods on three miles of creek, finding an open stretch of water shouldn't be a problem. And third, because DePuy is a spring creek, the water temperature will be cool, even if the air temperature isn't. But this isn't one of the pay lakes my mom took me to as a kid. The fee only entitles me to wade and cast. I have to pay, even if I don't catch any fish.

From the public's perspective, Montana has the most generous—many would say *fairest*—stream-use laws in the nation. If you don't trespass to get there, you can fish or float or recreate in some other way in any river or stream, subject only to the state's rules and regulations for those things. So, as a matter of law, the people who own the land around DePuy Spring Creek can't charge me to fish—they can only make me pay to use their roads and land to access the stream. They don't own the river or the ground under its water. The law is similar back in Michigan, but only for *navigable* rivers, sometimes causing you to navigate the poorly defined concept of what constitutes a navigable river, such as might happen when debating a landowner in a Carhartt jacket stained with the blood of some animal he recently dressed out:

"Hey, you, get da hell off a my property!"

"But I have a right to be in any river that can be used to float a log down it."

"I da know 'bout logs, but dis river can float a body, buddy."

In some states, if a landowner has property on both sides of a river, touching the bottom with your foot, oar, or anchor is considered trespassing. My friend Jarek—the skunk trapper—spent one March testing out the Peach State as a destination to retire. His fishing luck was terrible until he parked by a rural bridge, entered the stream, and within a few hundred yards began catching trout that looked like the forbidden spawn of a tarpon and Saint Bernard. He released most of the behemoths but gutted two of the smaller ones for dinner. As he returned to his car, a pickup truck leading a funnel of dust roared across the field in his direction, horn blaring.

"You don't belong on my property!"

"I can walk back in river if you like."

"No! No! You can't be in my river either!"

"Why is that? I park at bridge and get in river there."

"Didn't you see the sign?"

"What sign?"

The guy explained how he owned the river and all the trout in it, and more important than that, how he charged people five-hundred dollars per day to fish there.

"I can pay fee, or work on your farm for a few days if you like," Jarek offered.

"No, I have called the police."

When the conservation officer arrived, she diffused the situation and showed the landowner that his sign was faded and covered by leaves. But Jarek had broken the law, so he paid the Georgia Department of Natural Resources a fine of four-hundred dollars, thereby saving the extra hundred he was willing to pay the guy for unknowingly trespassing in his river.

Despite Montana's public-friendly policy, deep holes and narrow culverts quash the opportunities for getting in and out of these Paradise Valley spring creeks. You could parachute in and hire Daniel Craig to get you out, but most people don't have the resources for that, so the families who own the land can cater to folks like me who are willing to forgo a dinner for two at the Capital Grille to rent a rod on their creek.

I check in at the main residence around 7:30 a.m. The house is a two-story manor of the Jeffersonian Classicism sort: something architecture buffs might describe as a fifty-foot-wide portico-style entry with four twenty-foot-high columns supporting a towering pediment centered by a signature half-moon window. For the rest of us, it's the kind of place you'd expect to see Scarlett O'Hara desperately ask Rhett Butler, "Where should I go? What should I do?"

A man named Daryl hands me a detailed map of the property as if he's assisting General Sherman in mapping out a plan of attack at Shiloh. Then he asks me to swear on a copy of the *Compleat Angler* to release every fish I catch, close every gate I open, pack out my trash, stay out of any building without a "welcome" sign, and keep my dog on a leash if I have one. I ask about stream etiquette, and he says to use common sense but then tells me it shouldn't be a problem today because they only have two other anglers signed in, and those two will be fishing together. I should be able to fish all day without seeing another person.

I drive from the mansion and pull into the first parking area adjacent to something the map calls Dick's Riffle. I wrestle on my waders, stand beside this famous stream, and check my leader and tippet for abrasions and nicks. They're clean and smooth, meaning the only relevant things with frays are my nerves. The Roman philosopher Seneca the Younger wrote, "It is not that we have a short time to live, but that we waste a lot of it. Life is long enough, and a sufficiently generous amount has been given to us for the highest achievements if it were all well invested." Or as my mom might have put it, "You aren't going to catch a fish standing here with your thumb up your nose. Go wet your line."

Satisfied with my oath of good behavior, Daryl told me the fish won't eat from the surface until later in the morning, so I might want to use an emerger or nymph pattern to start. I figure Daryl knows what he's talking about, so I tie on a tiny soft hackle with a little pinch-on foam indicator above that. I'm not sure this will work, but by putting something on my line, I no longer have my thumb up my nose. I walk downstream to a footbridge, cross, then head back upstream to a moderate-sized pool below a midstream island. Some soft water appears to have depth along the river-right bank, so I cast the bobber and dropper far upstream and along the bank, then take in line to keep in touch as it bobs and weaves its way back to me. I lift when the bobber bobs more than it weaves. The line tightens and zips across the surface as a rainbow trout scrambles toward the island with my fly in its mouth.

The first fish of the day is always noteworthy. But I paid a hundred dollars to fish three miles of a Paradise Valley spring creek, and every foot I gain on this fish lifts a pound of pressure off my shoulders. After going fishless on *the* spring creek, I've asked the fish gods to show mercy today, and it appears they might. I'm a little worried about the rainbow burrowing into the weeds, but other than that, this is the perfect place to fight and land this trout. My knees shake the way Sunny's would in a thunderstorm, so when the fish is in my net, I kneel in the river, bowing to the trout like Galahad might greet Arthur. It's a thick rainbow in the mid-teens, with an army-green back, asphalt freckles, redwood stripe down its side, and a burnt-sienna blush on its cheek, looking for all the world as though it came to life on an easel in James Prosek's studio. I let out a sigh, knowing the spray of a hundred-dollar skunk will not douse me today. Catching fish might not be the only thing I'm after here, but it's one of them.

I'm not exclaiming, "Veni, vidi, vici!" like Julius Caesar after the Battle of Zela, and I know better than to turn my confidence knob to eleven, but I feel pretty good for the next half-hour or so. I cast the same fly the same way in similar water, but when no more fish cooperate in the pool below Dick's Riffle, I walk the bank downstream to look for rings or snouts or any other signs of fish. "Even a blind hen finds a grain of corn," my mom used to say, and I'm starting to feel the urge to cluck. Luck is a fickle mistress who teases, taunts, and turns on you faster than a beagle when you try to clean its ears. I look at my watch, and it's only been forty minutes since I caught that first fish. Sure, the clock's ticking for my day on DePuy, but I can fish until dark. I need to relax.

I get back in my truck and drive the gravel road along a wide section the map calls Dick's Pond, which predictably feeds water into Dick's Riffle. I park just after the road crosses the river and walk a trail upstream along the bank. A lone trout holds its position in the center of the creek, softly sneaking something from the surface. I crawl on my hands and knees to look closer and assess the situation. The large trout is eating with the timing of a metronome. *Eat two three four, eat two three four, eat two three four.* I can't see the flies it's eating, so I take that as a clue: "Okay, Galileo, I think you should use a tiny fly," I tell myself. My Uncle Floyd liked to say there's nothing wrong with talking to yourself until you start answering. I tie the tiny fly to my 7X tippet without saying a word.

I have the fish positioned for a quartering upstream cast, pretty much the way Tom Rosenbauer says I should in *The Orvis Fly-Fishing Guide.* Aware that this fish has an elite spring-creek education—as opposed to those free stoners I'm used to chasing—I stay on my knees and make two false casts well behind the trout. On my third forward cast, I put the fly precisely three feet above where the fish used to be. "Be sure to get upstream, so your fly leads your tippet over the fish," I suddenly remember Bob DeMott coaching me. "It's easy to spook these fish with your line." I'm glad Uncle Floyd isn't here to hear what I say to myself next.

Another fish rises close to the far bank, about ten yards downstream. I step into the creek, mimicking the pelican I saw catching the trout on

Hebgen Lake with Patrick and Bob—I move slowly and deliberately like a ninja warrior closing in to attack a samurai without warning. My heart rate quickens with every step, and when I sneak within casting range, one false cast drops the fly about ten feet upstream of the fish. The rainbow trout elevates toward the surface, drifts backward with my fly, then nothing. I make another cast, even better than my first, but still nothing. Two more casts and two more nothings. "Hey, Copernicus, maybe the fish wants a different tiny fly."

I read somewhere that a tiny hair's ear nymph doctored with floatant sometimes works in this situation, and I happen to have a few in size 20 and 22. I tie on the size 20, brush in some Frog's Fanny, and put it on the same path I'd put the other fly. The fish elevates, drifts back, and sucks the fly from the surface. For a reason known only to the trout and its highly efficient lentil-sized brain, the fish runs upstream for about fifty feet, then turns and steadily follows my line straight to my net. It's smaller than my first DePuy trout but a doppelgänger in every other way.

The creek's sleepy surface begins to awaken with dimples and rings, especially downstream in a stretch of heavy vegetation near the road crossing. It's like that moment in May at Overture Hall in Madison, Wisconsin, when the lights dimmed, the crowd hushed, and John Prine began to pick and sing "Six O'Clock News." Even though I paid for the moment, I can't believe it's happening. I redress the tiny nymph with floatant, land it about three yards before the nearest trout, then watch it disappear into a slight crevice in the water's surface. The big rainbow shakes its head twice, then barrel rolls toward me like the Red Baron in a dogfight. When I gather up the slack, the fish dives, pitches, then accelerates downstream away from me. The snap of the 7X tippet rings and echoes in the late morning air.

I tie on a smaller nymph, work in the floatant powder, then cast toward another DePuy rainbow. Determined to avoid repeating my mistake, I give the trout plenty of space after it takes my fly. So much that it burrows deep into the weeds, removing another of my flies from the tippet. My flies are vanishing like cash in a casino, and after I lose two more fish and flies, the kid's advice from the shop swarms my mind: "Give this thing a try. I got my biggest fish of the year there on one of these two days ago."

I clip the leader back to 4X and tie on the flamboyant conglomeration of hair, fur, rubber legs, and purple foam. I don't target a rising fish but cast it straight upstream into the middle of the creek, where it lands with an ungraceful plop. Launching a lure like this isn't the technical angling of a spring creek specialist—it's a defiant act of desperate sacrilege. Like in a scene from *Jaws*, a wake closes in on my plug from ten feet away. *Ten, nine, eight, seven, six, five, four, three, two, one, liftoff!* My rod bends with the weight of a bull-necked brown nearly as long as a newborn baby, and I strain to use all of the strength in the 4X tippet to keep this fish out of the weeds. With the trout in the wide basket of my Iverson net, I marvel at its splendor: merlot spots flank its muscular body, interspersed among woodsmoke freckles with steel-gray bands. They say beauty is in the eye of the beholder, but your eye would need to be made of ice to mistake this fish for anything less.

I make several more fruitless casts with the purple foam bait before turning my attention back to the fish in the weeds by the road crossing. I extend the leader with 6X tippet this time, but still lose my remaining hair's ear nymphs. One fish breaks off on the hook set, and two more tunnel their way to freedom in the grass. Partly disheartened and partly exhausted, I make a sandwich back at the Suburban, then drive to the fly shop for advice and some size 20 and 22 hair's ear nymphs.

Evan and James greet me and ask how I did so far.

"I had a great morning, but I lost more than I landed fishing over that weed bed near the culvert bridge above Dick's Pond."

"That's a tough spot. What did you get 'em on?"

"Size 20 and 22 hair's ear nymphs, fished dry. But I'm all out now. Do you have any?"

"I don't think so, but we have some small pheasant tails that might work."

"Did you try the purple hopper?"

"As a matter of fact, I did. I got pissed about losing fish on 7X tippet, so I tied that thing on and caught a big brown on my first cast."

"Nice!"

"Later today, a small tan comparadun should work. Do you have some of those?"

I have several, but I still have Evan put a few of those in the plastic cup with the pheasant tails.

My afternoon on DePuy is slow, but I find rising fish around 6 p.m. in a flat stretch below a place the map calls Betty's Riffle. I enter the creek between a pair of islands and use stealthy downstream casts to take four brilliant rainbows on the tan comparaduns. A few fish resist my allure, but for the most part, I'm dialed in and catching nearly every trout that can be caught. I focus so intensely on my casting that I don't notice a thunderstorm rolling into the valley. The first blast flushes me from the river like a merganser. Using the Suburban's cockpit as a waiting room, I check my phone for messages and see one from Bob DeMott:

I'm sorry to tell you this, but Jerry Dennis's dad died today.

I know Jerry's had time to prepare, but the pain of witnessing the end of the life that gave you yours is not something preparation can erase or dull.

In Jerry's story, "The Christmas Gift," he tells of helping his childhood friend Tony shoot and catch a dinner of baked grouse and pike fillets for Tony's family on the first Christmas Eve after his young friend's father had died. Tony's harvest brought joy to what would have otherwise been a somber and silent night for his mother, brothers, and sister. In the story, Jerry reflects on the mixed emotions of gratitude and guilt he experienced when he later celebrated his own family's Christmas Eve dinner surrounded by warmth and abundance:

I watched my father as if I had never seen him: A big man at the head of the table, his sleeves rolled up, laughing at someone's joke while he used a carving knife and fork to slice the turkey into thick white slabs. I was never so grateful to have him home.

After Jerry unwrapped his new twenty-gauge shotgun the following morning, he cleaned and oiled his old twelve-gauge—the one he let Tony use to shoot the grouse—and wrapped it as a gift for his friend. The gun was a Dennis family heirloom—passed from father to son for at least two generations. Something Jerry's father expected Jerry would pass on to his children. But when Jerry's dad saw what he was doing, his only question was, "What about shells?" Then he helped Jerry wrap two boxes.

After the storm passes, the eastern sky glows like the petals of an Oriental lily, and the Absaroka peaks shine like polished copper. A porcelain-white swan drifts below the island, and the creek's surface reflects a sheen of antique brass and clay. Several trout feed, but I take a seat on a wooden bench overlooking the water and send a text to my friend:

> *Jerry, Bob just told me your father passed away. I am so sorry for you and your family. I'm sitting beside DePuy now, asking the fish gods to help you find comfort.*

A few minutes later, my phone vibrates against my chest.

> *Thanks. Those are the gods I turn to.*

CHAPTER 24

I Only Want to Catch
That First Fish Again

Look at me, I am old, but I'm happy.

—Yusuf / Cat Stevens

The shortest route from the airport to the Slide Inn is about ninety-five miles through Ennis. I want Daniel—and me, too—to see more of Montana, so I take the route along the Gallatin River, adding fifteen extra miles and a half hour to the drive. It's the more scenic path, but "more scenic" in this part of Montana is like "more sandy" in the Sahara, "more snowy" in the Arctic, or "more quiet" in space. In the winter, skiers traveling from Bozeman to Big Sky use this route like a conveyor, and because of the large number of fatal accidents, some people call it the gauntlet of death. But even in the summer, it can be a wildlife gauntlet, with one-quarter of all crashes involving bear, elk, moose, sheep, or some other animal. Still, I decide the rewards outweigh the risks, and we drive south on US Highway 191.

As we wind upstream alongside the Gallatin, I tell Daniel this is where Robert Redford filmed most of the casting scenes in *A River Runs Through It*. "What's that?" he asks. When I was a kid, personal computers were some engineer's dream, televisions had four channels, watches told time, and we dialed phones by rotating a wheel with our fingers. Daniel grew up in a world of instant information and perceived gratification, so he never caught the fishing bug like I did. Of course, it's possible—even likely—that my mom did a better job of exposing me than I have of exposing him.

We drive through Yellowstone Park for twenty miles, including six of those in Wyoming, ultimately dropping into the West Yellowstone valley and turning right onto Highway 287. As we drive along Hebgen Lake, I tell Daniel about the day Bob and I caught gulpers with Patrick. "Is a gulper a trout?" he asks. I explain how the fish make a gulping sound when they eat mayflies from the surface, and before he asks, I tell him what a mayfly is. I see the same look of surprise, awe, and disbelief on his face that mine must have had when I first saw the mountain slide on the other side of Quake Lake. A little farther down the road, he asks, "How did that tree grow in the middle of the river?" and before I respond, he answers his own question.

"Is this it?" Daniel asks as I turn left into the parking area for the Slide Inn.

"Yes," I say, worrying that I've somehow let him down with my decisions.

"It's wonderful," he says.

When I park in front of our cabin, a couple come out from the unit next to ours and introduce themselves as Bob and Mary Hendrix. Bob has a career in real estate, but more important than that, he knows bamboo rods the way Hemingway knew brevity and Van Gogh knew color. Mary is an award-winning artist, and her watercolor painting of Bob DeMott with a cutthroat trout is on the cover of his book *Angling Days*.

"How do we distinguish between the two Bobs?" Daniel asks later.

"I don't know. What do you suggest?"

"How about Cali Bob for this one?" Daniel says, in reference to Bob and Mary being from California.

"Sounds good, but just between the two of us, okay?"

I Only Want to Catch That First Fish Again

Later, we'll learn that in their circle, Bob Hendrix is Bobster One, and Bob DeMott is Bobster Two. But for this trip, Daniel and I will distinguish them as Cali Bob and Writer Bob.

After we move our things into the cabin, Daniel takes time to catch up on texts and emails. As I've had for most of my adult life, he now has a job where vacation means he can be out of sight but never out of mind. While I watch him focus on the tiny LCD screen, my inner Harry Chapin laments, *He's grown up just like me. My boy is just like me.*

When he finishes replying, forwarding, deleting, composing, and saving, we drive to the Driftwaters Resort for dinner. I order us a couple of mugs of Gallatin Pale Ale, and before we have them half-finished, Joyce and Al, and a few of the other folks from their fly-fishing club visit our table. I'm yesterday's news now—Daniel is the new guy. So they mostly ignore me and fawn over him, just as they should. After we finish our burgers, we drive back to the cabin, where I ask Daniel what he thinks about Irish cream or similar liqueurs. "What's that?" he asks. I put a few cubes of ice in two stainless steel Yeti wine glasses and pour a wee dram of Orphan Girl into each.

"This is the best drink I've ever had," he says.

"I know, it's good, isn't it?"

We talk about life in general, and his girlfriend, Alicia, in particular. Shortly after Roxanne and I met her, I sat Daniel down and feigned one of the most serious father-to-son talks we've ever had.

"Son, your mother and I want you to know we think the world of Alicia. But more important than that, you need to know that if you screw this up, we're going to adopt her and kick you out of the family."

A father never means something like that to his son, but exaggeration is the neon sign of advice. When we finish our first glasses of Orphan Girl, Daniel asks me to talk about fly fishing. I suspect he's luring me into refilling our cups, and I gladly take the bait. This time, I pour each of us two wee drams, then tell him fly fishing is fishing the way God intended it to be.

"Why, Son, do you think a man of my means and acclaim would drive to Montana to fish for three weeks?"

"You know, Mom asked me the same thing yesterday."

"What did you tell her?"

"I told her I had no idea."

"Well, tomorrow, I'll give you the introductory course, and the day after that, we'll complete your education."

The next day, Daniel catches up on work in the early morning while we have a continental breakfast of yogurt, muffins, and other confections we bought in Bozeman. Before lunch, we spend some time talking with Kelly Galloup in his shop, and by "some time," I mean over an hour.

"That guy is amazing!" Daniel says when we get back to our cabin.

"I know, isn't he?"

"Dad, if he wasn't in fly fishing, he'd be running a prominent Silicon Valley company," which is high praise from a kid—an accomplished young man, actually—who works for one of the most successful start-ups in the world.

Shortly after noon, we meet the two Bobs at Three Dollar Bridge, and Daniel suits up with my backup waders, boots, and hat. Most backup equipment earns its status by serving reliably as the primary equipment for years. That's true for my waders and boots. But my backup hat is nearly brand new and will become the starter only if a strong wind steals the ratty one from my head or the last few threads holding it together finally evaporate from existence. Daniel and I stay relatively close to the bridge while the Bobs walk farther downstream—Cali Bob a little farther than Writer Bob. It's been several years since Daniel has cast a fly rod, but he gets the line out on the water nicely. The problem happens once his line, leader, tippet, and fly are on the surface. So I show him how to mend line in the air and on the water, and he gets some nice drifts through fishy-looking runs. After an hour of no "bites," as he calls them, we take a seat on the log Bob took me to twelve days ago.

"What did you think about the note Mom wrote for us the day Sunny died?" I ask him.

"It was beautiful. I didn't know she could write like that," he says.

"Your mother is a woman of many talents, Son."

I point downstream to the place I sat that day and tell him about the double rainbow that curved above the bridge. Just then, a guy with a black-and-white border collie appears from the brush and begins fishing in the same spot. The dog is calm and attentive in a way Sunny could never be in a place like this.

"Did you ever take Sunny fishing with you?" Daniel asks.

"What do you think?"

"Yeah, there's no way he'd stay out of the river, right?"

"Nope."

"And he'd probably get so excited he'd poop in the water, wouldn't he?"

"Yep."

"Why did he do that?"

"I don't know for sure, but do you ever have to poop when you're in a bookstore or library?"

"Yes, I do! Why is that?"

"Jerry Dennis told me he thinks it's because we feel comfortable, safe, and completely relaxed around books. Maybe Sunny got the same feeling around water. Or maybe he just got so excited he crapped himself."

"Look at that," Daniel says.

The guy across the river holds his rod high to pressure a fish, and his dog glides down to his side to watch. He brings the fish in quickly, with the skill of someone who's done this many times before. When he corrals the trout in his net, he and his dog strain their necks to see what's in the bag, then follow the fish with their eyes as it swims away. The guy holds out his hand with his palm toward the sky, and the dog slaps its paw down upon it the way a guide might congratulate a client. He waves at us, and we raise our fists with thumbs pointing toward the sky. It's a modern symbol of approval that has evolved from the signal for a Roman gladiator to die. A strange evolution on the surface until you consider how Bugs Bunny convinced a nation that a "Nimrod" was a bumbling fool instead of a revered and mighty hunter.

When the Bobs return, the four of us stand beside the river, sharing details of the day. Writer Bob caught a few small fish, he says, but Cali Bob fooled a seventeen-inch rainbow on a dry fly a little over a mile downstream. In the middle of our conversation, I see a fly box floating down the river. When I teach optics to my engineering students, I use a specific example to help them understand Fermat's principle of least time. Because you move slower in the water than on the ground, the quickest path between a position on land and in water is not a straight line. If possible, you should take a bent course that keeps you on the ground longer than in the water. Cali Bob apparently knows this principle too, but unlike the professor who teaches it, he puts it into practice. So whereas my straight-line attempt to get to the flies fails, he hurries downstream on dry land first, then enters the water and scoops the box with his net.

The box holds more colorful and heavily weighted nymphs than I've ever seen. Its flies are meticulously arranged, and the underside of the lid contains some sort of table of contents written in Italian. The Bobs want to fish a little more, so Daniel and I walk upstream, asking everyone we see if they've lost a box of nymphs. No one claims it, so we walk to the Suburban, pop the tops on a couple of Miller Lites, and wait for the Bobs to return to the parking area. Later, when we are just about to leave, we hear the voices of two men speaking Italian as they walk through the lot. We ask if they've lost a fly box, and the international look of relief on their faces provides the answer.

After showering at our cabin, I buy two bottles of red wine from Kelly in his shop. "Is that a good wine?" I ask. "It's the best *forking* wine you'll find in this valley," Kelly says. Then Daniel and I join Cali Bob, Mary, and Rodger Gaulding for dinner at Writer Bob and Kate's cabin. More accurately, it's Rodger's cabin. He's the landlord, but tonight, like us, he's a dinner guest. Bob has prepared the main course from cuts of elk and antelope that Danny Lahren—Jim Harrison's longtime fishing guide—has given him. Paraphrasing Aldo Leopold, there is a danger in a society believing that dinner comes from a grocery store. I don't hunt, so Daniel has had limited exposure to wild game, which is yet another folder in my file cabinet of regret.

"What is this? It's delicious!" Daniel says to Bob.

"That piece is antelope, and the other is elk," Bob tells him. "Which do you like best?"

"I can't decide. They're both fantastic."

~——~

Daniel and I get up early the following day and drive to Varney Bridge, where we leave the Suburban and ride with Justin Edge back to McAtee

Bridge to begin our float. On our way out from Varney Bridge to Highway 287, we see a few antelope standing in a field, seemingly oblivious and unafraid of our presence on the road.

"We had antelope and elk meat for dinner last night. Antelope must be relatively easy to hunt," I suggest to Justin.

"Why do you think that?" he asks.

"Well, they seem like pretty easy targets in the field."

When Justin slows down his truck, the antelope lose the carefree appearance they had when we were driving at the speed they're used to seeing on the road.

"Open your door," he says.

The instant I do, the antelope bolt away and out of sight in seconds.

"Still seem like easy targets?"

When Justin launches his boat above McAtee Bridge, it's as clear as freshly polished crystal that this is not a secret place. Guides and clients scurry about like teachers and children in an elementary school playground. I tell Daniel to take the bow seat and listen to everything Justin tells him.

"If anything seems to contradict something you think I've told you in the past, do what Justin says and forget what I said."

Justin rigs our rods with foam hoppers on a 3X tippet. The current in this river is like an unrelenting boxer—constantly bobbing, weaving, jabbing, and punching. If, or when, we hook a good fish, we'll need to keep tight to the reins, and anything less than 3X would invite failure. Justin goes over the dos and don'ts with us.

"Do keep your legs locked in the braces."

"Don't get your fly stuck in any part of my body."

"Do cast ahead toward the likely looking spots."

"Don't cast backward once we've passed a spot. That'll cause you to miss the next likely place for a fish."

"Other than that, have fun and enjoy the Madison River."

It's cool in the morning, and Justin says the hopper fishing might be slow early but should heat up with the air. As will be the case many times throughout the day, he's right. Still, Daniel casts with a falcon's focus, unwavering and uncomplaining.

"How are you doing up there?" I ask.

"Great. Even though I haven't gotten a bite, I feel like I'll get one at any moment."

"See that rock coming up on your left?" Justin asks. "Get ready to put your fly in front of it so it'll drift right beside it."

Daniel makes what appears to me to be a perfect cast. But the trout that is almost certainly hunkered beside the rock disagrees. Not only does Justin avoid hitting the uncountable number of boulders above and just below the river's surface, he continuously keeps us in position to cast to all the likely lies for a fish. He does this with a seemingly subconscious awareness, much the way we walk from our beds to the bathroom in the dark. We don't consciously count the steps between obstacles and turns, but we get it right every time.

Daniel has two small fish slash at his fly, or give him a "nibble," as he says, but other than that, the morning goes as Justin predicted. Then, at about 12:30, Justin tells me to cast far to the right side of the boat into what looks like a bland stretch of water in the middle of the river. He's kept the boat close to our left shore to make it easier for Daniel to cast to the likely structure, so this is a more manageable cast for me to make than for him.

"Wait, wait, wait," Justin says after my fly lands. Then *boom*, it happens. The rainbow rolls twice on the surface, then burrows into the deeper water of the run.

"Keep tight," Justin coaches as he oars the boat into a slack pocket in the shade of some shrubs along the bank. He gets the trout in the net, and we all celebrate the relief of the day's first fish. It's a muscular trout, between fifteen and sixteen inches long, with a brilliant, dense pattern of freckles on its tail.

"There's nothing like a wild fish in a river like the Madison," Justin says.

"Look at those riffles. Everywhere these fish go, they're on a treadmill, exercise bike, rowing machine, or you name it. The concept of a leisurely meal isn't in their vocabulary."

"Speaking of leisurely meals," Daniel says, "are you guys hungry?"

"Do you want some fried chicken?" Justin asks Daniel.

"Are you kidding? That would be great."

We anchor in some soft water along the shore, and much like I converted the drift boat into a suitable place for a nap two weeks ago, Justin converts it into a makeshift diner. He sets a spread of chicken, bread, and coleslaw on top of a battle-scarred cooler that appears to have survived two fires and five or six bear attacks. While Daniel works on his third piece of chicken, I ask Justin how this river handles all the fishing pressure it sees.

"See this boat coming down the river?" he asks.

"Yeah."

"They probably won't catch a fish the entire time we can see them, but I promise you they will float within casting range of several. This is a tough river to post up and hammer a hole. We've probably passed by a hundred fish that you could catch if you floated slower and put multiple casts on each of them. But it doesn't work that way here. It's really hard to pound this river."

Just like Justin said it would, the fishing heats up after lunch. The two biggest fish are a harvest-gold brown, just under twenty inches, and a bubblegum-striped rainbow, two inches over that magic mark. Unfortunately, every fish Daniel hooks gets off—the largest would have easily been the biggest fish of the day and the biggest of my trip. About one river mile from Varney Bridge, I land the last fish I'll catch today, and neither Daniel nor I take another cast after that.

That evening, we eat dinner at the Grizzly Bar with Writer Bob, Kate, Cali Bob, Mary, and Rodger. The Bobs and Rodger fished the Ruby River during the day, and as they unanimously agree, it was a complete bust.

"These guys are all excellent fishermen," I tell Daniel. "Sometimes, it just happens that way."

After dinner, everyone exchanges handshakes and hugs, and I promise Bob and Kate that I'll come back. "Do that and bring Daniel again," they say.

We drive to Bozeman in the morning and find a local restaurant for breakfast. While we eat, I tell Daniel I interviewed for a faculty position at Montana State University when he was young.

"Did they offer you the job?"

"Yes."

"So, I could have grown up here?"

The butterfly effect has always intrigued Daniel—I can see the wheels spinning behind his eyes. He wouldn't have gone to school at Michigan State, so he wouldn't have met the people who ultimately introduced him to Alicia. Sunny was born near Madison, Wisconsin, so he would have been someone else's dog. From this perspective, his world would have been a completely different place, and I know these are the things he's thinking about.

"If you had taken that job, you wouldn't have taken this trip."

Touché.

I drop Daniel off at the terminal, hug him, and promise to give one to his mother on his behalf when I get home.

"I love you, Dad."

"I love you too, Son."

I had built two extra days into my schedule to fish after Daniel left. So I take Interstate 90 toward Livingston, planning to exit, check into the Super 8, and fish for a day or two. But I drive past the ramp, over the Yellowstone River, and head east toward and beyond the sign that says *Billings 114*. After three weeks of a trip that took nearly fifty-eight years to make, I don't want to catch another fish in Montana. I only want to catch that first fish again.

ACKNOWLEDGMENTS

Even on days when candy bar–sized slabs of silicon and copper conspired with satellites to pinpoint my location and track my every move, I'd have been lost without the lodestar who orients my needle toward true north. Like an invisible force at a distance, my wife, Roxanne, guided me throughout this journey.

Every fire needs a little spark and a lot of oxygen. Bob DeMott struck flint against steel alongside the Au Sable River, then fanned the flames with kindness and generosity until they blazed a brilliant blue. I would still be thousands of casts away from Montana without his support.

A day with Jerry Dennis makes you think the human qualities of compassion, integrity, talent, and perception are as abundant as the infinity of irrational numbers between zero and one. They aren't, but I forget that when I'm around him. Without his encouragement, I would have found neither the courage nor the words to tell this story.

Aristotle said, "The aim of art is to represent not the outward appearance of things, but their inward significance." Few outdoor artists do this as well as Bob White—who is as fine a person as he is an artist. Having his work introduce this book and all of its chapters is an honor and thrill.

Every journey needs a knowledgeable wagon master and a few reliable scouts. Jerry Kustich advised my expedition plan, while Dave Delisi, Todd Tanner, and Justin Edge helped refine it. I would have been a drifting schooner on a windless sea without them.

Much like a fallen tree in the woods, no manuscript tells a story until someone reads it. I am indebted to a wonderful group of beta readers who, beyond some of the people I've already mentioned, include Kathy Scott, Mick Sheridan, and the incomparable Nick Lyons.

A book doesn't exist until a dedicated team does the hard work of turning a rough draft into a quality finished product. And that process doesn't begin until an editor like Gene Brissie believes in a story and then turns it over to the skilled minds and eyes of people like Brittany Stoner, Felicity Tucker, Lori Hobkirk, and Gavin Robinson. I am grateful to them and everyone at Lyons Press for what this book has become.

And finally, to the State of Montana and all the people and groups who have fought—and continue to fight tirelessly—for the fragile water that gives life to these stories. If we lose this fight, we lose it all.